CORINTHIAN
COLLEGES, INC.

Emergency Planning and Security Measures I

Matthew Pope, CPP

PEARSON
Custom
Publishing

HOMELAND
SECURITY
SPECIALIST

Cover Photo Courtesy of AP/Wide World Photos.

Printed in the United States of America

10 9 8 7 6 5 4

ISBN 0-536-83364-8

2004420181

LM/LD

Please visit our web site at www.pearsoncustom.com

PEARSON CUSTOM PUBLISHING
75 Arlington Street, Suite 300, Boston, MA 02116
A Pearson Education Company

Contents

CHAPTER FOUR: PREPARING FOR DISASTER: CONTINGENCY AND BUSINESS CONTINUITY PLANNING

Contents

CHAPTER EIGHT: CHALLENGES TO THE COMMUNITY

BIOGRAPHIES

Prologue:

Prevention. Every facet, every component, every principle related to emergency planning and security measure implementation can and should be summed up by that one word. Your study to become a homeland security specialist should always bring you back to prevention. Images of lights and sirens flashing as first responders race to an emergency scene, or dashing heroically into a burning structure to carry victims out to safety may be exciting and even romantic, but they are not what we as homeland security specialists are concerned with.

If we are racing to a crisis scene it means that something bad has already happened: property has been seriously damaged, day-to-day operations have been disrupted, people have been hurt or killed. The greatest act of service and heroism we will provide is to devote ourselves night and day to preventing a chance for loss. Prevention is ninety percent of a security specialist's job—to seal up an organization, community, facility or enterprise against attack, loss, intrusion, violence, waste or disclosure.

After prevention, we are concerned with the earliest possible detection of incipient problems and the rapid and proper notification of qualified responders. If and when the system breaks down and an opportunity for loss is exploited, then we must be able to effectively contain a crisis when it occurs, control every aspect of the scene in order to mitigate further loss or damage, and to effectively communicate a coordinated emergency response effort.

If western societies are to ever truly embrace this new millennium notion of homeland security, then we are going to have to learn to understand, appreciate and even laud the efforts of the preventative professional. In western medicine, for example, we often use the phrase "preventative medicine" to describe the early diagnosis and treatment of disease—that is discovering and initiating a recovery program when a disease is in an early and less destructive phase than had it been allowed to progress. While this is certainly a step in the right direction for the medical profession, to characterize this style of treatment as "preventative" is probably a misnomer. The disease was not in fact prevented; it was just discovered and treated early. The patient and his/ her family still had to undergo the anxiety of being diagnosed, the sometimes unpleasant and arduous therapy process, and the costs and hardships associated with extensive medical treatment.

Truly preventative medicine would be more focused on a complete examination of the risk factors facing a young child: family history, environmental realities, inborn allergies or anomalies and the an appropriate prescription of lifestyle choice education; stress management; mind and body care; immunization; etc. Too often in the west we are more focused on diagnosing and treating symptoms and prescribing drugs late in the game to repair a lifetime of environmental exposures, stress fatigue on the body, or poor lifestyle choices. In fact, so conditioned are we to think in this reactive manner that most of us venerate and laud the ability of the medical professional to diagnose disease and then perform the proper surgical or therapeutic procedure. Rarely, however, do we congratulate the school nurse or physical education teacher who may have inspired a group of children to devote a lifetime to making healthier choices.

This same reactive thought process permeates our security and emergency planning as well. The need for homeland security education—such as the material found in this text—is based on the fact that there has never before been a concerted education process in the true principles of security. Criminal justice and fire science curriculums have historically focused more on the tactical aspects of law enforcement and incident scene containment expending the majority of the study on what to do once a law is broken or a fire breaks out, in other words, after the system has broken down.

The effective security specialist should be like a good chess player—always looking several steps ahead of his or her opponent using a dynamic strategy to predict and preempt the adversary. The characteristics of a homeland security specialist are patience, focus, strategic thinking, planning, anticipation—and to some extent—a strong dislike of losing; because, when you lose, someone or something will be lost, either in some or in part, and no amount of proficiency in response will recover it exactly as it was.

1 *Introduction to Homeland Security*

Overview:

Homeland security, not unlike "terrorism", is a concept that is easily recognized but not necessarily universally understood. To some the term refers only to a massive new federal agency within the U.S. government that has pulled together 22 separate smaller agencies responsible for various aspects of domestic security.

To others "homeland security" is the first truly concerted effort to provide a domestic security screen across the North American continent, using technology, innovation and public/private partnerships to protect the borders, and cities of our national homes. Still others would define "homeland security" as enlisting and coordinating public safety and private security organizations as the first line of defense and response in community protection against terrorism, disaster and other forms of catastrophic loss.

Homeland security deals with large themes. In many respects it harkens back to the activist philosophy of "think globally, act locally." To begin your preparation in assuming a role as a homeland security specialist and first responder for community level disasters, we will spend the first chapter discussing the need, history and goals of this new millennium concept: homeland security.

Chapter Objectives:

- *Explain the historical events that directly prompted the creation of a Department of Homeland Security*
- *List the challenges presented to planners in developing a comprehensive homeland security strategy*
- *State and explain the six critical mission areas and four foundations of the U.S.' Homeland Security Strategy*
- *Articulate the social, political and economic challenges presented to the United States, Canada and the west following the terrorist attacks of September 11, 2001*
- *Identify the agencies in the U.S. and Canada responsible for homeland security and aerospace defense*
- *Explain the significance of NATO's Article 5 and when it was first invoked for the first time in history*

Homeland Security Defined

Resources:[1]

- Three and a half million square miles of land
- Over two thousand miles of the longest undefended border in the world
- 290 million people
- Two of the ten largest cities in world, and nine cities with populations in excess of one million people
- 22 major shipping ports
- 407 long runway airports
- A $10.5 trillion gross domestic product
- A $2 trillion budget
- 104 nuclear power reactors[2]
- Vast deposits of coal, copper, lead, molybdenum, phosphates, uranium, bauxite, gold, iron, mercury, nickel, potash, silver, tungsten, zinc, petroleum, natural gas, timber
- A massive industrial base consisting of leading steel, petroleum, automotive, high technology, entertainment; finance, mining, aerospace and defense sectors
- Much of the world's wheat, grain, soy and beef supply

Politically:

- The leading provider of financial and military aid to some of the world's most controversial governments and troubled regions including Colombia, Egypt, Saudi Arabia, and Israel
- The world's largest military and economic power with bases and corporate interests spread throughout the globe
- The only nation to have ever used atomic weapons in warfare against civilian population centers
- A fundamental tenet of "separation of church and state" which infuriates militant religious movements domestically and abroad
- An open and mobile society with a high expectation of privacy among the citizenry and a premium placed on individual liberties
- A citizenry that makes up less than five percent of the world's population but consumes approximately one fourth of the Earth's natural resources [3]
- A level of wealth, a standard of living, and a vast global presence that sometimes evokes envy and resentment

The preceding describes the United States of America in the early twenty-first century. Imagine if it was your job to develop a comprehensive security plan for this collection of people, resources and ideologies. If that thought feels like a daunting prospect then you are beginning to appreciate the challenge of homeland security.

The concept of a federal agency and a coordinated national effort towards the overall security of the domestic homeland had been considered for many years. Unfortunately, it took the deaths of 3,000 people in New York City, Washington, and Pennsylvania on the morning of September 11th, 2001 and the subsequent anthrax- letter attacks for this concept to become a reality.

The creation of the Department of Homeland Security has been the largest reorganization within the United States federal government since the sweeping reforms initiated by Franklin Roosevelt's "New Deal" in the 1930's. Twenty-two federal agencies were consolidated to form this new department, which now consists of approximately 183,000 employees organized into five major directorates, with a yearly budget of $36.2 Billion.[4]

The Secret Service; Immigration and Naturalization Service; Border Patrol; Customs Service; Coast Guard; Transportation Security Administration; Federal Emergency Management Agency; Office of Domestic Preparedness; Federal Protective Agency—and even more obscure entities such as the Animal and Plant Health Inspection Service and Plum Island Animal Disease Center—are all separate federal agencies that, under the Homeland Security Act of 2002 and amendments to the National Security Act of 1947, were merged into the new massive U.S. Department of Homeland Security. DHS cut across several departments such as Treasury, Justice, Transportation, Health and Human Services and even Agriculture to pull together multiple federal agencies with various responsibilities for providing security and emergency preparedness.[5]

The U.S. Department of Homeland Security is a particularly unique study in the need for, and the logistical reality of, forming such an organization. The federal government of the United States is one of the most sectionalized institutions in the world, consisting of: three separate branches—judicial, legislative and executive; fourteen distinct departments, each with its own cabinet level secretary; and then, literally hundreds of agencies and offices carrying out separate missions. As a result of this sub-dividing, there are many times when agencies, which should be cooperating, end up either inadvertently competing with one another, or failing to coordinate operations—assuming another agency is addressing important issues when in fact no one is.

The government's approach to homeland security prior to 9/11 was a great example of this phenomenon. There were critical failures in intelligence sharing, cooperation and counter-terrorism coordination. Security was defined many different ways and responsibility was given to many different agencies.

The ability of terrorists to successfully coordinate such a massive attack in the United States with such relative ease, and the resultant public outcry, prompted the federal government to address the need for better sharing of intelligence information and streamlining of federal agencies responsible for security. With the passage of the Homeland Security Act of 2002 former Pennsylvania governor Tom Ridge became the Nation's first Secretary of Homeland Security and the agency was tasked with the following critical mission areas.[6]

1) Intelligence and Warning

   Terrorism depends on surprise. With it, a terrorist attack has the potential to do massive damage to an unwitting and unprepared target. Without it, the terrorists stand a good chance of being preempted by authorities, and even if they are not, the damage that results from their attacks is likely to be less severe. The United States will take every necessary action to avoid being surprised by another terrorist attack. We must have an intelligence and warning system that can detect terrorist activity before it manifests itself in an attack so that proper pre-emptive, preventive, and protective action can be taken.

   The National Strategy for Homeland Security identifies five major initiatives in this area:

   • Enhance the analytic capabilities of the FBI;

   • Build new capabilities through the Information Analysis and Infrastructure Protection Division of the proposed Department of Homeland Security;

   • Implement the Homeland Security Advisory System;

   • Utilize dual-use analysis to prevent attacks; and

   • Employ "red team" techniques.

2) Border and Transportation Security

   America historically has relied heavily on two vast oceans and two friendly neighbors for border security, and on the private sector for most forms of domestic transportation security. The increasing mobility and destructive potential of modern terrorism has required the United States to rethink and renovate fundamentally its systems for border and transportation security. Indeed, we must now begin to conceive of border security and transportation security as fully integrated requirements because our domestic transportation systems are inextricably intertwined with the global transport infrastructure. Virtually every community in America is connected to the global transportation network by the seaports, airports, highways, pipelines, railroads, and waterways that move people and goods into, within, and out of the Nation. We must therefore promote the efficient and reliable flow of people, goods, and services across borders, while preventing terrorists from using transportation conveyances or systems to deliver implements of destruction.

   The National Strategy for Homeland Security identifies six major initiatives in this area:

   • Ensure accountability in border and transportation security;

   • Create "smart borders;"

   • Increase the security of international shipping containers;

   • Implement the Aviation and Transportation Security Act of 2001;

Figure 1 U.S. DHS Organization- ca. 2003

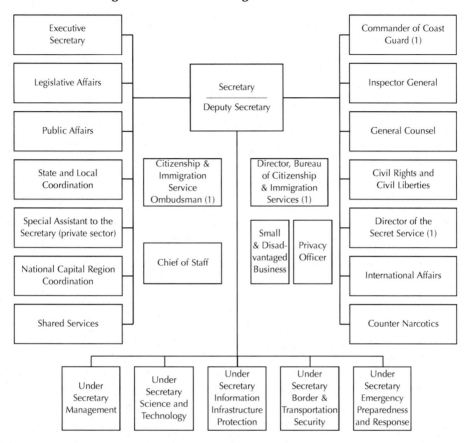

- Recapitalize the U.S. Coast Guard; and
- Reform immigration services.

The President proposed to Congress that the principal border and transportation security agencies—the Immigration and Naturalization Service, the U.S. Customs Service, the U.S. Coast Guard, the Animal and Plant Health Inspection Service, and the Transportation Security Agency—be transferred to the new Department of Homeland Security. This organizational reform will greatly assist in the implementation of all the above initiatives.

3) Domestic Counter-terrorism

The attacks of September 11 and the catastrophic loss of life and property that resulted have redefined the mission of federal, state, and local law enforcement authorities. While law enforcement agencies will continue to investigate and prosecute criminal activity, they should now assign priority to preventing and interdicting terrorist activity within the United States. The Nation's state and local law enforcement officers will be critical in this effort. Our Nation will use all legal means—both traditional and nontraditional—to identify, halt, and, where appropriate, prosecute terrorists in the United States. We will pursue not only the individuals directly involved in terrorist activity but also their sources of support: the people and organizations that knowingly fund the terrorists and those that provide them with logistical assistance.

Effectively reorienting law enforcement organizations to focus on counter terrorism objectives requires decisive action in a number of areas. The National Strategy for Homeland Security identifies six major initiatives in this area:

- Improve intergovernmental law enforcement coordination;
- Facilitate apprehension of potential terrorists;
- Continue ongoing investigations and prosecutions;
- Complete FBI restructuring to emphasize prevention of terrorist attacks;
- Target and attack terrorist financing; and
- Track foreign terrorists and bring them to justice.

4) Protection of Critical Infrastructure and Key Assets

Our society and modern way of life are dependent on networks of infrastructure—both physical networks such as our energy and transportation systems and virtual networks such as the Internet. If terrorists attack one or more pieces of our critical infrastructure, they may disrupt entire systems and cause significant damage to the Nation. We must, therefore, improve protection of the individual pieces and interconnecting systems that make up our critical infrastructure. Protecting America's critical infrastructure and key assets will not only make us more secure from terrorist attack, but will also reduce our vulnerability to natural disasters, organized crime, and computer hackers.

America's critical infrastructure encompasses a large number of sectors. The U.S. government will seek to deny terrorists the opportunity to inflict lasting harm to our Nation by protecting the assets, systems, and functions vital to our national security, governance, public health and safety, economy, and national morale.

The National Strategy for Homeland Security identifies eight major initiatives in this area:

- Unify America's infrastructure protection effort in the Department of Homeland Security;
- Build and maintain a complete and accurate assessment of America's critical infrastructure and key assets;
- Enable effective partnership with state and local governments and the private sector;

- Develop a national infrastructure protection plan;
- Secure cyberspace;
- Harness the best analytic and modeling tools to develop effective protective solutions;
- Guard America's critical infrastructure and key assets against "inside" threats; and
- Partner with the international community to protect our transnational infrastructure.

5) Defending Against Catastrophic Threats

The expertise, technology, and material needed to build the most deadly weapons known to mankind—including chemical, biological, radiological, and nuclear weapons—are spreading inexorably. If our enemies acquire these weapons, they are likely to try to use them. The consequences of such an attack could be far more devastating than those we suffered on September 11—a chemical, biological, radiological, or nuclear terrorist attack in the United States could cause large numbers of casualties, mass psychological disruption, contamination and significant economic damage, and could overwhelm local medical capabilities.

Currently, chemical, biological, radiological, and nuclear detection capabilities are modest and response capabilities are dispersed throughout the country at every level of government. While current arrangements have proven adequate for a variety of natural disasters and even the September 11 attacks, the threat of terrorist attacks using chemical, biological, radiological, and nuclear weapons requires new approaches, a focused strategy, and a new organization.

The National Strategy for Homeland Security identifies six major initiatives in this area:

- Prevent terrorist use of nuclear weapons through better sensors and procedures;
- Detect chemical and biological materials and attacks;
- Improve chemical sensors and decontamination techniques;
- Develop broad-spectrum vaccines, anti-microbials, and antidotes;
- Harness the scientific knowledge and tools to counter terrorism; and
- Implement the Select Agent Program.

6) Emergency Preparedness and Response

We must prepare to minimize the damage and recover from any future terrorist attacks that may occur despite our best efforts at prevention. An effective response to a major terrorist incident—as well as a natural disaster—depends on being prepared. Therefore, we need a comprehensive national system to bring together and coordinate all necessary response assets quickly and effectively. We must plan, equip, train, and exercise many different response units to mobilize without warning for any emergency.

Many pieces of this national emergency response system are already in place. America's first line of defense in the aftermath of any terrorist attack is its first responder community—police officers, firefighters, emergency medical providers, public works personnel, and emergency management officials. Nearly three million state and local first responders regularly put their lives on the line to save the lives of others and make our country safer.

Yet multiple plans currently govern the federal government's support of first responders during an incident of national significance. These plans and the government's overarching policy for counter terrorism are based on an artificial and unnecessary distinction between "crisis management" and "consequence management." Under the President's proposal, the Department of Homeland Security will consolidate federal response plans and build a national system for incident management in cooperation with state and local government. Our federal, state, and local governments would ensure that all response personnel and organizations are properly equipped, trained, and exercised to respond to all terrorist threats and attacks in the United States. Our emergency preparedness and response efforts would also engage the private sector and the American people.

The National Strategy for Homeland Security identifies twelve major initiatives in this area:

- Integrate separate federal response plans into a single all-discipline incident management plan;
- Create a national incident management system;
- Improve tactical counter terrorist capabilities;
- Enable seamless communication among all responders;
- Prepare health care providers for catastrophic terrorism;
- Augment America's pharmaceutical and vaccine stockpiles;
- Prepare for chemical, biological, radiological, and nuclear decontamination;
- Plan for military support to civil authorities;
- Build the Citizen Corps;
- Implement the First Responder Initiative of the Fiscal Year 2003 Budget;
- Build a national training and evaluation system; and
- Enhance the victim support system.

The National Strategy for Homeland Security also describes four foundations—unique American strengths that cut across all of the mission areas, across all levels of government, and across all sectors of our society. These foundations—law, science and technology, information sharing and systems, and international cooperation—provide a useful framework for evaluating our homeland security investments across the federal government.

Law

Throughout our Nation's history, we have used laws to promote and safeguard our security and our liberty. The law will both provide mechanisms for the government to act and will define the appropriate limits of action.

The National Strategy for Homeland Security outlines legislative actions that would help enable our country to fight the war on terrorism more effectively. New federal laws should not preempt state law unnecessarily or overly federalize the war on terrorism. We should guard scrupulously against incursions on our freedoms.

The Strategy identifies twelve major initiatives in this area:

Federal level

- Enable critical infrastructure information sharing;
- Streamline information sharing among intelligence and law enforcement agencies;
- Expand existing extradition authorities;
- Review authority for military assistance in domestic security;
- Revive the President's reorganization authority; and
- Provide substantial management flexibility for the Department of Homeland Security.

State level

- Coordinate suggested minimum standards for state driver's licenses;
- Enhance market capacity for terrorism insurance;
- Train for prevention of cyber attacks;
- Suppress money laundering;
- Ensure continuity of the judiciary; and
- Review quarantine authorities.

Science and Technology

The Nation's advantage in science and technology is a key to securing the homeland. New technologies for analysis, information sharing, detection of attacks, and countering chemical, biological, radiological, and nuclear weapons will help prevent and minimize the damage from future terrorist attacks. Just as science has helped us defeat past enemies overseas, so too will it help us defeat the efforts of terrorists to attack our homeland and disrupt our way of life.

The federal government is launching a systematic national effort to harness science and technology in support of homeland security. We will build a national research and development enterprise for homeland security sufficient to mitigate the risk posed by modern terrorism. The federal government will consolidate most federally funded homeland security research and development under the Department of Homeland Security to ensure strategic direction and avoid duplicative efforts. We will create and implement a long-term research and development plan that includes investment in revolutionary capabilities with high-payoff potential. The federal government will also seek to harness the energy and ingenuity of the private sector to develop and produce the devices and systems needed for homeland security.

The National Strategy for Homeland Security identifies eleven major initiatives in this area:

- Develop chemical, biological, radiological, and nuclear countermeasures;
- Develop systems for detecting hostile intent;
- Apply biometric technology to identification devices;
- Improve the technical capabilities of first responders;
- Coordinate research and development of the homeland security apparatus;
- Establish a national laboratory for homeland security;
- Solicit independent and private analysis for science and technology research;
- Establish a mechanism for rapidly producing prototypes;
- Conduct demonstrations and pilot deployments;
- Set standards for homeland security technology; and
- Establish a system for high-risk, high-payoff homeland security research.

Information Sharing and Systems

Information systems contribute to every aspect of homeland security. Although American information technology is the most advanced in the world, our country's information systems have not adequately supported the homeland security mission. Databases used for federal law enforcement, immigration, intelligence, public health surveillance, and emergency management have not been connected in ways that allow us to comprehend where information gaps or redundancies exist. In addition, there are deficiencies in the communications systems used by states and municipalities throughout the country; most state and local first responders do not use compatible communications equipment. To secure the homeland better, we must link the vast amounts of knowledge residing within each government agency while ensuring adequate privacy.

The National Strategy for Homeland Security identifies five major initiatives in this area:

- Integrate information sharing across the federal government;
- Integrate information sharing across state and local governments, private industry, and citizens;

- Adopt common "meta-data" standards for electronic information relevant to homeland security;
- Improve public safety emergency communications; and
- Ensure reliable public health information.

International Cooperation[7]

In a world where the terrorist threat pays no respect to traditional boundaries, our strategy for homeland security cannot stop at our borders. America must pursue a sustained, steadfast, and systematic international agenda to counter the global terrorist threat and improve our homeland security. Our international anti-terrorism campaign has made significant progress since September 11. The full scope of these activities will be further described in the forthcoming National Security Strategy of the United States and the National Strategy for Combating Terrorism. The National Strategy for Homeland Security identifies nine major initiatives in this area:

- Create "smart borders";
- Combat fraudulent travel documents;
- Increase the security of international shipping containers;
- Intensify international law enforcement cooperation;
- Help foreign nations fight terrorism;
- Expand protection of transnational critical infrastructure;
- Amplify international cooperation on homeland security science and technology;
- Improve cooperation in response to attacks; and
- Review obligations to international treaties and law.

Costs of Homeland Security[8]

The national effort to enhance homeland security will yield tremendous benefits and entail substantial financial and other costs. Benefits include reductions in the risk of attack and their potential consequences. Costs include not only the resources we commit to homeland security but also the delays to commerce and travel. The United States spends roughly $100 billion [$100,000 million] per year on homeland security. This figure includes federal, state, and local law enforcement and emergency services, but excludes most funding for the armed forces.

The responsibility of providing homeland security is shared between federal, state and local governments, and the private sector. In many cases, sufficient incentives exist in the private market to supply protection. Government should fund only those homeland security activities that are not supplied, or are inadequately supplied, in the market. Cost sharing between different levels of government should reflect the principles of federalism. Many homeland security activities, such as intelligence gathering and border security, are properly accomplished at the federal level. In other circumstances, such as with first responder capabilities, it is more appropriate for state and local governments to handle these responsibilities.

In 2004, Homeland Security was one of very few items in the U.S. Federal Government's budget that received an increase—approximately nine percent or $3.6 billion—for FY05.[9] Even in the difficult economic conditions of 2004, the federal government felt that the need for improved homeland security spending was the critical. Where the Department of Homeland Security will go next, and what it may evolve into over time remains to be seen. Whether the new department will endure or be repealed in years to come; whether it will continue to see increases in federal dollars and budget share, or will face cuts; whether the DHS will remain focused on its charter missions or will expand and adapt to take on new roles is a matter now for time and history. Regardless, the Homeland Security Act of 2002; the creation of the federal Department of Homeland Security and even the introduction of the phrase *"homeland security"* into the public vernacular reflects a shift of the American mindset not seen for almost half a century- a sign of the times that an age of innocence and a sense of insulation from a hostile world is gone, if not for good, than at least for a foreseeable future.

9/11 was unique as a terrorist attack. The traditional aim of a terrorist is to violently underscore a point about a perceived injustice—often centered on an acute issue such as Israeli settlements in Palestine, the presence of British troops in Northern Ireland, or to reverse laws around abortion or gun ownership. The hijackers and planners of 9/11, however, never issued a statement or specified a cause. American support of Israel; the presence of U.S. troops in Saudi Arabia; American aid to repressive regimes in the Arab world; fear of western influenced globalization were all formative causes to al-Qaeda to be sure; however, the language, writings and doctrine of the fanatics involved in the 9/11 plot all seemed murkier than these straightforward, geo-political/sociological motives.

The 9/11 hijackers wrote in personal diaries and last wills about the rewards of martyrdom—promises of an eternity in paradise with a cadre of 72 virgins each—if they should take their own lives while at the same time murdering their "enemies". In the warped theology of al-Qaeda, all Americans were fair game—civilians, women, children, and the elderly. Not only was it permissible to murder any and all Americans (and their collaborators), but God actually demanded it. The motives of the 9/11 hijackers didn't seem to land on practical matters of politics, but rather on dark, apocalyptic visions of a holy war between the forces of God and Satan, with themselves on the side of righteousness and their enemies as the dehumanized incarnations of evil. Thus, while all acts of terrorism are senseless, 9/11 took on a particular note of nihilistic gloom.

9/11 was also unique in the sense that the whole world experienced the attacks together. Terrorists typically rely on media coverage to enhance their ability to intimidate and broadcast their agenda. Most times however, we only see the aftermath with journalists and cameras arriving after the explosion or shooting has taken place. 9/11 was filmed from start to finish. The whole world watched as the first tower burned. Millions were tuned in when United Airlines 175 slammed into the south tower. We saw the Pentagon smoldering; heard the tapes of anguished but resolved voices calling loved ones from cell phones sensing their doom; we saw both towers come down. 9/11 was a long, agonizing and traumatic experience for millions, with every second recorded and broadcast repeatedly. The attacks of 9/11 unfolded over a period of hours, letting the enigma and horror of the event bore into the collective consciousness of civilized people everywhere. For sheer effect it is without equal in the annals of terrorism.

9/11 was also a spectacular attack in the original sense of the word—to cause a spectacle. 9/11 was in a strange way original; designed to be more than just a bombing or a hijacking, but also to create a morbid sense of drama. Terrorists seek to use symbolism in their attacks, but September 11th was designed to create something that would not only kill and injure on a grand scale, but would also create indelible and unsettling visuals. The surreal image of an aluminum jumbo jet's fuselage being swallowed up by the World Trade Center before erupting in a vicious orange ball-of-flame; the notion that commercial airliners and office buildings would suddenly be turned into the scene of life and death struggles ; the realization that the Nation's capital city and the central headquarters of the world's most powerful military could be effectively attacked using a civilian jet liner, created a deeply disturbing and unnerving sense . The exploitation of our freedom and mobility, the helplessness and horror we felt, the nagging mystery of who was doing this and why conspired to make an eerie, and outraging point.

Finally, September 11th was unique in its lethality. The death toll surpassed the only other coordinated attack of that magnitude on U.S. soil—the Pearl Harbor bombing of December 7th, 1941. 9/11 stands alone as the most deadly terror attack in history.

Courtesy of AP/Wide World Photos.

Mass Anxiety and the Terror Formula: "Super-Terrorism"

9/11 was a new form of terrorism, a type of "super-terrorism." Following the Second World War, the United States and the Soviet Union redefined geo-politics by emerging as "super-powers": nation states characterized by large populations and geographic territories; leadership in several strategic alliances; enormous military, naval and air forces; powerful economies and industrial bases; nuclear arsenals sufficient to obliterate all life on earth many times over; and unquestioned status as the predominant global champions of opposing ideologies (democracy and the free-market economy versus Marxism-Leninism and the command economy). In much the same way, al-Qaeda has ushered in the super-terrorist organization.

Al-Qaeda operates as a loose-knit yet well coordinated global network, decentralized enough that the myriad of cells which compose the network are able to melt virtually unnoticed into target populations, yet synchronized enough to carry out simultaneous attacks against disparate targets hundreds of miles a part. Al-Qaeda is well financed, with numerous surreptitious revenue streams and money laundering schemes. Recruits are trained at fairly sophisticated bases in third world nations throughout the globe. Al-Qaeda, at least prior to the U.S. led attack on Afghanistan commencing October 7, 2001, was the largest terrorist network ever, complete with a command structure and communications network.

More than anything however, al-Qaeda possesses a certain degree of morbid "vision". Al-Qaeda sends a profound message with every attack. They invest a great deal of time in researching particular targets so as to ensure that their point is plainly understood without the formality of having to issue a statement. Some suggest that al-Qaeda's practice of not issuing a statement reflects the group's intense hatred and pseudo-religious apocalyptic theology letting the bitterness and the horror of the act itself be the only "statement." Other terrorism experts suggest the purpose of not issuing a statement is more practical—to generate a sense of anxiety and insecurity by increasing the mysteriousness of the attack.

The terror formula is simple: "kill 10, terrorize 10,000." As their title implies, the purpose of a *terrorist* is to *terrorize* "to fill with terror; to coerce by threat or violence."[10] For terrorism to be truly successful, knowledge of an attack and the resultant fear must reach a much larger audience then merely those present at the scene. Terrorism not only relies upon media coverage, but also in a perverse way, actually courts it. Not unlike celebrity publicists or marketing agencies, terrorist planners invest a great deal of time and energy in determining which attacks will generate maximum interest and impact. Terrorists must study media behavior to decide what sort of attack will seize and capture the media's often fleeting attention span. Sadly, in the United States, where the population is highly acclimated to sensationalist imagery, an attack the size and scale of 9/11 was really the first event to capture long-term media attention, to mobilize civic leaders and ordinary citizens to act, and to advance terrorism as a serious consideration for the public.

Al-Qaeda had been active in operations against the U.S. for eight years prior to 9/11, including the 1993 bombing of the World Trade Center, which was the first attempt to bring the twin towers down. The 1996 Air Force barracks bombing at Khobar towers in Saudi Arabia; the synchronized 1998 bombings of the U.S. embassies in Kenya and Tanzania; and the year 2000 suicide attack on the naval ship U.S.S. Cole in Yemen were all al-Qaeda operations targeted at the United States. In 1998, the chief organizer and spiritual leader of al-Qaeda, Osama bin Laden, issued a "fatwa" (which could be translated as a "religious edict" or "commandment") to his followers to "kill Americans- including civilians- wherever you find them."

Osama bin Laden is the son of an extremely wealthy Saudi businessman and construction contractor. The Bin Laden Group is a very lucrative construction concern in the Saudi kingdom. According to Saudi law, polygamy(a man having several wives) is legal. Bin Laden's father had nine wives and a total of 52 children. Osama grew up in this rather large and extended family and likely felt rather overlooked competing with fifty-one siblings for his father's attention. In 1979, a younger Osama found a cause to give his here-to-for pampered life some sense of significance: the struggle of Islamic rebels in Afghanistan against Soviet troops who were sent to uphold the unpopular communist government of that nation. Bin Laden packed up his share of the millions his father had doled out to his children and left for Afghanistan. There he used his fortunes and ties to his father's construction business to begin funding various humanitarian projects for the people of Afghanistan.

Eventually bin Laden joined the direct fighting and soon he was regarded as a hero of the native Afghani resistance known as the *Muhajadeen.* Following the 1989 defeat of the Soviets in Afghanistan, international attention on the war torn region waned and soon bin Laden was without an enemy to distinguish himself against. Afghanistan fell into chaos for several years with Muhajadeen elements fracturing into regional-tribal clans where they began battling for control of the nation. From 1989 onward, bin Laden began setting his sites on more global objectives, inculcating and training his followers with an apocalyptical, pseudo-theological campaign against "non-believers" and secular societies. He formed a new network that was given only the vague and ominous name "the base", which in Arabic is translated as "al- Qaeda."

When Saddam Hussein ordered Iraqi forces into the tiny, oil-rich Arab nation of Kuwait in August 1990, the Kingdom of Saudi Arabia feared that they might be invaded next. As home to two of Islam's holiest sites: the cities of Mecca and Medina; bin Laden proposed to the Saudi government, perhaps unrealistically, to raise a legion of Muhajadeen fighters to defend Saudi Arabia against Saddam Hussein. Bin Laden regarded Hussein as a non-believer and a decadent secularist unworthy of leading an Arab nation or even being a "fellow Muslim."[11] The Saudi government declined bin Laden's offer and opted instead to invite the American military in to defend the Saudi kingdom. This infuriated bin Laden who felt the Kingdom of Saudi Arabia and the holy sites of Islam should not be protected by westerners. Bin Laden began preaching against the United States and the Saudi government, a move that eventually resulted in the revocation of his Saudi citizenship. His ire at the U.S., the West and cooperative Arab governments manifested itself as a fiery mix of literal interpretation of Islamic law known as "Wahibbism" and violent militancy.

Al-Qaeda emerged as a functioning terror network when it staged its first concerted operations in 1992 and 1993. On the 29th of December 1992, a bomb detonated at the Gold Mohur Hotel in Aden, Yemen. U.S. military personnel on their way to support the on-going humanitarian mission in Somalia had recently stayed at the hotel. Although the bombing was planned too late to impact the servicemen who had been there, two Australian tourists were killed.

Al Qaeda ambitiously raised the stakes for international terrorism by conducting its next attack within the United States. On February 26, 1993 operatives drove a truck loaded with a massive bomb into an underground parking garage at the World Trade Center in Manhattan. Six people were killed and almost a thousand were wounded when the bomb exploded. The subsequent investigation and trail of captured suspects revealed that the attackers hoped to cause a structural failure below the south tower, collapsing it in to the north tower- bringing both skyscrapers down.

Al-Qaeda showed up significantly again during American military operations in Somalia in 1993. Although the October 3, 1993 raid on Mogadishu's Bakara market by U.S. Special Forces resulted in the successful capture of several influential Somali figures, resistance fighters using rocket-propelled grenades (RPG's) shot down two U.S. Army Blackhawk helicopters. The loss of the helicopters significantly complicated the mission and ultimately resulted in the deaths of 18 American soldiers. Muhajadeen in Afghanistan had developed the tactic of using RPG's as surface-to-air weapons against slow flying helicopters during the Soviet invasion. The ability of the Somalis to do the same thing suggested the presence of al-Qaeda in Mogadishu. Two years later in November 1995,al-Qaeda placed a truck bomb at a Saudi military training facility in Riyadh, killing seven Americans and two Indians.

Bin Laden returned to Afghanistan in 1996 after being banned by the Saudi government. At about that same time the Islamic extremist Taliban movement seized control of the country.[12] Bin Laden was believed to be a chief financier and supporter of the Taliban, who in turn offered him political sanctuary and a base of operations for al-Qaeda.

August 7th, 1998 two powerful car bombs exploded almost simultaneously in front of the U.S. Embassies in Dar es Salaam, Tanzania and Nairobi, Kenya. Two hundred twenty-four people, mostly African citizens working as part of the  embassy staff, were murdered and another 5,000 were injured. A few weeks later the U.S. fired a salvo of 70 Tomahawk cruise missiles from navy ships into al-Qaeda facilities and training camps in the Sudan and Afghanistan. Although the attacks missed bin Laden, they did injure and kill several key al Qaeda operatives and rattled the Taliban government of Afghanistan. Taliban leader Mullah Omar scolded bin Laden in the aftermath of the cruise missile attacks and warned him not to initiate any more threatening actions or statements against the United States from inside the country. Bin Laden said he would comply, but the pledge did not last long.

On October 12, 2000 a Navy destroyer, the U.S.S. Cole, was performing routine refueling operations at a port near Aden, Yemen when a small boat packed with explosives rammed it. Seventeen American sailors were killed.

Then of course, September 11th, 2001, the world was changed forever when al-Qaeda carried out the most brazen terror attack in history. There have been subsequent lethal attacks by al-Qaeda in Riyadh, Casablanca, Kabul, Jakarta, Baghdad, Istanbul, Bali, Mombassa, Kerbala and Madrid. There is an equally long list of failed al-Qaeda attempts and disrupted attacks since 1989. al-Qaeda has murdered an estimated 4,000 people around the globe and has injured approximately 8,300.

Of course, al-Qaeda is not the only terrorist organization in the world, and the network itself is, in many respects, an amalgam of smaller, affiliated terror groups. Hundreds of terrorist groups ranging from 20to 2,000 members operate in all corners of the globe and claim to advocate all manner of ideological and political agendas. Other major terrorist groups include, the *Al-Aqsa Martyr's Brigade* in the West Bank and Gaza Strip; *Hamas* in the occupied territories of Palestine; *Islamic Jihad* which operates throughout the Middle East; *Armed Islamic Group* in Algeria; *Sendero Luminoso ("Shining Path")* in Peru; *Revolutionary Armed Forces* (FARC) in Colombia; *Abu Sayyaf* in the Philippines; and the *Irish Republican Army* in northern Ireland.* This of course is just a small fraction of known terrorist organizations operating in the world.

Courtesy of AP/Wide World Photos.

Although the history of terrorism dates back hundreds, if not thousands, of years, the period from the 1960 on has seen a steady rise in the concerted and consistent use of terror as a tool for social, political and religious change.

The advent of al-Qaeda has created new and very serious phenomena for the homeland security specialist. The super-terrorist group has: a global organization with thousands of adherents operating independently and yet with an unified ideology; a command staff; decentralized planning capabilities; a communications network which includes rather sophisticated technology such as steganography; training programs and facilities; a vast recruiting network; surreptitious, lucrative and far reaching financing streams; a particular fondness for large scale, dramatic attacks; and a willingness to be patient.

In this new millennium, all homeland security specialists—frontline security agents and supervisors, first responders, intelligence operatives and disaster recovery planners—will all have to be familiar with the mindset, tactics and objectives of the super-terrorist organization. Whatever you are assigned to protect and defend or wherever you find yourself in the community, you will always have to be thinking and planning in much the same way a terrorist would, asking yourself:

- What vulnerabilities could be exploited?
- What targets are of high symbolic and media interest value?
- What manner of attack would produce the greatest damage with the least risk of the attacker exposing himself before hand?
- What would seem suspicious, unusual or out-of-place?
- Are the security measures in place sufficient to stop someone who is intent on killing himself as part of the attack?
- Have I witnessed any activity that would seem consistent with my facility or community being under surveillance?

Use of the Media

The media is a key concern for all security specialists. The media can be a great asset in alerting the general public or calming widespread alarm by managing information. At the same time, if used irresponsibly or ineffectively, the media may contribute to mass panic, or be exploited by terrorists as a tool. As mentioned in a previous section, terrorists often court the media as a means of increasing the reach of their attacks and to generate publicity for their cause. In fact, without public exposure it is doubtful terrorism would retain much value as a practice. Terrorism, in its modern incarnation, is really almost entirely dependent on media coverage. The dramatic practice of hijacking commercial airlines, for example, became very popular only after the advent of satellite television broadcasting when stories could be beamed around the world live-time. There is some speculation that the targets were chosen specifically by the 9/11 hijackers to underscore a point about America's vulnerability.

In 1974, the scholar Brian Jenkins stated, "Terrorism is theater"[13], and he was correct. A lethal form of theater to be sure, but as homeland security specialists it is important for us to understand that the objective of the terrorist is not solely to maim and kill, but also to do it in a manner that will inure the greatest media exposure and message proliferation. The creation of panic and fear; to instill a sense of chaos and disorder; and to discredit a government and ideology—these are the goals of the terrorist. The media obviously can be an unwitting accomplice in the achievement of these goals. 9/11 is a paramount example. Many of us remember the first broadcasts of World Trade Center One, the north tower, burning after a low flying airplane struck it. In their frenzy to break and carry this dramatic story, scores of news agencies were broadcasting, and millions of viewers tuned in when the second plane hit the south tower. We collectively shared the moment. Many of those who were watching the second strike live shared the same experience of confusion, not realizing for a few moments what had happened, and the slow dread of understanding that this could not possibly be an accident.

News agencies are often aware that they are being exploited, especially during live broadcasts when it is impossible to predict and edit events. The pressure to generate subscriber-ship and ratings usually compels media organizations to carry the story because that is ultimately how they succeed. Terrorists are aware of this media tendency and use it to further their aims. Like good advertisers, terrorists typically plot and plan their attacks based on what will generate maximum interest and attention. Panic and hysteria become "force multipliers" to their attacks, especially when the media reports only partial facts about the terrorist attack, leaving the public imagination to fill in the rest.

In 1995 when the Aum Shinrikyo cult released deadly Sarin gas in the Tokyo subway system, twelve people were killed and just over 1,000 were admitted into hospitals and treated for illness related to Sarin poisoning. Altogether, however, 5,500 people showed up in various Tokyo hospital emergency rooms. The majority of them falsely believed they had been poisoned. The panic caused by early media images of chaos and death in the subways resulted in an additional 4,000 people developing psychosomatic symptoms and needing to be rushed to the hospital.[14] These imaginary symptoms caused very real problems as you might imagine, as overworked hospital staff now had the additional headache and burden of having to triage and diagnose actual illness from hysterical illness.

Following the anthrax letter attacks of October of 2001, a panic ensured in the U.S. Although only 23 people were actually sickened by anthrax and there were five fatalities, there were millions of "psychological causalities" throughout the country, with thousands of calls to 9-1-1 to report on mysterious white powders and unsolicited mailings that the public would normally just ignore.[15]

The scars of terrorism are not found only at the scene of the attack, but also in the post-traumatic stress, the sleep disorders, the anxiety, depression and malaise found throughout the affected public. Studies conducted by the National Organization for Research at the University of Chicago found that while, by in large, Americans responded quite resiliently to the 9/11 attacks, a full eight percent of people of the U.S. and fifteen percent of the people living in New York exhibited significant symptomology of Post Traumatic Stress Disorder (PTSD), a serious psychological condition affecting persons exposed to a profound or sustained crisis (i.e. combat veterans, disaster survivors, victims of violent crimes, etc.). Far beyond the immediate tragic loss of 9/11, millions more became, in effect, psychological casualties. For many of these causalities the trauma of the event was experienced only through the exhaustive media coverage.

The media may also be an effective tool in combating terrorism. In the same way that broadcast coverage of attacks can multiply the residual anxiety of terrorism, the media may also allow government agencies the ability to disseminate messages of reassurance and guidance to the general public. During the Second World War, U.S. President Franklin Roosevelt would have regular "fireside chats" broadcast via radio to millions of Americans. The mental image conjured up of the wise and grandfatherly Roosevelt sitting in a cozy salon next to a crackling fire was very comforting to a nation at war and recovering from economic depression. One of the factors that psychologists believe contributed to the resiliency of Americans in coping with September 11th, even in New York and Washington, DC, was the public celebration of the heroism around 9/11 as well. Although the continuous broadcasting of the horror of the attacks likely contributed to the mass trauma, the almost equally continuous media coverage of emergency workers' heroism, the unity of Americans and people around the world waving flags and holding candle light vigils, prayer services and images such as a united Congress singing "God Bless America" likely accelerated the healing process as well.

Media broadcasting may also be effective in deterring terrorist attacks. Terrorists by definition enjoy the element of surprise. Thorough news coverage of terror warnings, especially when accompanied by instructions for simple things the public can do to protect themselves and their communities create a heightened awareness, may be disquieting to terrorist planners. Terrorists seem to be sensitive to feeling that they are being watched or scrutinized before hand. Capture and incarceration before carrying out an operation is an inglorious result for someone intent on achieving esteem through martyrdom or successful terror attack. Increased media attention to terror threats or use of the media to alert the general public to be more vigilant may cause terrorists to abort missions. Finally, a better-informed public may be more likely to report suspicious activity and objects such as backpacks left unattended or persons.

Legislative changes: USA PATRIOT Act

After September 11th, as well as the subsequent anthrax letter attacks, America's denial regarding terrorism quickly shifted to a state of near hysteria. Suddenly the fear of terrorism was everywhere and all manner of funds and ideas were being advanced to combat the threat. Among the changes that came quickly on the heels of 9/11 was the enactment of sweeping new security legislation. On October 24th, 2001—six weeks after the attacks in New York, Washington, DC and Pennsylvania, and in the midst of the anthrax letter attacks—House Resolution 3162, the USA PATRIOT *(Uniting and Strengthening America by Providing Appropriate Tools Required to Intercept and Obstruct Terrorism)* Act was overwhelmingly passed in Congress and was signed into law the next day by the President. Soon after its passing, the act began generating controversy. Some felt the PATRIOT Act was an overdue expansion of resources needed by law enforcement to investigate and prosecute terrorists—an expansion that could have helped prevent the 9/11 terrorist attacks. Others feared that the act represented: an encroachment on basic civil liberties; was hastily passed during a time of great anxiety; and, was a dangerous over-reaction that served more as an impediment to the U.S. Constitution than to future acts of terrorism.

Since its enactment there have been a lot of misconceptions about the PATRIOT Act. Within the 342-page legislation, the PATRIOT Act addresses a broad range of concerns related to combating terrorism. This chapter will conduct an in-depth examination of the provisions of the PATRIOT Act, but to begin with, it is important that we separate fact from fiction regarding the more controversial aspects of the PATRIOT Act.

What the USA PATRIOT Act does:

1. Instructs and facilitates means for the Federal Bureau of Investigation (FBI) and Central Intelligence Agency (CIA) to share information related to terrorist activity;

2. Enables the FBI to directly access federal judges on the highly secretive Foreign Intelligence Service Act (FISA) court, and to secure FISA court orders for businesses to hand over records that the FBI suspects may be related to terrorism;

3. Greatly eases the definition of "probable cause" for searches and surveillance. Under the PATRIOT Act federal agents need to only articulate that the business records sought are "related to a terrorism investigation or intelligence probe."

4. Codifies the "delayed notification" of searches. Delayed notifications have been used in the past for the investigation of organized crime. The PATRIOT Act however, makes delayed notification a written federal law instead of a general, unwritten *rule-of-thumb* used on a limited, case-by-case basis. This allows prosecutors to request a

"reasonable delay period" from judges in notifying people that federal agents have searched their homes or businesses. If a probe is terminated because the subject is found not to be involved in terrorism or an effective case can not be proven, the subject may never be notified, meaning that he or she will never know their home or business has been searched.

5. Allow agents to secure "roving wire taps", which involves tapping various electronic devices the subject uses.

What the USA PATRIOT Act does NOT do:

1. After 9/11, thousands of people in the United States, mostly of Middle Eastern descent, were detained under a special authority given to the U.S. Department of Justice (DOJ). Because of the prolonged nature of this detention without subjects necessarily having the opportunity to appear before a judge, and the ambiguity of some of the reasons given for detaining suspects, this action has raised concerns that public anxiety over terrorism could erode the concept of Due Process as articulated in the sixth amendment of the Bill of Rights. This detention power was afforded to the DOJ by immigration law and not the USA PATRIOT Act

2. The PATRIOT Act did not grant the President the authority to detain 650 Taliban and al-Qaeda combatants captured in Afghanistan. The authority to hold enemy combatants until the succession of hostilities is an interpretation of executive war powers as articulated in the Constitution

3. Similarly, two enemy combatants have also been detained in a U.S. Navy brig without having charges levied against them or access to attorneys. This is also an application of executive war powers, although it is currently being challenged in the U.S. Supreme Court.

4. The PATRIOT Act contains no provisions regarding military tribunals being called to adjudicate terrorism charges against non-citizens being held by the U.S. This power is granted to the U.S. Department of Defense.

5. The U.S. Attorney General did alter rules for investigators post 9/11 to enter houses of worship and attend rallies while conducting terrorism probes. This was done internally at the DOJ and is not written in to the PATRIOT Act

The USA PATRIOT Act is a far-reaching piece of legislation, which addresses many disparate pieces of counter-terrorism concepts and attempts to codify them into one sweeping law. The PATRIOT Act does deal extensively with technology-based investigations and in many ways serves as an excellent bench mark for the types of questions and challenges facing investigators in a technology environment.

More than creating a lot of new laws, the USA PATRIOT Act amended a great deal of existing legislation. Included in the U.S. law specifically amended by the PATRIOT Act are:

- Electronic Communications Privacy Act
- Computer Fraud and Abuse Act
- Foreign Intelligence Surveillance Act
- Family Education Rights and Privacy Act
- Pen Register and Trap and Trace Statute
- Money Laundering Act
- Immigration and Nationality Act
- Bank Secrecy Act
- Right to Financial Privacy Act
- Fair Credit Reporting Act
- Title III of the Federal Wiretap Statute

War on Terrorism

September 20, 2001: The President proposes a new Office of Homeland Security.

October 7, 2001: The President announces Operation Enduring Freedom to dismantle the Taliban regime in Afghanistan, which is harboring al Qaeda.

October 8, 2001: The President establishes the Office of Homeland Security in the Executive Office of the President and appoints Pennsylvania Governor Tom Ridge as Director.

November 19, 2001: The President signs the Aviation and Transportation Security Act, creating the Transportation Security Administration.

October 4, 2002: Six suspected members of the al Qaeda terrorist network operating near Buffalo are indicted.

November 25, 2002: President Bush signs the Homeland Security Act of 2002, establishing the Department of Homeland Security.

January 17, 2003: The U.S. State Department reopens the U.S. Embassy in Kabul, Afghanistan. The embassy had been closed for over 25 years.

January 7, 2003: Congress creates the Select Committee on Homeland Security with authorizing and oversight responsibility for the new Department of Homeland Security.

January 24, 2003: President Bush swears in Tom Ridge as the first Secretary of the Department of Homeland Security.

March 1, 2003: Khalid Sheikh Mohammed, the alleged architect of the September 11th attacks is captured in Pakistan.

March 17, 2003: Homeland Security Department commences Operation Liberty Shield, an increase in protective measures to defend the homeland.

May 1, 2003: The Terrorist Threat Integration Center begins operation.

May 12, 2003: Homeland Security Department launches Top Off II, a week long national training exercise for emergency preparedness and response.

June 8, 2003: Acting on a tip from U.S. authorities, Thai police arrest Narong Penanam, who tried to sell cesium-137 to make a "dirty bomb."

June 19, 2003: Lyman Faris, the Ohio truck driver who plotted with Osama Bin Laden to cut the cables on the Brooklyn Bridge, pleads guilty.

June 24, 2003: House passes the first ever Homeland Security Appropriations bill, approving $29.4 billion to bolster homeland security, bringing funding for First Responders to more than $20 billion since 9/11.

July 16, 2003: House passage of Project Bioshield to help prevent and inoculate for bio-terror attack.

August 12, 2003: Arrest in Newark of Hemant Lakhani, London arms dealer who tried to smuggle surface-to-air missiles.

September 2, 2003: Secretary Ridge announces the "One Face at the Border" initiative to unify the border inspection process.

September 23, 2003: Authorities arrest Rusman Gunawan, the brother Of Al Qaeda operative Riduan Isamuddin, in Pakistan and 14 students who were with him were also arrested on charges of suspected terrorism.

October 1, 2003: President Bush signs the first Homeland Security Appropriations bill into law.

October 30, 2003: HR 2886, The Department of Homeland Security Financial Accountability Act is reported favorably out of the Homeland Security Committee

November 20, 2003: HR 3266, The Faster and Smarter Funding for First Responders Act of 2003 passes unanimously in the House -Homeland Security's Subcommittee on Emergency Preparedness and Response.

November 20, 2003: The Homeland Security Department released final rules to allow the customs and border protection directorate to collect information necessary to identify high-risk cargo shipments bound for the United States.

November 26, 2003: Mohammed Hamdi al-Ahdal, a top al Qaeda leader in Yemen, is captured. Al-Ahdal was one of the top 20 al Qaeda members at large, and is suspected of planning the bombing of the USS Cole in 2000.

February 24, 2004: The Department of Homeland Security releases their strategic plan, "Securing Our Homeland."

March 1, 2004: The one-year anniversary of the creation of Department of Homeland Security.

March 11, 2004: Terrorist bombings on commuter trains in Madrid, Spain take hundreds of lives in the deadliest terrorist attack on a European target since Word War II.

March 14, 2004: In Spain, Jose Luis Rodriguez Zapatero of the Socialist Party is elected Prime Minister, ousting the ruling Popular Party. The result, it is said, reflects voter backlash against Prime Minister Jose Aznar's strong support for the action in Iraq.

Stock Market/Economic Impact

Given the immeasurable cost in human suffering, it may seem distasteful to put the 9/11 attacks in the context of money. As security specialists though, we must look at terrorism, or any type of loss and disruption, in terms of the total impact, including economic. 9/11 shut down the New York Stock Exchange for four business days—an unprecedented event. Of the two airlines directly affected by the attacks one had to declare chapter eleven, bankruptcy protection and the other was pressed to cut four billion dollars in operating costs to stay financially solvent. The federal government issued a $15 billion bail-out of the airline industry and almost one year later the industry as a whole was still operating at a loss of almost $3.6 billion. Hospitality and entertainment industries were hurt badly as people shied away from travel. The loss to New York City alone was totaled in the billions in missing tourism and travel revenues, and of course the enormous property, rental and retail loss of the World Trade Center facilities. Factor in healthcare, worker's compensation, insurance, productivity losses, increases in public and private security, and clean up and the total costs related to the 9/11 terrorist attacks are nothing short of astronomical.

The vitality of a national economy is largely driven by the psychological comfort of the general population. When people feel confident and optimistic they will tend to spend more, incur debt and invest. When the public feels insecure and unsure about the future, people are more likely to save up and hold their money close. Many economists estimated that the U.S. economy began a recession in March of 2001. There is a general sense that the unsettling events of 9/11, and subsequent corporate scandals, profoundly exaggerated the depth and length of the recession, exacerbating anxiety from the "dot-com" burst and the natural cooling of the 1990's stock market, prolonging sluggish economic conditions and staving off recovery for a longer than necessary period.

Being the son of a billionaire businessman and himself a financier and millionaire, Osama bin Laden was no stranger to stock market forces and the movement of wealth. The selection of the World Trade Center in Manhattan's financial district as a target suggests that al-Qaeda was deliberately seeking to make a point about the vulnerability of the American economic might. Economic disruption is an important goal of al-Qaeda. One of the purposes of the 9/11 attacks was not solely to cause loss of life and damage, but to negatively impact the financial vitality of a free-market nation like the United States.

The following is an excerpt from an October 2001 report on the economy by the Board of Governors for the United States Federal Reserve.

Retail sales followed much the same pattern throughout the country. In the week following the attack, consumer spending dropped sharply for all items except those that were likely purchased in preparation for possible additional attacks. Sales of groceries, security devices, and bottled water increased; purchases of insurance also rose. One to two weeks later, consumer buying picked up somewhat, although in most Districts it was weaker than in early September. Contacts in the Chicago District note that the weakness is the result of fundamental economic causes prevailing before the attack, higher unemployment, and falling stock prices, rather than the attack itself.

The grounding of aircraft caused some very short-run effects. For example, the transport of fresh vegetables from the West Coast to the East Coast was disrupted somewhat. The supply chain of parts to manufacturers also was interrupted but appeared to recover quickly from dislocations in air transportation, as air cargo was promptly rerouted through ground networks.

All Districts except Boston and Kansas City report sharp declines in the hotel, airline, and tourism industries. In many Districts, demand dropped sharply immediately following the attack but later rebounded partially. Some cancelled conventions have been rescheduled. In Manhattan, Broadway theaters have noted some pickup in attendance after a sharp drop-off in mid-September. However, large layoffs in the airline industry may be the result of previously observed weakness in the industry, which was then amplified by the attack. Manhattan lost roughly 7 percent of its office space in the September 11 attack, but an estimated four percent will be repaired in upcoming months. Despite the damage, however, office availability increased slightly on balance in September.

The attack is likely to have a longer-term effect on manufacturing. Aircraft orders are down sharply, causing layoffs in the aircraft and aircraft parts industries in the Boston, Kansas City, and San Francisco regions. There has been an increase in demand for security products and data storage devices produced in the Cleveland and San Francisco Districts. Boston reports a large rise in insurance demand, while Atlanta, Dallas, and San Francisco report an increase in insurance premiums. The Atlanta and Chicago Districts report a fall in business productivity due to increased security precautions.

Consumer Spending

Retail sales softened in September and early October in all Districts except St. Louis, where sales were flat, and Minneapolis, where sales were considered normal, and Richmond, where sales returned to pre-attack levels. In the New York District, recent sales were well below levels of a year ago. Almost all regions reported that discount chains were doing much better than specialty stores, and luxury items did poorly. The softer sales tempered the retail sector's forecasts for the holiday season. Most Districts report sales expectations that are both more uncertain and lower than they had been in August.

Automobile sales were much weaker during the first weeks of September, but all Districts, except Boston and New York, report a rebound in sales because of zero-percent financing options that are being offered. In most cases, sales were back to normal, except in the San Francisco and Atlanta Districts, where they were weaker than normal. Atlanta and Chicago also mention that sales of trucks were down.

Manufacturing

Industrial activity was generally weak throughout the country in September and early October. The only exceptions were New York, which reports some pickup in activity, and Richmond, which reports steady activity. Most Districts mention that shipments and orders are weaker than the year before, and, indeed, than in early September. The continued weakness in manufacturing has contributed to pessimism about when orders will improve, as many Districts report that they do not expect a turnaround until 2002.

The weakness is broadly based. The industries affected by lower shipments and orders include high-tech industries, such as semiconductors in the Boston, Dallas, and San Francisco regions, as well as the more traditional heavy industries such as steel in the Chicago and Cleveland regions. In spite of robust auto sales, the auto parts industries in the Boston, Cleveland, Dallas, and St. Louis Districts all reported difficult times. The resource-based industries such as lumber reported mill closures in the regions of Atlanta, Dallas, and San Francisco. A few industries are doing well. Cement in the Dallas region, some textiles in the Richmond region, and luxury goods in Cleveland report some gains.

Real Estate and Construction

Construction generally slowed during September and early October, although there were exceptions in some locations and in some types of construction. Commercial construction weakened in the Atlanta, Boston, Cleveland, Kansas City, and San Francisco regions and in the western Kentucky portion of the St. Louis region. Some commercial and industrial projects were put on hold in the Chicago, Dallas, Minneapolis, Richmond, and San Francisco Districts. Office builders were less active than in the past in the Atlanta, Cleveland, and Richmond regions, as well as in the city of St. Louis. Commercial vacancies rose in the Atlanta, Chicago, Kansas City, and San Francisco Districts. New York, in spite of the attack, still experienced a slight up-tick in vacancies. Office building held steady in the Cleveland District.

Residential construction rose only in Philadelphia and some areas of the St. Louis region. It held steady in the Cleveland and Minneapolis Districts and fell in the Atlanta, Boston, Chicago, Dallas, Kansas City, New York, Richmond and San Francisco Districts and some portions of the St. Louis region. In Boston, the decline followed a strong summer, so that on a year-over-year basis, construction activity was still up. In the Richmond and New York regions, the decline was seen in the construction of luxury homes. New York also reports a decline in rents in Manhattan.

Agriculture and Natural Resources

Most of the year's crops have now been harvested. Corn and soybean harvests were good in the Richmond and St. Louis regions and in the southern part of the Cleveland region, but were below normal in the Chicago and Kansas City regions and in the northern part of the Cleveland region. Prices for cattle and hogs are low. Kansas City reports that the winter wheat crop is in the ground ahead of schedule. Atlanta reports a poor cotton harvest. Minneapolis and Dallas report weather-related poor crop yields, but San Francisco notes that West Coast harvests have generally been good.

Decreases in oil and natural gas prices have led to a decline of drilling activity in the Dallas and Kansas City Districts. Decreases in steel production have caused several iron ore mines to close in the Minneapolis District.

Financial Services and Credit

Banks experienced greater mortgage refinancing activity in response to lower interest rates across Districts. New mortgage lending was also reported to have increased in all but four districts: Kansas City and San Francisco, where loan activity generally decreased in most categories, and Boston and Dallas. Atlanta, Cleveland, New York, Philadelphia, and St. Louis report consumer loans were down. Cleveland, Philadelphia, and St. Louis report increases in commercial lending, and Chicago, New York, Richmond, and St. Louis report decreases in these loans.

The Chicago, Cleveland, New York, and San Francisco Districts report that loan delinquencies were up, and credit standards were reportedly higher in the Atlanta, Kansas City, and New York Districts. Non-performing loans were higher in the Philadelphia and St. Louis Districts.

Employment

Many Districts report layoffs in a wide variety of jobs. Large manufacturing layoffs are reported in the Boston, Dallas, Kansas City, Chicago, Philadelphia, San Francisco, and St. Louis regions. In the service sector, hotel, tourism, and airline industries laid off people throughout the country. In addition, the Dallas, Richmond, and Philadelphia Districts saw cutbacks in the retail sector, and New York reports layoffs in the financial services industry. The West Coast's media and advertising industry also experienced large layoffs.

Wages and Prices

Most Districts report little or no change in wages. Manufacturers were reducing salaries in the Boston District, and wages were down in parts of the San Francisco District. Steady wages or no wage pressure are reported in the Chicago, Kansas City, New York, and Richmond regions, as well as among temporary workers in the Minneapolis region. The Atlanta, Cleveland, and Dallas Districts report that wage pressures had subsided or were subdued. Dallas and San Francisco also report an increase in health care costs.

Most Districts report steady or declining consumer prices. Districts reporting steady retail prices included Kansas City and Richmond. San Francisco reports steady prices except for declining prices in apparel. Districts reporting lower retail prices included Atlanta, Boston, Chicago, and Dallas. The prices for manufactured goods also fell in the Chicago, Dallas, and New York regions, while they were steady in the Atlanta, Kansas City, Richmond, and San Francisco regions.

Input prices are reported as decreasing or holding steady, except in Cleveland, where they were mixed. Districts reporting price declines included Boston, Chicago, Dallas, Minneapolis, and New York. Those reporting steady prices were Atlanta, Kansas City, and San Francisco.

The Organization of North American Homeland Security Apparatus

Security is often a simple matter of "extending the perimeter." The large perimeter of defending the North American homeland is protected by a number of civilian, law enforcement and military agencies throughout Canada and the United States.

Figure 4   Members and Regions of North American Aerospace Defense

Courtesy of NORAD/Air Force Public Affairs

Courtesy of NORAD/Air Force Public Affairs

Courtesy of NORAD/Air Force Public Affairs

U.S. Department of Homeland Security[17]

The National Strategy for Homeland Security and the Homeland Security Act of 2002 served to mobilize and organize our nation to secure the homeland from terrorist attacks. This exceedingly complex mission requires a focused effort from our entire society if we are to be successful. To this end, one primary reason for the establishment of the Department of Homeland Security was to provide the unifying core for the vast national network of organizations and institutions involved in efforts to secure our nation. In order to do this better and to provide guidance to the 180,000 DHS men and women who work every day on this

Courtesy of AP/Wide World Photos

important task, the Department developed its own high-level strategic plan. The vision and mission statements, strategic goals and objectives provide the framework guiding the actions that make up the daily operations of the department.

Vision

Preserving our freedoms, protecting America . . . we secure our homeland.

Mission

We will lead the unified national effort to secure America. We will prevent and deter terrorist attacks and protect against and respond to threats and hazards to the nation. We will ensure safe and secure borders, welcome lawful immigrants and visitors, and promote the free-flow of commerce.

Strategic Goals

Awareness—Identify and understand threats, assess vulnerabilities, determine potential impacts and disseminate timely information to our homeland security partners and the American public.

Prevention—Detect, deter and mitigate threats to our homeland.

Protection—Safeguard our people and their freedoms, critical infrastructure, property and the economy of our Nation from acts of terrorism, natural disasters, or other emergencies.

Response—Lead, manage and coordinate the national response to acts of terrorism, natural disasters, or other emergencies.

Recovery—Lead national, state, local and private sector efforts to restore services and rebuild communities after acts of terrorism, natural disasters, or other emergencies.

Service—Serve the public effectively by facilitating lawful trade, travel and immigration.

Organizational Excellence—Value our most important resource, our people. Create a culture that promotes a common identity, innovation, mutual respect, accountability and teamwork to achieve efficiencies, effectiveness, and operational synergies.

U.S. Northern Command (NORCOM)

The Department of Defense established U.S. Northern Command in 2002 to consolidate under a single unified command existing missions that were previously executed by other military organizations.

The command's mission is homeland defense and civil support, specifically:

Conduct operations to deter, prevent, and defeat threats and aggression aimed at the United States, its territories, and interests within the assigned area of responsibility; and

As directed by the President or Secretary of Defense, provide military assistance to civil authorities including consequence management operations.

U.S. Northern Command plans, organizes, and executes homeland defense and civil support missions, but has few permanently assigned forces. The command will be assigned forces whenever necessary to execute missions as ordered by the President.

Approximately 500 civil service employees and uniformed personnel representing all service branches provide this essential unity of command.

North American Air Defense Command (NORAD)

Three regions, two countries, one team responsible for protecting the airspace of two vast countries. North American Aerospace Defense Command's area of responsibility stretches from Clear, Alaska, to the Florida Keys, and from St. John's Newfoundland, to San Diego, Calif. Thousands of U.S. and Canadian military members have worked side-by-side in both countries for more than 40 years to protect North America against an aerospace attack. Aerospace warning and control are the cornerstones of the NORAD mission.

To perform its twin missions of aerospace warning and aerospace control, NORAD consists of three regions: Alaskan NORAD Region (ANR), Canadian NORAD Region (CANR), and the Continental U.S. NORAD Region (CONR).

CONR is further broken into three sectors: Western Air Defense Sector at McChord AFB, Wash.; Northeast Air Defense Sector at Rome, N.Y.; and Southeast Air Defense Sector at Tyndall AFB, Fla., which is also the headquarters for CONR.

CANR's headquarters is in Winnipeg, Manitoba, and the Canadian Air Defence Sector is located in North Bay, Ontario. ANR's headquarters is located at Elmendorf AFB, Alaska, adjacent to Anchorage.

The Department of Public Safety & Emergency Preparedness: Canada

On December 12, 2003, Prime Minister Paul Martin announced restructuring changes to government on Securing Canada's Public Health and Safety. While globalization offers enhanced opportunities for Canada, it also brings new risks, including new threats of disease, international criminal activity and terrorism.

The Government of Canada must play a fundamental role in securing the public health and safety of Canadians, while ensuring that all Canadians continue to enjoy the benefits of an open society. The government will achieve these goals by making the following changes to integrate federal activities under strong leadership, maximize the effectiveness of interagency cooperation, and increase accountability to all Canadians:

1. Creating a new Minister of Public Safety and Emergency Preparedness, to integrate into a single portfolio the core activities of the existing Solicitor General portfolio that secure the safety of Canadians and other activities required to protect against and respond to natural disasters and security emergencies;

2. Integrating the Office of Critical Infrastructure Protection and Emergency Preparedness (currently in the Department of National Defence) into the Public Safety and Emergency Preparedness portfolio to maximize emergency preparedness and responses to natural disaster and security emergencies, as well as improving connections to provincial and territorial emergency preparedness networks, and by adding the National Crime Prevention Centre to actively support crime prevention activities;

3. Increasing National Defence Reserves available for civil preparedness, including capacity to deal with natural disasters and local emergencies;

4. Creating a Canada Border Services Agency to build on the Smart Border Initiative and the important progress that has been made in expediting trade and travel while enhancing security with respect to high risk arrivals, and continue to work in close collaboration with business, labour, immigrant and refugee groups, and other important stakeholders in pursuing these changes;

5. Protecting the interests of immigrants and refugees remains the responsibility of Citizenship and Immigration, which will continue to be present at all major airports and land crossings to issue immigration benefits, to greet new Canadians and to make immigration determinations that will be based on existing criteria. There will be consultations with stakeholders to fully define this presence;

6. Reforming the refugee determination process to create a more predictable and streamlined system, including a reformed appointment process to ensure the quality and effectiveness of the Immigration and Refugee Board;

7. Creating an independent arm's length review mechanism for the RCMP's activities with respect to national security. The mechanism will be designed in a way that respects the important principle of the independence of the police in relation to law enforcement and criminal investigations;

8. Creating a new position of National Security Advisor to the Prime Minister in the Privy Council Office, to be responsible for intelligence and threat assessment integration and interagency cooperation, and to assist the Minister of Public Safety and Emergency Preparedness in the development and overall implementation of an integrated policy for national security and emergencies, to be referred to the appropriate House Standing Committee;

9. Creating a new Canada Public Health Agency, under the Minister of Health, Intergovernmental Affairs, and Minister responsible for Official Languages, following consultations with provincial and territorial governments, to address public health risks and coordinate a national response to health crises, assisted by the Minister of State (Public Health);

10. Establishing a new Cabinet Committee on Security, Public Health, and Emergencies, chaired by the Minister of Public Safety and Emergency Preparedness, to manage national security and intelligence issues and activities and coordinate government-wide responses to all emergencies, including public health, natural disasters and security;

11. Proposing a National Security Standing Committee in the House of Commons whose members would be sworn-in as Privy Councillors so that they could be briefed on national security issues; and

12. Rationalizing responsibility for marine safety and security policy under the Minister of Transport to consolidate responsibility for security in all transportation sectors and creating the Coast Guard as a special operating agency in the Fisheries and Oceans department.

Study: The North Atlantic Treaty Organization (NATO) Article Five: "An Attack Against One is an Attack Against All"—invoked for the first time on September 12, 2001

What is NATO?[18]

The North Atlantic Treaty Organisation (NATO) is an alliance of 26 countries from North America and Europe committed to fulfilling the goals of the North Atlantic Treaty signed on 4 April 1949. In accordance with the Treaty, the fundamental role of NATO is to safeguard the freedom and security of its member countries by political and military means. NATO is playing an increasingly important role in crisis management and peacekeeping.

What is Article 5?[19]

Article Five of the North Atlantic Treaty Organization- Signed in Washington, DC on April 4th, 1949.

"The Parties agree that an armed attack against one or more of them in Europe or North America shall be considered an attack against them all and consequently they agree that, if such an armed attack occurs, each of them, in exercise of the right of individual or collective self-defence recognised by Article 51 of the Charter of the United Nations, will assist the Party or Parties so attacked by taking forthwith, individually and in concert with the other Parties, such action as it deems necessary, including the use of armed force, to *restore and maintain the security of the North Atlantic area.*"

The decision:

On 12 September, NATO decided that, if it is determined that the attack against the United States was directed from abroad, it shall be regarded as an action covered by Article 5 of the Washington Treaty.

This is the first time in the Alliance's history that Article 5 has been invoked.

Article 5 of the Washington Treaty:

The Parties agree that an armed attack against one or more of them in Europe or North America shall be considered an attack against them all and consequently they agree that, if such an armed attack occurs, each of them, in exercise of the right of individual or collective self-defense recognized by Article 51 of the Charter of the United Nations, will assist the Party or Parties so attacked by taking forthwith, individually and in concert with the other Parties, such action as it deems necessary, including the use of armed force, to restore and maintain the security of the North Atlantic area.

Any such armed attack and all measures taken as a result thereof shall immediately be reported to the Security Council. Such measures shall be terminated when the Security Council has taken the measures necessary to restore and maintain international peace and security.

NATO's Strategic Concept recognizes the risks to the Alliance posed by terrorism.

What does Article 5 mean?

Article 5 is at the basis of a fundamental principle of the North Atlantic Treaty Organization. It provides that if a NATO Ally is the victim of an armed attack, each and every other member of the Alliance will consider this act of violence as an armed attack against all members and will take the actions it deems necessary to assist the Ally attacked.

This is the principle of collective defense.

Article 5 and the case of the terrorist attacks against the United States:

The United States has been the object of brutal terrorist attacks. It immediately consulted with the other members of the Alliance. The Alliance determined that the US had been the object of an armed attack. The Alliance therefore agreed that if it was determined that this attack was directed from abroad, it would be regarded as covered by Article 5. NATO Secretary General, Lord Robertson, subsequently informed the Secretary-General of the United Nations of the Alliance's decision.

Article 5 has thus been invoked, but no determination has yet been made whether the attack against the United States was directed from abroad. If such a determination is made, each Ally will then consider what assistance it should provide. In practice, there will be consultations among the Allies. Any collective action by NATO will be decided by the North Atlantic Council. The United States can also carry out independent actions, consistent with its rights and obligations under the UN Charter.

Allies can provide any form of assistance they deem necessary to respond to the situation. This assistance is not necessarily military and depends on the material resources of each country. Each individual member determines how it will contribute and will consult with the other members, bearing in mind that the ultimate aim is to "to restore and maintain the security of the North Atlantic area".

By invoking Article 5, NATO members have shown their solidarity toward the United States and condemned, in the strongest possible way, the terrorist attacks against the United States on 11 September.

If the conditions are met for the application of Article 5, NATO Allies will decide how to assist the United States(many Allies have clearly offered emergency assistance). Each Ally is obliged to assist the United States by taking forward, individually and in concert with other Allies, such action as it deems necessary. This is an individual obligation on each Ally and each Ally is responsible for determining what it deems necessary in these particular circumstances.

No collective action will be taken by NATO until further consultations are held and further decisions are made by the North Atlantic Council.

Reprinted from http://www.nato.int/issues/faq, April 23, 2004, North Atlantic Treaty Organisation.

Discussion Questions:

1) The U.S. Department of Homeland Security has an annual budget of $_____ billion and pulled together _____ different federal agencies with security responsibilities.

2) The _____ Act of 2002 and certain revisions to the _____ Act of 1947 legally established the Department of Homeland Security

3) Which of the following is NOT a critical mission area of the Department of Homeland Security?

   (a) Intelligence and Warning

   (b) Border and Transportation Security

   (c) Protection of Critical Infrastructure and Key Assets

   (d) Traffic Law Enforcement at Border Crossings

4) Al Qaeda, as a defined terrorist organization, has been conducting operations against the United States since at least

   (a) 1896

   (b) 1968

   (c) 1992

   (d) 2001

5) On October 12, 2000 al Qaeda conducted a successful suicide-bombing run against...

   (a) The Bakara Market in Mogadishu, Somalia

   (b) The U.S. Navy Destroyer *U.S.S. Cole*

   (c) The Gold Mohur Hotel in Aden, Yemen

   (d) The parking garage of the World Trade Center in Manhattan

6) Generally terrorists have very little use for or interest in media coverage of their attacks

   True   False

7) Al Qaeda was successful in negatively impacting the U.S. economy with the terrorist attacks of September 11th, 2001.

   True   False

8) The USA PATRIOT Act took a very long time to pass through the U.S. Congress following the terrorist attacks of September 11th, 2001

   True   False

9) The USA PATRIOT Act provided the U.S. Department of Justice with the authority to indefinitely hold "enemy combatants" at Guantanomo Bay, Cuba

   True   False

10) Article 5 of the North Atlantic Treaty Organization's charter states that "attack against one is an attack against _____".

Answers

1) $36.2; 22

2) Homeland Security; National Security

3) D

4) C

5) B

6) False

7) True

8) False

9) False

10) All

Endnotes

[1] "United States of America," *Central Intelligence Agency- The World Fact Book 2003*, 2003

[2] US Nuclear Regulatory Commission

[3] Denny, Charlotte, Paul Brown, and Tim Radford. "The Shackles of Poverty," The Guardian, August 2002.- Posted on www.sierraclub.org/population/consumption- website of The Sierra Club

[4] "DHS Budget in Brief," *U.S. Department of Homeland Security;* Feb. 2004; www.dhs.gov/dhspublic

[5] "DHS Organization," *U.S. Department of Homeland Security;* 2003; www.dhs.gov/dhspublic

[6] *The National Strategy for Homeland Security;* The White House, U.S. Government Press, 2003

[7] Ibid

[8] Ibid

[9] "Department of Homeland Security," *Budget of the United States Government: Fiscal Year 2005*, United States Office of Budget and Management, 2004

[10] The Merriam-Webster Dictionary, Pocket Books, NY, NY

[11] Douglas Jehl, "Ex- Saudi Chief of Intelligence Casts Doubt on Iraq- Qaeda Tie", *The New York Times* Service, November 22, 2001

[12] Kasra Naji, Reuters, "Taliban Wants Bin Laden to Stop Making Anti- U.S. Threats", *Cable News Network*, August 24th, 1998

[*] The IRA has been in a state of relative dormancy since a cease fire accord in July 1997.

[+] Steganography—the hiding of a message in hyper-text transfer protocol image (i.e. a picture on a website) such that it may only be read by browsers who know a specific DOS command to decode the message

[13] Council on Foreign Relations, Terrorism and the Media, *Terrorism Q&A*, 2004

[14] Robyn Pangi, After the Attack: *The Psychological Impact of Terrorism*, Executive Session of Domestic Preparedness, John F. Kennedy School of Government, Harvard University, August 2002

[15] Ibid

[16] www.whitehouse.gov/homeland security

[17] National Strategy for the Protection of Critical Infrastructures and Key Assets

[18] North Atlantic Treaty Organisation Official Homepage, http://www.nato.int/issues/faq, April 23, 2004

[19] Ibid

2 Critical Infrastructures and Key Assets

Overview:

Before you can develop an emergency plan and implement security counter-measures, you must first determine what it is you need to protect and what the threats are to it. The National Strategy for Protection of Critical Infrastructures and Key Assets is this type of large-scale risk assessment. In protecting the homeland, the first consideration for planners was to determine what are the critical systems that must be kept protected and operational in order to prevent a catastrophic shut down of society.

These most important considerations are regarded as "critical infrastructure and key assets"—the facilities and systems upon which our day-to-day health, safety, well- being and comfort directly depend.

Chapter Objectives:

- *Define critical infrastructure and key assets*
- *Explain the major points of the National Strategy for Protection of Critical Infrastructures and Key Assets*
- *State the strategic objectives of National Strategy for Protection of Critical Infrastructures and Key Assets*

What are "Critical Infrastructure and Key Assets?"

The critical infrastructure and key assets of a nation are those things, which provide for the basic maintenance and continuity of public health, safety and standard of living. These are the things that drive, direct and operate the basic necessities of our day-to-day lifestyle as well as our ability to function effectively. Critical infrastructure and key assets include:

- Federal, state, municipal government facilities
- Defense installations
- Public safety mechanisms (police, fire, emergency medical services)
- Hospitals, healthcare, trauma centers, emergency shelters
- Banks, financial institutions and financial transfer systems
- Telecommunications systems
- Computer networks and information technology systems
- Highways, roads and thoroughfares
- Airports
- Seaports
- Public transit
- Electrical power plants and grids
- Coal, oil, and other energy
- Nuclear power plants and facilities
- Mainframes and information hubs
- Water treatment, aqueducts and reservoirs
- Agriculture and food distribution
- Sewage and sewage treatment
- Corporate and private enterprise

Currently in the United States eighty-five percent of all critical infrastructure is managed by private enterprise. These private management concerns are also responsible for providing security to the facilities. One of the great challenges of providing for the security of critical infrastructure is coordinating a cohesive strategy and developing consistent standards for these vast and disparate resources. The public and private sectors must work together to develop standards for security in much

**Figure 6 Government buildings, power plants,
shipping—all examples of "critical infrastructure"**

the same way that years ago the federal as well as state and local governments began partnering with industry to develop cohesive occupational health and safety guidelines.

An important first step in identifying critical infrastructures and developing standardized security requirements in the U.S. Federal Government's National Strategy for Protection of Critical Infrastructures and Key Assets.

The National Strategy for Protection of Critical Infrastructures and Key Assets

The National Strategy for Physical Protection of Critical Infrastructures and Key Assets serves as a critical bridge between the National Strategy for Homeland Security and a national protection plan to be developed by the Department of Homeland Security. The strategic objectives that underpin the national infrastructure and key asset protection effort include:

Courtesy of PhotoDisc/Getty Images, Inc.

• Identifying and assuring the protection of those infrastructure and assets we deem most critical;

• Providing timely warning and assuring the protection of those infrastructures and assets that face a specific, imminent threat; and

• Assuring the protection of other infrastructures and assets that may become targets over time by pursuing specific initiatives and enabling a collaborative environment between the public and private sector.

Executive Order on Critical Infrastructure Protection

By the authority vested in me as President by the Constitution and the laws of the United States of America, and in order to ensure protection of information systems for critical infrastructure, including emergency preparedness communications, and the physical assets that support such systems, in the information age, it is hereby ordered as follows:

Section 1. Policy

(a) The information technology revolution has changed the way business is transacted, government operates, and national defense is conducted. Those three functions now depend on an interdependent network of critical information infrastructures. The protection program authorized by this order shall consist of continuous efforts to secure information systems for critical infrastructure, including emergency preparedness communications, and the physical assets that support such systems. Protection of these systems is essential to the telecommunications, energy, financial services, manufacturing, water, transportation, health care, and emergency services sectors.

(b) It is the policy of the United States to protect against disruption of the operation of information systems for critical infrastructure and thereby help to protect the people, economy, essential human and government services, and national security of the United States, and to ensure that any disruptions that occur are infrequent, of minimal duration, and manageable, and cause the least damage possible. The implementation of this policy shall include a voluntary public-private partnership, involving corporate and nongovernmental organizations.

Sec. 2. Scope.
To achieve this policy, there shall be a senior executive branch board to coordinate and have cognizance of Federal efforts and programs that relate to protection of information systems and involve:

(a) cooperation with and protection of private sector critical infrastructure, State and local governments, critical infrastructure, and supporting programs in corporate and academic organizations;

(b) protection of Federal departments, and agencies, critical infrastructure; and

(c) related national security programs.

Sec. 3. Establishment.
I hereby establish the "President's Critical Infrastructure Protection Board" (the "Board").

Sec. 4. Continuing Authorities.
This order does not alter the existing authorities or roles of United States Government departments and agencies. Authorities set forth in 44 U.S.C. Chapter 35, and other applicable law, provide senior officials with responsibility for the security of Federal Government information systems.

(a) Executive Branch Information Systems Security. The Director of the Office of Management and Budget (OMB) has the responsibility to develop and oversee the implementation of government-wide policies, principles, standards, and guidelines for the security of information systems that support the executive branch departments and agencies, except those noted in section 4

(b) of this order. The Director of OMB shall advise the President and the appropriate department or agency head when there is a critical deficiency in the security practices within the purview of this section in an executive branch department or agency. The Board shall assist and support the Director of OMB in this function and shall be reasonably cognizant of programs related to security of department and agency information systems.

(c) National Security Information Systems. The Secretary of Defense and the Director of Central Intelligence (DCI) shall have responsibility to oversee, develop, and ensure implementation of policies, principles, standards, and guidelines for the security of information systems that support the operations under their respective control. In consultation with the Assistant to the President for National Security Affairs and the affected departments and agencies, the Secretary of Defense and the DCI shall develop policies, principles, standards, and guidelines for the security of national security information systems that support the operations of other executive branch departments and agencies with national security information.

(d) Policies, principles, standards, and guidelines developed under this subsection may require more stringent protection than those developed in accordance with subsection 4(a) of this order.

(e) The Assistant to the President for National Security Affairs shall advise the President and the appropriate department or agency head when there is a critical deficiency in the security practices of a department or agency within the purview of this section. The Board, or one of its standing or ad hoc committees, shall be reasonably cognizant of programs to provide security and continuity to national security information systems.

(f) Additional Responsibilities: The Heads of Executive Branch Departments and Agencies. The heads of executive branch departments and agencies are responsible and accountable for providing and maintaining adequate levels of security for information systems, including emergency preparedness communications systems, for programs under their control. Heads of such departments and agencies shall ensure the development and, within available appropriations, funding of programs that adequately address these mission areas. Cost-effective security shall be built into and made an integral part of government information systems, especially those critical systems that support the national security and other essential government programs. Additionally, security should enable, and not unnecessarily impede, department and agency business operations.

Sec. 5. Board Responsibilities.

Consistent with the responsibilities noted in section 4 of this order, the Board shall recommend policies and coordinate programs for protecting information systems for critical infrastructure, including emergency preparedness communications, and the physical assets that support such systems. Among its activities to implement these responsibilities, the Board shall:

(a) Outreach to the Private Sector and State and Local Governments. In consultation with affected executive branch departments and agencies, coordinate outreach to and consultation with the private sector, including corporations that own, operate, develop, and equip information, telecommunications, transportation, energy, water, health care, and financial services, on protection of information systems for critical infrastructure, including emergency preparedness communications, and the physical assets that support such systems; and coordinate outreach to State and local governments, as well as communities and representatives from academia and other relevant elements of society.

   (i) When requested to do so, assist in the development of voluntary standards and best practices in a manner consistent with 15 U.S.C. Chapter 7;

   (ii) Consult with potentially affected communities, including the legal, auditing, financial, and insurance communities, to the extent permitted by law, to determine areas of mutual concern; and

   (iii) Coordinate the activities of senior liaison officers appointed by the Attorney General, the Secretaries of Energy, Commerce, Transportation, the Treasury, and Health and Human Services, and the Director of the Federal Emergency Management Agency for outreach on critical infrastructure protection issues with private sector organizations within the areas of concern to these departments and agencies. In these and other related functions, the Board shall work in coordination with the Critical Infrastructure Assurance Office (CIAO) and the National Institute of Standards and Technology of the Department of Commerce, the National Infrastructure Protection Center (NIPC), and the National Communications System (NCS).

(b) Information Sharing. Work with industry, State and local governments, and nongovernmental organizations to ensure that systems are created and well managed to share threat warning, analysis, and recovery information among government network operation centers, information sharing and analysis centers established on a voluntary basis by industry, and other related operations centers. In this and other related functions, the Board shall work in coordination with the NCS, the Federal Computer Incident Response Center, the NIPC, and other departments and agencies, as appropriate.

(c) Incident Coordination and Crisis Response. Coordinate programs and policies for responding to information systems security incidents that threaten information systems for critical infrastructure, including emergency preparedness communications, and the physical assets that support such systems. In this function, the Department of Justice, through the NIPC and the Manager of the NCS and other departments and agencies, as appropriate, shall work in coordination with the Board.

(d) Recruitment, Retention, and Training Executive Branch Security Professionals. In consultation with executive branch departments and agencies, coordinate programs to ensure that government employees with responsibilities for protecting information systems for critical infrastructure, including emergency preparedness communications, and the physical assets that support such systems, are adequately trained and evaluated. In this function, the Office of Personnel Management shall work in coordination with the Board, as appropriate.

(e) Research and Development. Coordinate with the Director of the Office of Science and Technology Policy (OSTP) on a program of Federal Government research and development for protection of information systems for critical infrastructure, including emergency preparedness communications, and the physical assets that support such systems, and ensure coordination of government activities in this field with corporations, universities, Federally funded research centers, and national laboratories. In this function, the Board shall work in coordination with the National Science Foundation, the Defense Advanced Research Projects Agency, and with other departments and agencies, as appropriate.

(f) Law Enforcement Coordination with National Security Components. Promote programs against cyber crime and assist Federal law enforcement agencies in gaining necessary cooperation from executive branch departments and agencies. Support Federal law enforcement agencies, investigation of illegal activities involving information systems for critical infrastructure, including emergency preparedness communications, and the physical assets that support such systems, and support coordination by these agencies with other departments and agencies with responsibilities to defend the Nation's security. In this function, the Board shall work in coordination with the Department of Justice, through the NIPC, and the Department of the Treasury, through the Secret Service, and with other departments and agencies, as appropriate.

(g) International Information Infrastructure Protection. Support the Department of State's coordination of United States Government programs for international cooperation covering international information infrastructure protection issues.

(h) Legislation. In accordance with OMB circular A-19, advise departments and agencies, the Director of OMB, and the Assistant to the President for Legislative Affairs on legislation relating to protection of information systems for critical infrastructure, including emergency preparedness communications, and the physical assets that support such systems.

(i) Coordination with Office of Homeland Security. Carry out those functions relating to protection of and recovery from attacks against information systems for critical infrastructure, including emergency preparedness communications, that were assigned to the Office of Homeland Security by Executive Order 13228 of October 8, 2001. The Assistant to the President for Homeland Security, in coordination with the Assistant to the President for National Security Affairs, shall be responsible for defining the responsibilities of the Board in coordinating efforts to protect physical assets that support information systems.

Sec. 6. Membership.

(a) Members of the Board shall be drawn from the executive branch departments, agencies, and offices listed below; in addition, concerned Federal departments and agencies may participate in the activities of appropriate committees of the Board. The Board shall be led by a Chair and Vice Chair, designated by the President. Its other members shall be the following senior officials or their designees:

   (i) Secretary of State;

   (ii) Secretary of the Treasury;

   (iii) Secretary of Defense;

   (iv) Attorney General;

   (v) Secretary of Commerce;

   (vi) Secretary of Health and Human Services;

   (vii) Secretary of Transportation;

   (viii) Secretary of Energy;

   (ix) Director of Central Intelligence;

   (x) Chairman of the Joint Chiefs of Staff;

   (xi) Director of the Federal Emergency Management Agency;

   (xii) Administrator of General Services;

   (xiii) Director of the Office of Management and Budget;

   (xiv) Director of the Office of Science and Technology Policy;

   (xv) Chief of Staff to the Vice President;

   (xvi) Director of the National Economic Council;

(xvii) Assistant to the President for National Security Affairs;

(xviii) Assistant to the President for Homeland Security;

(xix) Chief of Staff to the President; and

(xx) Such other executive branch officials as the President may designate.

Members of the Board and their designees shall be full-time or permanent part-time officers or employees of the Federal Government.

(b) In addition, the following officials shall serve as members of the Board and shall form the Board's Coordination Committee:

(i) Director, Critical Infrastructure Assurance Office, Department of Commerce;

(ii) Manager, National Communications System;

(iii) Vice Chair, Chief Information Officers' (CIO) Council;

(iv) Information Assurance Director, National Security Agency;

(v) Deputy Director of Central Intelligence for Community Management; and

(vi) Director, National Infrastructure Protection Center, Federal Bureau of Investigation, Department of Justice.

(c) The Chairman of the Federal Communications Commission may appoint a representative to the Board.

Sec. 7. Chair.

(a) The Chair also shall be the Special Advisor to the President for Cyberspace Security. Executive branch departments and agencies shall make all reasonable efforts to keep the Chair fully informed in a timely manner, and to the greatest extent permitted by law, of all programs and issues within the purview of the Board. The Chair, in consultation with the Board, shall call and preside at meetings of the Board and set the agenda for the Board. The Chair, in consultation with the Board, may propose policies and programs to appropriate officials to ensure the protection of the Nation's information systems for critical infrastructure, including emergency preparedness communications, and the physical assets that support such systems. To ensure full coordination between the responsibilities of the National Security Council (NSC) and the Office of Homeland Security, the Chair shall report to both the Assistant to the President for National Security Affairs and to the Assistant to the President for Homeland Security. The Chair shall coordinate with the Assistant to the President for Economic Policy on issues relating to private sector systems and economic effects and with the Director of OMB on issues relating to budgets and the security of computer networks addressed in subsection 4(a) of this order.

(b) The Chair shall be assisted by an appropriately sized staff within the White House Office. In addition, heads of executive branch departments and agencies are authorized, to the extent permitted by law, to detail or assign personnel of such departments and agencies to the Board's staff upon request of the Chair, subject to the approval of the Chief of Staff to the President. Members of the Board's staff with responsibilities relating to national security information systems, communications, and information warfare may, with respect to those responsibilities, also work at the direction of the Assistant to the President for National Security Affairs.

Sec. 8. Standing Committees.

(a) The Board may establish standing and ad hoc committees as appropriate. Representation on standing committees shall not be limited to those departments and agencies on the Board, but may include representatives of other concerned executive branch departments and agencies.

(b) Chairs of standing and ad hoc committees shall report fully and regularly on the activities of the committees to the Board, which shall ensure that the committees are well coordinated with each other.

(c) There are established the following standing committees:

   (i) Private Sector and State and Local Government Outreach, chaired by the designee of the Secretary of Commerce, to work in coordination with the designee of the Chairman of the National Economic Council.

   (ii) Executive Branch Information Systems Security, chaired by the designee of the Director of OMB. The committee shall assist OMB in fulfilling its responsibilities under 44 U.S.C. Chapter 35 and other applicable law.

   (iii) National Security Systems. The National Security Telecommunications and Information Systems Security Committee, as established by and consistent with NSD-42 and chaired by the Department of Defense, shall serve as a Board standing committee, and be redesignated the Committee on National Security Systems.

   (iv) Incident Response Coordination, co-chaired by the designees of the Attorney General and the Secretary of Defense.

   (v) Research and Development, chaired by a designee of the Director of OSTP.

(vi) National Security and Emergency Preparedness Communications. The NCS Committee of Principals is renamed the Board's Committee for National Security and Emergency Preparedness Communications. The reporting functions established above for standing committees are in addition to the functions set forth in Executive Order 12472 of April 3, 1984, and do not alter any function or role set forth therein.

(vii) Physical Security, co-chaired by the designees of the Secretary of Defense and the Attorney General, to coordinate programs to ensure the physical security of information systems for critical infrastructure, including emergency preparedness communications, and the physical assets that support such systems. The standing committee shall coordinate its work with the Office of Homeland Security and shall work closely with the Physical Security Working Group of the Records Access and Information Security Policy Coordinating Committee to ensure coordination of efforts.

(viii) Infrastructure Interdependencies, co-chaired by the designees of the Secretaries of Transportation and Energy, to coordinate programs to assess the unique risks, threats, and vulnerabilities associated with the interdependency of information systems for critical infrastructures, including the development of effective models, simulations, and other analytic tools and cost-effective technologies in this area.

(ix) International Affairs, chaired by a designee of the Secretary of State, to support Department of State coordination of United States

Government programs for international cooperation covering international information infrastructure issues.

(x) Financial and Banking Information Infrastructure, chaired by a designee of the Secretary of the Treasury and including representatives of the banking and financial institution regulatory agencies.

(xi) Other Committees. Such other standing committees as may be established by the Board.

(d) Subcommittees. The chair of each standing committee may form necessary subcommittees with organizational representation as determined by the Chair.

(e) Streamlining. The Board shall develop procedures that specify the manner in which it or a subordinate committee will perform the responsibilities previously assigned to the Policy Coordinating Committee. The Board, in coordination with the Director of OSTP, shall review the functions of the Joint Telecommunications Resources Board, established under Executive Order 12472, and make recommendations about its future role.

Sec. 9. Planning and Budget

(a) The Board, on a periodic basis, shall propose a National Plan or plans for subjects within its purview. The Board, in coordination with the Office of Homeland Security, also shall make recommendations to OMB on those portions of executive branch department and agency budgets that fall within the Board's purview, after review of relevant program requirements and resources.

(b) The Office of Administration within the Executive Office of the President shall provide the Board with such personnel, funding, and administrative support, to the extent permitted by law and subject to the availability of appropriations, as directed by the Chief of Staff to carry out the provisions of this order. Only those funds that are available for the Office of Homeland Security, established by Executive Order 13228, shall be available for such purposes. -To the extent permitted by law and as appropriate, agencies represented on the Board also may provide administrative support for the Board. The National Security Agency shall ensure that the Board's information and communications systems are appropriately secured.

(c) The Board may annually request the National Science Foundation, Department of Energy, Department of Transportation, Environmental Protection Agency, Department of Commerce, Department of Defense, and the Intelligence Community, as that term is defined in Executive Order 12333 of December 4, 1981, to include in their budget requests to OMB funding for demonstration projects and research to support the Board's activities.

Sec. 10. Presidential Advisory Panels.

The Chair shall work closely with panels of senior experts from outside of the government that advise the President, in particular: the President's National Security Telecommunications Advisory Committee (NSTAC) created by Executive Order 12382 of September 13, 1982, as amended, and the National Infrastructure Advisory Council (NIAC or Council) created by this Executive Order. The Chair and Vice Chair of these two panels also may meet with the

Courtesy of PhotoDisc/Getty Images, Inc.

Board, as appropriate and to the extent permitted by law, to provide a private sector perspective.

(a) NSTAC. The NSTAC provides the President advice on the security and continuity of communications systems essential for national security and emergency preparedness.

(b) NIAC. There is hereby established the National Infrastructure Advisory Council, which shall provide the President advice on the security of information systems for critical infrastructure supporting other sectors of the economy: banking and finance, transportation, energy, manufacturing, and emergency government services. The NIAC shall be composed of not more than 30 members appointed by the President. The members of the NIAC shall be selected from the private sector, academia, and State and local government. Members of the NIAC shall have expertise relevant to the functions of the NIAC and generally shall be selected from industry Chief Executive Officers (and equivalently ranked leaders in other organizations) with responsibilities for the security of information infrastructure supporting the critical sectors of the economy, including banking and finance, transportation, energy, communications, and emergency government services. Members shall not be full-time officials or employees of the executive branch of the Federal Government.

(i) The President shall designate a Chair and Vice Chair from among the members of the NIAC.

(ii) The Chair of the Board established by this order will serve as the Executive Director of the NIAC.

(c) NIAC Functions. The NIAC will meet periodically to:

(i) enhance the partnership of the public and private sectors in protecting information systems for critical infrastructures and provide reports on this issue to the President, as appropriate;

(ii) propose and develop ways to encourage private industry to perform periodic risk assessments of critical information and telecommunications systems;

(iii) monitor the development of private sector Information Sharing and Analysis Centers (ISACs) and provide recommendations to the Board on how these organizations can best foster improved cooperation among the ISACs, the NIPC, and other Federal Government entities;

(iv) report to the President through the Board, which shall ensure appropriate coordination with the Assistant to the President for Economic Policy under the terms of this order; and

    (v) advise lead agencies with critical infrastructure responsibilities, sector coordinators, the NIPC, the ISACs, and the Board.

(d) Administration of the NIAC.

    (i) The NIAC may hold hearings, conduct inquiries, and establish subcommittees, as appropriate.

    (ii) Upon the request of the Chair, and to the extent permitted by law, the heads of the executive branch departments and agencies shall provide the Council with information and advice relating to its functions.

    (iii) Senior Federal Government officials may participate in the meetings of the NIAC, as appropriate.

    (iv) Members shall serve without compensation for their work on the Council. However, members may be allowed travel expenses, including per diem in lieu of subsistence, as authorized by law for persons serving intermittently in Federal Government service (5 U.S.C. 5701-5707).

    (v) To the extent permitted by law, and subject to the availability of appropriations, the Department of Commerce, through the CIAO, shall provide the NIAC with administrative services, staff, and other support services and such funds as may be necessary for the performance of the NIAC's functions.

(e) General Provisions.

    (i) Insofar as the Federal Advisory Committee Act, as amended (5 U.S.C. App.), may apply to the NIAC, the functions of the President under that Act, except that of reporting to the Congress, shall be performed by the Department of Commerce in accordance with the guidelines and procedures established by the Administrator of General Services.

    (ii) The Council shall terminate 2 years from the date of this order, unless extended by the President prior to that date.

    (iii) Executive Order 13130 of July 14, 1999, is hereby revoked.

Sec. 11. National Communications System.

Changes in technology are causing the convergence of much of telephony, data relay, and internet communications networks into an interconnected network of networks. The NCS and its National Coordinating Center shall support use of telephony, converged information, voice networks, and next generation networks for emergency preparedness and national security communications functions assigned to them in Executive Order 12472. All authorities and assignments of responsibilities to departments and agencies in that order, including the role of the Manager of NCS, remain unchanged except as explicitly modified by this order.

Sec. 12. Counter-intelligence.

The Board shall coordinate its activities with those of the Office of the Counter-intelligence Executive to address the threat to programs within the Board's purview from hostile foreign intelligence services.

Sec. 13. Classification Authority.

I hereby delegate to the Chair the authority to classify information originally as Top Secret, in accordance with Executive Order 12958 of April 17, 1995, as amended, or any successor Executive Order.

Sec. 14. General Provisions.

    (a) Nothing in this order shall supersede any requirement made by or under law.

    (b) This order does not create any right or benefit, substantive or procedural, enforceable at law or equity, against the United States, its departments, agencies or other entities, its officers or employees, or any other person.

GEORGE W. BUSH
THE WHITE HOUSE,
October 16, 2001.

Critical infrastructure tends to have a dual implication. Just as important as the protection of physical assets, there is an equal emphasis on developing strategies, technologies and processes to protect the information infrastructure as well.

The Department of Homeland Security is concurrently developing plans and strategies to better improve cyber-security as well as physical infrastructure.

U.S. Department of Homeland Security Improves America's Cyber Security Preparedness—Unveils National Cyber Alert System

For Immediate Release
Office of the Press Secretary
January 28, 2004

WASHINGTON, D.C.—The National Cyber Security Division (NCSD) of the Department of Homeland Security (DHS) today unveiled the National Cyber Alert System, an operational system delivering to Americans timely and actionable information to better secure their computer systems.

As part of this program, Homeland Security is making available a series of information products targeted for home users and technical experts in businesses and government agencies. These e-mail products will provide timely information on computer security vulnerabilities, potential impact, and action required to mitigate threats, as well as PC security "best practices" and "how to" guidance.

"The President's National Strategy to Secure Cyberspace provides a framework for the public and private sectors to work together to secure cyberspace, "said Frank Libutti, Under Secretary of Homeland Security for Information Analysis and Infrastructure Protection. " The National Cyber

---

Security Division's mission is to serve as a focal point for implementing the National Strategy and protecting the American People."

"The development and initial operating capability of the National Cyber Alert System elevates awareness and helps improve America's IT security posture," said Amit Yoran, director of the National Cyber Security Division. "We are focused on making the threats and recommended actions easier for all computer users to understand, prioritize, and act upon. We recognize the importance and urgency of our mission and are taking action."

Homeland Security National Cyber Alert System

This new National Cyber Alert System is America's first coordinated national cyber security system for identifying, analyzing, and prioritizing emerging vulnerabilities and threats. Managed by the United States Computer Emergency Readiness Team (US-CERT), a partnership between NCSD and the private sector, the National Cyber Alert System provides the first infrastructure for relaying graded computer security update and warning information to all users.

The system evolves previous framework models such as CERT/CC Advisories and other similar efforts in the private sector. It provides actionable information to empower all citizens (from computer security professionals to home computer users with basic skills) to better secure their portion of cyberspace. The National Cyber Alert System provides credible and timely information on cyber security issues and allows DHS to provide both technical and easy to understand information on a timely basis.

The new National Cyber Alert System security suite of products includes:

- Cyber Security Tips: Targeted at non-technical home and corporate computer users, the bi-weekly Tips provide information on best computer security practices and "how-to" information. How to Access: Sign up at www.us-cert.gov.

- Cyber Security Bulletins: Targeted at technical audiences, Bulletins provide bi-weekly summaries of security issues, new vulnerabilities, potential impact, patches and work-arounds, as well as actions required to mitigate risk. How to Access: Sign up at www.us-cert.gov.

- Cyber Security Alerts: Available in two forms—regular for non-technical users and advanced for technical users—Cyber Security Alerts provide real-time information about security issues, vulnerabilities, and exploits currently occurring. Alerts encourage all users to take rapid action. How to Access: Sign up at www.us-cert.gov.

All information products are available on a free subscription basis and are delivered via push e-mail. Home users can also access Cyber Security Tips and Cyber Security Alerts from US-CERT affiliates including StaySafe Online (www.staysafeonline.info).

About the National Cyber Security Division

The National Cyber Security Division (NCSD) is part of Information Analysis and Infrastructure Protection in the Department of Homeland Security. NCSD is charged with coordinating the implementation of the National Strategy to Secure Cyberspace and serves as the single National point of contact for the public and private sector regarding cyber security issues. NCSD is also charged with identifying, analyzing, and reducing cyber threats and vulnerabilities; disseminating threat warning information; coordinating incident response; and providing technical assistance in continuity of operations and recovery planning. NCSD's US-CERT serves as a focal point—bridging public and private sector institutions—to advance computer security preparedness and response.

3 First Responders

Overview:

At the start of this text we discussed the importance for prevention. The importance of the security specialists' mission to focus on prevention must remain firmly fixed in his or her mind. Homeland security specialists must never let up on their dedication to preventing catastrophic losses before they escalate into a situation requiring a large coordinated response.

That being said, there will be times when knowing how to respond will be absolutely necessary. It is unrealistic to think that every contingency can be avoided. Thus a large part of your education and development must be preparing yourself as a first responder.

This chapter will begin the discussion by defining who are first responders, what they do and how they work to contain and control emergency situations when such critical events arise.

Chapter Objectives:

- *Define which professional and volunteer occupations are considered to be "first responders"*
- *Explain the first responders' responsibilities in an emergency*
- *Explain the reasons why mutual aid agreements are both beneficial and necessary*
- *Explain the significance of Title 29 of the Code of Federal Regulations (CFR) part 1910 "Right to Know" and "Hazard Identification"*
- *State the importance of Material Safety Data Sheets (MSDS) to first responders*
- *State the principles of scene safety*

"First Responder" defined

Just as the name implies, a first responder is a professional or trained volunteer who is responsible for moving rapidly and immediately to the scene of an emergency. The first responder's responsibilities vary based on position or professional specialty, but first responders, as a whole, generally perform the following key functions at an emergency scene:

Courtesy of Corbis Images.

- Assessing initial scene
- Establishing response priorities
- Evacuating persons still in harm's way
- Establishing an element of security and control
- Containing and eliminating remaining threats
- Containing and mitigating further loss and destruction
- Treating and transporting the injured

First responders generally include the following professionals[3]:

Firefighters

Every year, fires and other emergencies take thousands of lives and destroy property worth billions of dollars. Firefighters help protect the public against these dangers by rapidly responding to a variety of emergencies. They are frequently the first emergency personnel at the scene of a traffic accident or medical emergency and may be called upon to put out a fire, treat injuries, or perform other vital functions.

During duty hours, firefighters must be prepared to respond immediately to a fire or any other emergency that arises. Because fighting fires is dangerous and complex, it requires organization and teamwork. At every emergency scene, firefighters perform specific duties assigned by a superior officer. At fires, they connect hose lines to hydrants, operate a pump to send water to high pressure hoses, and position ladders to enable them to deliver water to the fire. They also rescue

Courtesy of Dorling Kindersley.

victims and provide emergency medical attention as needed, ventilate smoke-filled areas, and attempt to salvage the contents of buildings. Their duties may change several times while the company is in action. Sometimes they remain at the site of a disaster for days at a time, rescuing trapped survivors and assisting with medical treatment.

Firefighters have assumed a range of responsibilities, including emergency medical services. In fact, most calls to which firefighters respond involve medical emergencies, and about half of all fire departments provide ambulance service for victims. Firefighters receive training in emergency medical procedures, and many fire departments require them to be certified as emergency medical technicians.

Firefighters work in a variety of settings, including urban and suburban areas, airports, chemical plants, other industrial sites, and rural areas like grasslands and forests. In addition, some firefighters work in hazardous materials units that are trained for the control, prevention, and cleanup of oil spills and other hazardous materials incidents.

Workers in urban and suburban areas, airports, and industrial sites typically use conventional firefighting equipment and tactics, while forest fires and major hazardous materials spills call for different methods.

In national forests and parks, *forest fire inspectors and prevention specialists* spot fires from watchtowers and report their findings to headquarters by telephone or radio. Forest rangers patrol to ensure travelers and campers comply with fire regulations. When fires break out, crews of firefighters are brought in to suppress the blaze using heavy equipment, handtools, and water hoses. Forest firefighting, like urban firefighting, can be rigorous work. One of the most effective means of battling the blaze is by creating fire lines through cutting down trees and digging out grass and all other combustible vegetation, creating bare land in the path of the fire that deprives it of fuel. Elite firefighters, called smoke jumpers, parachute from airplanes to reach otherwise inaccessible areas.

This can be extremely hazardous because the crews have no way to escape if the wind shifts and causes the fire to burn toward them.

Between alarms, firefighters clean and maintain equipment, conduct practice drills and fire inspections, and participate in physical fitness activities. They also prepare written reports on fire incidents and review fire science literature to keep abreast of technological developments and changing administrative practices and policies.

Most fire departments have a fire prevention division, usually headed by a fire marshal and staffed by *fire inspectors*. Workers in this division conduct inspections of structures to prevent fires and ensure fire code compliance. These firefighters also work with developers and planners to check and approve plans for new buildings. Fire prevention personnel often speak on these subjects in schools and before public assemblies and civic organizations.

Some firefighters become *fire investigators*, who determine the origin and causes of fires. They collect evidence, interview witnesses, and prepare reports on fires in cases where the cause may be arson or criminal negligence. They often are called upon to testify in court.

Firefighters spend much of their time at fire stations, which usually have features common to a residential facility like a dormitory. When an alarm sounds, firefighters respond rapidly, regardless of the weather or hour. Firefighting involves risk of death or injury from sudden cave-ins of floors, toppling walls, traffic accidents when responding to calls, and exposure to flames and smoke. Firefighters may also come in contact with poisonous, flammable, or explosive gases and chemicals, as well as radioactive or other hazardous materials that may have immediate or long-term effects on their health. For these reasons, they must wear protective gear that can be very heavy and hot.

Work hours of firefighters are longer and vary more widely than hours of most other workers. Many work more than 50 hours a week, and sometimes they may work even longer. In some agencies, they are on duty for 24 hours, then off for 48 hours, and receive an extra day off at intervals. In others, they work a day shift of 10 hours for 3 or 4 days, a night shift of 14 hours for 3 or 4 nights, have 3 or 4 days off, and then repeat the cycle. In addition, firefighters often work extra hours at fires and other emergencies and are regularly assigned to work on holidays. Fire lieutenants and fire captains often work the same hours as the firefighters they supervise. Duty hours include time when firefighters study, train, and perform fire prevention duties.

Police Officers

People depend on police officers and detectives to protect their lives and property. Law enforcement officers, some of whom are State or Federal special agents or inspectors, perform these duties in a variety of ways, depending on the size and type of their organization. In most jurisdictions, they are expected to exercise authority when necessary, whether on or off duty.

Courtesy of Corbis Images.

Uniformed police officers who work in municipal police departments of various sizes, small communities, and rural areas have general law enforcement duties including maintaining regular patrols and responding to calls for service. They may direct traffic at the scene of a fire, investigate a burglary, or give first aid to an accident victim. In large police departments, officers usually are assigned to a specific type of duty. Many urban police agencies are becoming more involved in community policing—a practice in which an officer builds relationships with the citizens of local neighborhoods and mobilizes the public to help fight crime.

Police agencies are usually organized into geographic districts, with uniformed officers assigned to patrol a specific area, such as part of the business district or outlying residential neighborhoods. Officers may work alone, but in large agencies they often patrol with a partner. While on patrol, officers attempt to become thoroughly familiar with their patrol area and remain alert for anything unusual. Suspicious circumstances and hazards to public safety are investigated or noted, and officers are dispatched to individual calls for assistance within their district. During their shift, they may identify, pursue, and arrest suspected criminals, resolve problems within the community, and enforce traffic laws.

Public college and university police forces, public school district police, and agencies serving transportation systems and facilities are examples of special police agencies. These agencies have special geographic jurisdictions or enforcement responsibilities in the United States. Most sworn personnel in special agencies are uniformed officers, a smaller number are investigators.

Some police officers specialize in such diverse fields as chemical and microscopic analysis, training and firearms instruction, or handwriting and fingerprint identification. Others work with special units such as horseback, bicycle, motorcycle or harbor patrol, canine corps, or special weapons and tactics (SWAT) or emergency response teams. A few local and special law enforcement officers primarily perform jail-related duties or work in courts. Regardless of job duties or location, police officers and detectives at all levels must write reports and maintain meticulous records that will be needed if they testify in court.

Sheriffs and deputy sheriffs enforce the law on the county level. Sheriffs are usually elected to their posts and perform duties similar to those of a local or county police chief. Sheriffs' departments tend to be relatively small, most having fewer than 25 sworn officers. A deputy sheriff in a large agency will have law enforcement duties similar to those of officers in urban police departments. Police and sheriffs' deputies who provide security in city and county courts are sometimes called bailiffs.

State police officers (sometimes called State troopers or highway patrol officers) arrest criminals Statewide and patrol highways to enforce motor vehicle laws and regulations. Uniformed officers are best known for issuing traffic citations to motorists who violate the law. At the scene of accidents, they may direct traffic, give first aid, and call for emergency equipment. They also write reports used to determine the cause of the accident. State police officers are frequently called upon to render assistance to other law enforcement agencies, especially those in rural areas or small towns.

State law enforcement agencies operate in every State except Hawaii. Most full-time sworn personnel are uniformed officers who regularly patrol and respond to calls for service. Others are investigators, perform court-related duties, or work in administrative or other assignments.

Detectives are plainclothes investigators who gather facts and collect evidence for criminal cases. Some are assigned to interagency task forces to combat specific types of crime. They conduct interviews, examine records, observe the activities of suspects, and participate in raids or arrests. Detectives and State and Federal agents and inspectors usually specialize in one of a wide variety of violations such as homicide or fraud. They are assigned cases on a rotating basis and work on them until an arrest and conviction occurs or the case is dropped.

The Federal Government maintains a high profile in many areas of law enforcement. *Federal Bureau of Investigation (FBI) agents* are the Government's principal investigators, responsible for investigating violations of more than 260 statutes and conducting sensitive national security investigations. Agents may conduct surveillance, monitor court-authorized wiretaps, examine business records, investigate white-collar crime, track the interstate movement of stolen property, collect evidence of espionage activities, or participate in sensitive undercover assignments. The FBI investigates organized crime, public corruption, financial crime, fraud against the government, bribery, copyright infringement, civil rights violations, bank robbery, extortion, kidnapping, air piracy, terrorism, espionage, interstate criminal activity, drug trafficking, and other violations of Federal statutes.

U.S. Drug Enforcement Administration (DEA) agents enforce laws and regulations relating to illegal drugs. Not only is the DEA the lead agency for domestic enforcement of Federal drug laws, it also has sole responsibility for coordinating and pursuing U.S. drug investigations abroad. Agents may conduct complex criminal investigations, carry out surveillance of criminals, and infiltrate illicit drug organizations using undercover techniques.

U.S. marshals and deputy marshals protect the Federal courts and ensure the effective operation of the judicial system. They provide protection for the Federal judiciary, transport Federal prisoners, protect Federal witnesses, and manage assets seized from criminal enterprises. They enjoy the widest jurisdiction of any Federal law enforcement agency and are involved to some degree in nearly all Federal law enforcement efforts. In addition, U.S. marshals pursue and arrest Federal fugitives.

U.S. Immigration and Naturalization Service (INS) agents and inspectors facilitate the entry of legal visitors and immigrants to the U.S. and detain and deport those arriving illegally. They consist of border patrol agents, immigration inspectors, criminal investigators and immigration agents, and detention and deportation officers. *U.S. Border Patrol agents* protect more than 8,000 miles of international land and water boundaries. Their missions are to detect and prevent the smuggling and unlawful entry of undocumented foreign nationals into the U.S., apprehend those persons found in violation of the immigration laws, and interdict contraband, such as narcotics. *Immigration inspectors* interview and examine people seeking entrance to the U.S. and its territories. They inspect passports to determine whether people are legally eligible to enter the United States. Immigration inspectors also prepare reports, maintain records, and process applications and petitions for immigration or temporary residence in the United States.

Bureau of Alcohol, Tobacco, and Firearms (ATF) agents regulate and investigate violations of Federal firearms and explosives laws, as well as Federal alcohol and tobacco tax regulations. *Customs agents* investigate violations of narcotics smuggling, money laundering, child pornography, customs fraud, and enforcement of the Arms Export Control Act. Domestic and foreign investigations involve the development and use of informants, physical and electronic surveillance, and examination of records from importers/exporters, banks, couriers, and manufacturers. They conduct interviews, serve on joint task forces with other agencies, and get and execute search warrants.

Customs inspectors inspect cargo, baggage, and articles worn or carried by people and carriers including vessels, vehicles, trains and aircraft entering or leaving the U.S. to enforce laws governing imports and exports. These inspectors examine, count, weigh, gauge, measure, and sample commercial and noncommercial cargoes entering and leaving the United States. Customs inspectors seize prohibited or smuggled articles, intercept contraband, and apprehend, search, detain, and arrest violators of U.S. laws.

U.S. Secret Service special agents protect the President, Vice President, and their immediate families; Presidential candidates; former Presidents; and foreign dignitaries visiting the United States. Secret Service agents also investigate counterfeiting, forgery of Government checks or bonds, and fraudulent use of credit cards.

The U.S. Department of State *Bureau of Diplomatic Security special agents* are engaged in the battle against terrorism. Overseas, they advise ambassadors on all security matters and manage a complex range of security programs designed to protect personnel, facilities, and information. In the U.S., they investigate passport and visa fraud, conduct personnel security investigations, issue security clearances, and protect the Secretary of State and a number of foreign dignitaries. They also train foreign civilian police and administer a counter-terrorism reward program.

Other Federal agencies employ police and special agents with sworn arrest powers and the authority to carry firearms. These agencies include the Postal Service, the Bureau of Indian Affairs Office of Law Enforcement, the Forest Service, the National Park Service, and the Federal Air Marshals.

Police work can be very dangerous and stressful. In addition to the obvious dangers of confrontations with criminals, officers need to be constantly alert and ready to deal appropriately with a number of other threatening situations. Many law enforcement officers witness death and suffering resulting from accidents and criminal behavior. A career in law enforcement may take a toll on officers' private lives.

Uniformed officers, detectives, agents, and inspectors are usually scheduled to work 40-hour weeks, but paid overtime is common. Shift work is necessary because protection must be provided around the clock. Junior officers frequently work weekends, holidays, and nights. Police officers and detectives are required to work at any time their services are needed and may work long hours during investigations. In most jurisdictions, whether on or off duty, officers are expected to be armed and to exercise their arrest authority whenever necessary.

The jobs of some Federal agents such as U.S. Secret Service and DEA special agents require extensive travel, often on very short notice. They may relocate a number of times over the course of their careers. Some special agents in agencies such as the U.S. Border Patrol work outdoors in rugged terrain for long periods and in all kinds of weather.

Emergency Medical Technicians and Paramedics

People's lives often depend on the quick reaction and competent care of emergency medical technicians (EMTs) and paramedics—EMTs with additional advanced training to perform more difficult pre-hospital medical procedures. Incidents as var-

ied as automobile accidents, heart attacks, drownings, childbirth, and gunshot wounds all require immediate medical attention. EMTs and paramedics provide this vital attention as they care for and transport the sick or injured to a medical facility.

In an emergency, EMTs and paramedics typically are dispatched to the scene by a 911 operator, and often work with police and fire department personnel. (Police and detectives and firefighting occupations are discussed elsewhere in the Handbook.) Once they arrive, they determine the nature and extent of the patient's condition while trying to ascertain whether the patient has preexisting medical problems. Following strict rules and guidelines, they give appropriate emergency care and, when necessary, transport the patient. Some paramedics are trained to treat patients with minor injuries on the scene of an accident or at their home without transporting them to a medical facility. Emergency treatment for more complicated problems is carried out under the direction of medical doctors by radio preceding or during transport.

EMTs and paramedics may use special equipment, such as backboards, to immobilize patients before placing them on stretchers and securing them in the ambulance for transport to a medical facility. Usually, one EMT or paramedic drives while the other monitors the patient's vital signs and gives additional care as needed. Some EMTs work as part of the flight crew of helicopters that transport critically ill or injured patients to hospital trauma centers.

At the medical facility, EMTs and paramedics help transfer patients to the emergency department, report their observations and actions to emergency room staff, and may provide additional emergency treatment. After each run, EMTs and paramedics replace used supplies and check equipment. If a transported patient had a contagious disease, EMTs and paramedics decontaminate the interior of the ambulance and report cases to the proper authorities.

Beyond these general duties, the specific responsibilities of EMTs and paramedics depend on their level of qualification and training. To determine this, the National Registry of Emergency Medical Technicians (NREMT) registers emergency medical service (EMS) providers at four levels: First Responder, EMT-Basic, EMT-Intermediate, and EMT-Paramedic. Some States, however, do their own certification and use numeric ratings from 1 to 4 to distinguish levels of proficiency.

The lowest-level workers—First Responders—are trained to provide basic emergency medical care because they tend to be the first persons to arrive at the scene of an incident. Many firefighters, police officers, and other emergency workers have this level of training. The EMT-Basic, also known as EMT-1, represents the first component of the emergency medical technician system. An EMT-1 is trained to care for patients at the scene of an accident and while transporting patients by ambulance to the hospital under medical direction. The EMT-1 has the emergency skills to assess a patient's condition and manage respiratory, cardiac, and trauma emergencies.

The EMT-Intermediate (EMT-2 and EMT-3) has more advanced training that allows the administration of intravenous fluids, the use of manual defibrillators to give lifesaving shocks to a stopped heart, and the application of advanced airway techniques and equipment to assist patients experiencing respiratory emergencies. EMT-Paramedics (EMT-4) provide the most extensive pre-hospital care. In addition to carrying out the procedures already described, paramedics may administer drugs orally and intravenously, interpret electrocardiograms (EKGs), perform endotracheal intubations, and use monitors and other complex equipment.

Mutual Aid—Federal, State and Local

The model of government in the United States deliberately separates powers among various branches, and between federal, state and local agencies. While these important distinctions are vital to the preservation of democracy, they do present certain logistical challenges to overcome in terms of coordinating security, intelligence and disaster readiness. To that end the U.S. Department of Homeland Security has drafted the following mutual aid agreement which proposes how the federal government may lawfully aid and assist local responders when coordinating a disaster and critical incident response.

U.S. Department of Homeland Security–Mutual Aid Agreement[4]

Mutual Aid Agreements: Support for First Responders outside Major Metropolitan Areas

Terrorists can strike anytime, anywhere. Crop dusters, power generating plants, dams and reservoirs, crops, livestock, trains and highways are among the resources that could be targets. Homeland security in the heartland is just as important as homeland security in America's largest cities.

First responders from communities outside major metropolitan areas who must protect large geographic areas with small populations face many response challenges. In fact, over half of our firefighters protect small or rural communities of fewer than 5,000 people. Many of these communities rely upon volunteer departments with scarce resources. Fewer than 10% of counties surveyed by the National Association of Counties said they are prepared to respond to a bioterrorist attack.

One of the best strategies to build capability in communities outside major metropolitan areas is to develop mutual aid agreements to share resources. First responders from smaller communities need assistance in organizing and developing the unified command and control procedures and protocols necessary for operationally sound mutual aid. These agreements will enable neighboring jurisdictions to share specialized resources, rather than duplicate them in every jurisdiction.

President Bush's 2003 budget provides $140 million to assist these communities in planning and establishing mutual aid agreements. While mutual cooperation and mutual aid agreements have existed over the years in support of civil defense, fire, and National Guard activities, this is the first time that the federal government has directly supported the establishment of mutual aid agreements with federal resources.

As an established mechanism for sharing or pooling limited resources to augment existing capabilities and supplementing jurisdictions that have exhausted existing resources due to disaster, mutual aid processes will help ensure that jurisdictions across the United States can benefit from each other's efforts to enhance their first response capabilities. Jurisdictions can use the funding provided under this initiative to create or improve their response capabilities, without duplicating their efforts. Many areas have little or no capability to respond to terrorist attack using weapons of mass destruction. Even the best prepared States and localities do not possess adequate resources to respond to the full range of terrorist threats we face.

Hazmat Awareness for First Responders

In industrial nations such as the United States and Canada, there are literally thousands of locations, facilities and systems that use, process, manufacture and transport hazardous materials (HAZMAT). As a first responder it is vitally important that you are aware of what HAZMAT is present at a site you will work at or respond to. The Occupational Health and Safety Administration (OSHA) under the Code of Federal Regulations 1910, defines the right to be aware of what HAZMAT is present, what its fundamental properties are and how to safely handle such materials. The frontline document of HAZMAT awareness is the Material Safety Data Sheet or MSDS. The MSDS will typically contain 16 key pieces of information:

1. Identification and content of the substance and manufacturer's contact information
2. Chemical composition and elements
3. Identification of hazards
4. First aid for exposure
5. Firefighting information
6. Accidental release measures
7. Handling and storage
8. Exposure controls and personal protection
9. Physical and chemical properties of the substance
10. Stability and reactivity
11. Toxicological (poisonous nature) information
12. Ecological/environmental impact
13. Disposal considerations
14. Transport information
15. Regulations
16. Additional information

Throughout your career as a first responder/security specialist you should always make it a first priority to locate, study and review the MSDS at your facility.

Right to Know—29 CFR Parts 1910, 1915, 1917, 1918, 1926, and 1928—MSDS

In order to ensure chemical safety in the workplace, information must be available about the identities and hazards of the chemicals. OSHA's Hazard Communication Standard (HCS) requires the development and dissemination of such information:

> Chemical manufacturers and importers are required to evaluate the hazards of the chemicals they produce or import, and

Prepare labels and material safety data sheets (MSDSs) to convey the hazard information to their downstream customers.

All employers with hazardous chemicals in their workplaces must have labels and MSDSs for their exposed workers, and train them to handle the chemicals appropriately.

Size-Up Concept

Another important safety concept for first responders is the size-up concept. The safety of the individual responder is paramount. A first responder is of no

---

DEPARTMENT OF LABOR

Occupational Safety and Health Administration
29 CFR Parts 1910, 1915, 1917, 1918, 1926, and 1928
Hazard Communication

AGENCY: Occupational Safety and Health Administration (OSHA); Labor.

ACTION: Final rule.

SUMMARY: The HCS requires employers to establish hazard communication programs to transmit information on the hazards of chemicals to their employees by means of labels on containers, material safety data sheets, and training programs. Implementation of these hazard communication programs will ensure all employees have the "right-to-know" the hazards and identities of the chemicals they work with, and will reduce the incidence of chemically—related occupational illnesses and injuries.

This modified final rule includes a number of minor changes and technical amendments to further clarify the requirements, and thereby help ensure full compliance and achieve protection for employees. In particular, the rule adds and clarifies certain exemptions from labeling and other requirements; modifies and clarifies aspects of the written hazard communication program and labeling requirements; clarifies and slightly modifies the duties of distributors, manufacturers, and importers to provide material safety data sheets (MSDSs) to employees; and clarifies certain provisions regarding MSDSs.

EFFECTIVE DATES: The amendments in this document will be effective on March 11, 1994.

FOR FURTHER INFORMATION CONTACT: Mr. James F. Foster, Office of Information and Consumer Affairs, Occupational Safety and Health Administration, 200 Constitution Avenue, NW., room N3647, Washington, DC 20210; telephone (202) 219–8151.

To aid in efforts to comply with the HCS, a single copy of the following documents may be obtained without charge from OSHA's Publications Office, room N3101 at the above address, (202) 219–4667: the Hazard

---

Communication Standard (a Federal Register reprint of today's publication); OSHA 3084, Chemical Hazard Communication, a booklet describing the requirements of the rule; OSHA 3117, Informacion Sobre Los Riesgos De Los Productos Quimicos, a Spanish translation of OSHA 3084; OSHA 3111, Hazard Communication Guidelines for Compliance, a booklet which reprints Appendix E of the standard to further help employers comply with the rule; and OSHA 3116, Information Sobre Riegos Normas De Cumplimiento, a Spanish translation of OSHA 3111.

OSHA 3104, Hazard Communication—A Compliance Kit (a step-by-step guide to compliance with the standard) is available from the Superintendent of Documents, U.S. Government Printing Office, Washington, DC 20402, (202) 783–3238; GPO Order No. 929–022–00000–9; $18–domestic; $22.50–foreign.

SUPPLEMENTARY INFORMATION: References to the rulemaking record are made in the text of this preamble. The Hazard Communication Standard docket, No. H–022, contains eight sub-dockets-H–022A, H–022B, H–022C, H–022D, H–022E, H–022F, H–022G, and H–022H. All of these docket files are part of the rulemaking record. However, in this document, no specific references are made to either Docket H–022C or H–022E (these files deal exclusively with the issue of trade secrets), or H–022F, H–022G, and H–022H. The following abbreviations have been used for citations to the other record files:

H–022, Ex.: Exhibit numbers in Docket H–022, which includes H–022A and H–022B, for exhibits collected for the original 1983 HCS for manufacturing.

Ex.: Exhibit numbers in H–022D for exhibits collected since the 1985 Court remand related to the expansion of the scope of industries covered. This docket includes the comments received in response to the August 8, 1988 proposal.

Tr.: Public hearing transcript page numbers. The hearing transcript pages from the December 1988 hearing are not numbered consecutively, i.e., each day begins again with page 1. Transcript references will thus include a reference to the day, and the page number for that day's testimony. The days are numbered as follows: December 6 is Day 1; December 7 is Day 2; December 8 is Day 3; December 9 is Day 4; December 12 is Day 5; December 13 is Day 6; and December 14 is Day 7. As an example, a reference to testimony which appears on page 65 of the transcript for December 8 will be indicated as "Tr. 3–65." Transcript references to hearings held between June 15 and July 31, 1982, are consecutively numbered, and will not have a prefix number identifying the day.

[59 FR 6126, Feb. 9, 1994

value if he or she is inattentive to his/her individual safety and in so doing becomes an additional victim at the scene.

Courtesy of PhotoDisc/ Getty Images, Inc.

Whenever arriving at an emergency scene the first responder must first size up the hazards present. Particularly the responder will want to address the following:

Body Substance Isolation (BSI)—Body fluids are a major potential hazard at an emergency scene. Human Immunodeficiency Virus (HIV), Hepatitis-B and Hepatitis-C are all infectious materials that can be found in the human blood and could pose a risk of exposure to first responders. In part 1030 of Title 29 Code of Federal Regulations 1910 the Occupational Health and Safety Administration (OSHA) discusses hazard recognition, exposure control and post exposure evaluation of blood borne pathogens.

PPE and Universal Precautions—Personal Protective Equipment and universal precautions are required for all first responders. Universal precautions are generally considered to be simple prophylaxis (barriers) designed to provide BSI for the responder by not letting fluids and viral microbial pass through to the responder's skin or mucous membranes (eyes, nose, mouth). Universal precautions consist of things such as latex gloves, facemasks, eye shields, and gowns. Proper donning and doffing of universal precautions will be covered in your emergency medical training.

Courtesy of Bettmann/ Corbis Images

Personal Protective Equipment (PPE) generally requires more advanced training for proper use. PPE includes chemical resistant suits and self-contained breathing apparatus.

Scene Safety—Be aware of the other hazards present. Terrorist bombing scenes for instance, sometimes have secondary explosive devices present specifically to take out first responders. At a violent crime event medical responders will wait until law enforcement has cleared the scene, verifying any dangerous subjects have been subdued. Open electrical sources, hazardous chemicals, fires, damaged structures, falling debris are all highly representative of the types of secondary mechanisms for injury or illness present at a disaster scene.

Professional first responders never run in to a scene. They always initiate a systematic, coordinated response, communicate with one another and ensure, to the best of their ability, the safety of the scene before entering the critically affected areas.

Request Additional Assistance—Finally, be prepared to request additional assistance. One of the greatest single safety measures a first responder can provide is the ability to call for appropriate trained additional resources. Know how to assess a scene so that you will know when to call for police, fire, medical, HAZMAT, etc.

Emergency Management[5]

Emergency management involves actions taken to prepare for, respond to, recover from, and mitigate against natural and man-made disasters. Emergency management agencies, like the New York City Office of Emergency Management, exist in cities throughout the United States. Many of the same processes and tools are used throughout the country to manage emergencies.

In preparing for and responding to disasters, emergency managers develop plans and work with agencies in their jurisdictions to implement those plans if the need arises, usually by holding drills and exercises to train for the response. Recovery involves clearing debris and restoring essential services to a community as well as providing assistance to disaster victims. Local emergency managers work with agencies in their jurisdictions and their State and Federal counterparts coordinate the recovery process. To reduce the impacts of disasters emergency managers implement mitigation measures. This can involve installing storm shutters in government facilities as well as working with homeowners to identify ways they can protect their property from hazards.

Conducting mitigation activities improves the sustainability of communities following a disaster, as less damage occurs saving taxpayers the cost of substantial reconstruction projects.

Recovery and Mitigation

The Recovery and Mitigation (R&M) Unit serves as the Agency's lead unit for recovery, mitigation, and infrastructure-related emergency planning.

Recovery

Recovery is the phase of emergency management that continues until all systems return to normal or as close to normal as possible.

The steps involved in any recovery effort following a disaster are usually expressed in terms of being short or long term. **Short-term recovery** focuses on restoring vital utilities and life support systems (e.g., power, water, sanitation, communications), transportation infrastructure, the removal of debris, and the assessment of damage. **Long-term efforts** begin after some degree of stabilization has been attained and focus on restoring public facilities and infrastructure.

Mitigation

Mitigation is any sustained action taken to reduce or eliminate long-term risk to people, property and the environment from the effects of both natural and man-made hazards. An efficiently managed hazard mitigation program can be a powerful resource in the combined efforts of the City, State, and Federal governments to end the cycle of repetitive disaster damage.

Who are the Players in Emergency Planning and Response?

FEMA[6]

FEMA is part of the Department of Homeland Security's Emergency Preparedness and Response Directorate. FEMA has more than 2,600 full time employees. They work at FEMA headquarters in Washington D.C., at regional and area offices across the country, the Mount Weather Emergency Operations Center, and the National Emergency Training Center in Emmitsburg, Maryland. FEMA also has nearly 4,000 standby disaster assistance employees who are available for deployment after disasters. Often FEMA works in partnership with other organizations that are part of the nation's emergency management system. These partners include state and local emergency management agencies, 27 federal agencies and American Red Cross.

DMORT[7]

The DMORT (Disaster Mortuary Operational Response Team) is a Federal Level Response team designed to provide mortuary assistance in the case of mass fatality and cemetery related incidents.

DMORT and other medical teams are sponsored by the United States Public Health Service and the Office of Emergency Preparedness /National Disaster Medical System and thousands of volunteers from across the country dedicated to helping those in need.

DMORT is composed of professionals from a variety of disciplines related to the safe, dignified and hygienic identification, recovery and processing of mass fatality incidents. A mass fatality is generally defined as any event exceeding local mortuary capabilities. DMORT specialists include:

- Medical Examiner/Coroners
- Forensic Pathologists
  —Forensic Anthropologists
  —Fingerprint Specialists
  —Forensic Odontologists
- Funeral Directors/Embalmers
- Dental Assistants
- X-ray Technicians
- Photographic Specialists
- Heavy Equipment Operators
- Mental Health Specialists
- DNA Specialists
- Computer Specialists
- Medical Records Technicians
- Transcriptionists
- Administrative support staff
- Security personnel
- Investigative personnel
- Evidence Specialists
- Facility Maintenance Personnel

DMAT[8]

Disaster Medical Assistance Team (DMAT) is a group of medical and support personnel designed to provide emergency medical care during a disaster or other unusual even.

DMATs deploy to disaster sites with adequate supplies and equipment to support themselves for a period of 72 hours while providing medical care at a fixed or temporary medical site. They may provide primary health care and/or augment overloaded local health care staff. DMATs are designed to be a rapid-response element to supplement local medical care until other Federal or contract resources can be mobilized, or the situation resolved.

Each DMAT deployable unit consists of approximately 35 individuals; however, teams may consist of more than three times this number to provide some redundancy for each job role. This insures that an adequate number of personnel are available at the time of deployment. The team is composed of medical professionals and support staff organized, trained, and prepared to activate as a unit.

DMATs are categorized according in four readiness levels:

- Level One—DMATs that are fully deployable within 8 hours of notification and can are self-sufficient for 72 hours. They are deployed with standardized equipment and supply sets to treat up to 250 patients per day.
- Level Two—DMATs that lack enough equipment to make them self-sufficient but are able to deploy and replace a Level One team utilizing and supplementing their equipment which is left on site.
- Level Three—DMATs that have local response capability only.
- Level Four—DMATs with a Memorandum of Understanding executed in some stage of development but have no response capability

NDMS[9]

The National Disaster Medical System is an asset sharing partnership designed to provide emergency medical assistance to States following a catastrophic disaster or other major emergency. The system is designed to care for victims of any incident that exceeds the medical care capability of the affected local and State resources. The Department of Health and Human Services in partnership with other Federal agencies such as the Department of Defense, Department of Veterans Affairs, and the Federal Emergency Management Agency administer the program. The NDMS has three primary objectives:

- To provide health, medical, and related social service response to a disaster area in the form of medical response units or teams and medical supplies and equipment;
- To evacuate patients who cannot be cared for in the affected area to designated locations elsewhere in the nation; and
- To provide hospitalization in Federal hospitals and a voluntary network of non-Federal acute care hospitals that have agreed to accept patients in the event of a national emergency.

NTSB[10]

The National Transportation Safety Board is an independent Federal agency charged by Congress with investigating every civil aviation accident in the United States and significant accidents in the other modes of transportation –railroad, highway, marine and pipeline–and issuing safety recommendations aimed at preventing future accidents. The Safety Board determines the probable cause of:

- All U.S. civil aviation accidents and certain public-use aircraft accidents;
- Selected highway accidents;

- Railroad accidents involving passenger trains or any train accident that results in at least one fatality or major property damage;
- Major marine accidents and any marine accident involving a public and a nonpublic vessel;
- Pipeline accidents involving a fatality or substantial property damage;
- Releases of hazardous materials in all forms of transportation; and
- Selected transportation accidents that involve problems of a recurring nature.

The NTSB is responsible for maintaining the government's database of civil aviation accidents and also conducts special studies of transportation safety issues of national significance. The NTSB provides investigators to serve as U.S. Accredited Representatives as specified in international treaties for aviation accidents overseas involving U.S.-registered aircraft, or involving aircraft or major components of U.S. manufacture.

The NTSB also serves as the "court of appeals" for any airman, mechanic or mariner whenever certificate action is taken by the Federal Aviation Administration or the U.S. Coast Guard Commandant, or when civil penalties are assessed by the FAA. For more information about this NTSB function, see the pages regarding the Administrative Law Judges and General Counsel.

The NTSB opened its doors on April 1, 1967. Although independent, it relied on the U.S. Department of Transportation (DOT) for funding and administrative support. In 1975, under the Independent Safety Board Act, all organizational ties to DOT were severed. The NTSB is not part of DOT, or affiliated with any of its modal agencies.

Since its inception in 1967, the NTSB has investigated more than 124,000 aviation accidents and over 10,000 surface transportation accidents. In so doing, it has become one of the world's premier accident investigation agencies. On call 24 hours a day, 365 days a year, NTSB investigators travel throughout the country and to every corner of the world to investigate significant accidents and develop factual records and safety recommendations.

The NTSB has issued more than 12,000 recommendations in all transportation modes to more than 2,200 recipients. Since 1990, the NTSB has highlighted some issues on a Most Wanted list of safety improvements. Although the NTSB does not regulate transportation equipment, personnel or operations, and the NTSB does not initiate enforcement action, its reputation for impartiality and thoroughness has enabled the NTSB to achieve such success in shaping transportation safety improvements that more than 82 percent of its recommendations have been adopted by those in a position to effect change. Many safety features currently incorporated into airplanes, automobiles, trains, pipelines and marine vessels had their genesis in NTSB recommendations.

Department of Transportation (DOT)—National Response Center[11]

The National Response System (NRS) is the government's mechanism for emergency response to discharges of oil and the release of chemicals into the navigable waters or environment of the United States and its territories. Initially, this system focused on oil spills and selected hazardous polluting substances discharged into the environment. It has since been expanded by other legislation to include hazardous substances and wastes released to all types of media.

The NRS functions through a network of interagency and inter-government relationships that were formally established and described in the National Oil and Hazardous Substances Pollution Contingency Plan (NCP). The NCP establishes three high level organizations and four special force components, which are described below.

Federal On-Scene Coordinators (FOSC)

The FOSC is a federal official, pre-designated by EPA for inland areas and by the Coast Guard for coastal or major navigable waterways. These individuals coordinate all federal containment, removal, disposal efforts, and resources during an incident. The FOSC also coordinates federal efforts with the local community's response. Anyone responsible for reporting releases should be aware of which FOSC has responsibility for the affected area. For locations near the coast or a major waterway, there may be both a Coast Guard and EPA FOSC with assigned responsibilities within jurisdictional boundaries of various state or local entities.

National Response Team (NRT)

The National Response Team's membership consists of 16 federal agencies with interest and expertise in various aspects of emergency response to pollution incidents. The NRT is a planning, policy, and coordinating body; providing national level policy guidance prior to an incident and does not respond directly to an incident. They can provide assistance to an FOSC during an incident, usually in the form of technical advice or access to additional resources and equipment at the national level.

Regional Response Team

The RRT's are the next organizational level in the federal response system. Currently, there are 13 RRTs, one for each of the ten federal regions, plus one each for Alaska, the Caribbean and the Pacific Basin. Each team maintains a Regional Contingency Plan and both the state and federal governments are represented. The RRTs are primarily planning, policy and coordinating bodies. They provide guidance to FOSCs through the Regional Contingency Plans and work to locate assistance requested by the FOSC during an incident. RRTs may also provide assistance to state and local governments in preparing, planning or training for emergency response.

The four special force components are:

Coast Guard National Strike Force (NSF)

The NSF is composed of three strategically located strike teams and a coordination center. The strike teams have specially trained personnel and are equipped to respond to major oil spills and chemical releases. The coordination center maintains a national inventory listing of spill response equipment and assists with the development and implementation of an exercise and training program for the National Response System. NSF capabilities are especially suited to incidents occurring in the marine environment, but also include site assessments, safety, action plan development and documentation for both

Coast Guard Public Information Assist Team (PIAT)

The PIAT is a highly skilled unit of public affairs specialists prepared to complement the existing public information capabilities of the Federal On-Scene Coordinator.

EPA Environmental Response Team (ERT)

The ERT is a group of specially trained scientists and engineers based in Edison, NJ and Cincinnati, OH. Its capabilities include multimedia sampling and analysis, hazard assessment, cleanup techniques and technical support.

Scientific Support Coordinators (SSC)

The National Oceanic and Atmospheric Administration (NOAA) provides SSC in coastal and marine areas. The SSC serves on the FOSC staff as the lead of a scientific team. This support team provides expertise in environmental chemistry, oil slick tracking, pollutant transport modeling, natural resources at risk, environmental tradeoffs of countermeasures and cleanup, information management, contingency planning and liaison to the scientific community and the natural resource trustees.

NEST[12]

Nuclear Emergency Support Teams are searchers and scientists who can locate and then conduct or support technical operations on a suspected nuclear device. NEST personnel and equipment are ready to deploy worldwide at all times.

Under the Atomic Energy Act, the Federal Bureau of Investigation (FBI) is responsible for investigating illegal activities involving the use of nuclear materials within the United States, including terrorist threats involving the use of special nuclear materials.

The NEST program was initiated in 1974 as a means to provide technical assistance to the FBI. A series of Executive Orders provides authority for NNSA to assist the FBI conduct, direct, and coordinate search and recovery operations for nuclear materials, weapons, or devices, and assist in identifying and deactivating an Improvised Nuclear Device (IND) or a Radiological Dispersal Device (RDD). Today's operations are guided by recent Presidential Decision Directives addressing the threat of weapons of mass destruction terrorism. Under this national policy, the FBI is the Lead Federal Agency (LFA) for terrorism response within the United States, the Department of State is the LFA for terrorism response outside the United States, and NNSA supports the LFA

Because a nuclear terrorist incident could arise with little or no warning, NEST response teams are prepared to deploy rapidly upon notification. If the crisis develops over time and information is available from intelligence efforts or other warnings, response teams may be alerted or activated for pre-deployment planning. All response team activations and deployments are directed by DOE headquarters-after coordination with other concerned agencies. This interagency process-may involve strict operational security to protect classified or sensitive details of the response operation. The FBI or State Department coordinates U.S. government assistance to support the resolution of the crisis with state and local officials or foreign governments.

American Red Cross[13]

Although the American Red Cross is not a government agency, its authority to provide disaster relief was formalized when, in 1905, the Red Cross was chartered by Congress to "carry on a system of national and international relief in time of peace and apply the same in mitigating the sufferings caused by pestilence, famine, fire, floods, and other great national calamities, and to devise and carry on measures for preventing the same." The Charter is not only a grant of power, but also an imposition of duties and obligations to the nation, to disaster victims, and to the people who generously support its work with their donations.

Red Cross disaster relief focuses on meeting people's immediate emergency disaster-caused needs. When a disaster threatens or strikes, the Red Cross provides shelter, food, and health and mental health services to address basic human needs. In addition to these services, the core of Red Cross disaster relief is the assistance given to individuals and families affected by disaster to enable them to resume their normal daily activities independently.

The Red Cross also feeds emergency workers, handles inquiries from concerned family members outside the disaster area, provides blood and blood products to disaster victims, and helps those affected by disaster to access other available resources.

State/Regional and Local Office of Emergency Services[14]

Many states, counties and cities have dedicated offices of emergency services. These offices typically report directly to the governor, sheriff or mayor. The following text is taken from the website of the city of San Francisco's OES.

The San Francisco Office of Emergency Services (OES) is the component of the Emergency Communications Department responsible for strategic emergency planning. The OES develops and manages the emergency plan for the City and County of San Francisco, coordinates all protective and relief services, trains emergency services, and implements all emergency plans and activities.

The Office of Emergency Services administers the following key programs to accomplish this mission:

> **Emergency Preparedness Program**—coordinates the City and County Emergency Operations Plan and provides training and technical assistance to other departments and agencies in the development of supporting agency plans.

> **Community Preparedness Program**—fosters neighborhood preparedness through community outreach and organization.

> **Emergency Operation Center Program**—maintains the EOC in a state of constant readiness and evaluates technological upgrades to improve EOC capabilities. The Emergency Operation Center is the central location for coordination of emergency response activities by the Mayor and designated department heads. The EOC serves as the location where damage information is assessed, the overall disaster situation is analyzed, and the City's response and recovery priorities are established.

Key City departments also maintain separate department operations centers off site that communicate with and report to the EOC.

> **Disaster Recovery Program**—coordinates reimbursements from the State of California and the Federal Government after declared disasters. In addition to these programs, the Director of the OES serves as the Executive Secretary of the City and County Disaster Council. The City and County Disaster Council is an organization of key department heads and City officials, members of the Board of Supervisors, and representatives of private organizations appointed by the Mayor. Chaired by the Mayor, the Disaster Council is responsible for the development of emergency plans and mutual aid agreements. It also recommends appropriate legislation to the Board of Supervisors. The Council meets at the call of the Mayor, usually twice a year in April and October.

> **Emergency Operations Plan**—the City and County of San Francisco's Emergency Operations Plan (EOP) describes how the City will manage and coordinate resources and personnel during periods of emergency.

This plan was developed by the Mayor's EOP Task Force, which began its work in July 1993. The Task Force was comprised of senior planners and managers of the Departments and Agencies that have key roles during periods of emergency. These Departments and agencies now constitute a standing committee responsible for on-going emergency planning activities.

> The EOP is a single volume document that effectively incorporates detailed emergency planning with lessons learned from past experiences such as the Loma Prieta earthquake, East Bay Hills fire, Northridge earthquake, Rodney King civil disturbance, Y2K and September 11th. The plan:

> • Conforms to the State mandated Standardized Emergency Management System (SEMS) and effectively restructures emergency

response at all levels in compliance with the Incident Command System (ICS).

- Establishes response policies and procedures, providing City and County of San Francisco Departments and agencies clear guidance for their own planning purposes. Describes and details steps necessary by key city officials to protect lives and property.
- Outlines coordination requirements.
- Provides a basis for unified training and response exercises to insure compliance and modernity.

The EOP is a living document. It is in constant revision and changes may be made immediately. The EOP Task Force is charged with the responsibility of reviewing and approving all such changes.

Below is a summary of chapters, annexes, and appendices:

Chapter 1. User's Guide. Provides a basic overview of the EOP, its supplemental Disaster Management Guide, and guidance for Departments to develop their supporting plans. It also contains a list of abbreviations, description of reference icons, and page layout information.

Chapter 2. Emergency Management. Provides the user an overview of emergency management as set forth by the State under SEMS. It defines key elements of San Francisco's interpretation and adaptations of SEMS. This chapter sets forth emergency response levels: 0,1,2,3. Finally, it graphically displays operational use of SEMS, ICS, Emergency Response Districts, and mutual aid.

Chapter 3. Emergency Operations Center (EOC) Organization. Outlines in detail the functions and organization of the EOC. Each section is identified by color tab consistent with the vests worn by EOC staff for Command & Policy, Plans, Operations, Logistics, and Finance.

Chapter 4. Emergency Command and Control Centers. Provides detailed information regarding disaster response facilities and sites, pre-designated disaster facilities, and Emergency Response Districts, along with an overview of the EOC and City Department and Agencies' Emergency Operations Centers (DOC). Because the plan is computerized, it allows for immediate changes to Operation Return sites, Casualty Collection Points, and pre-designated State and Federal staging area, also contained in this chapter.

Chapter 5. Quick Reference. Contains the entire text of the Disaster Management Guide, a pocket guide designed for key City and County of San Francisco officials to assist them in performance of their duties and insuring continuity during periods of emergency.

Chapter 6. Communications. Outlines reliability concerns, policies, current systems to include State and Federal. This chapter describes EOC and City and County of San Francisco personnel recall procedures. The chapter provides a general overview of radio frequencies although not all encompassing for operational reasons. It also contains information (still incomplete) of the mobile communications as well as fixed alert and warning systems.

Chapter 7. Public Information. Establishes public information policies and procedures tailored to the City and County of San Francisco. The chapter describes a public information organization to work in coordination with a Joint Information Center. It provides detailed contact data for City and County of San Francisco and surrounding Bay Area counties. Further, the chapter describes media access rights, procedures for initiating emergency broadcasts, and depicts sample text for radio.

Chapter 8. Recovery Operations. This chapter outlines operational tasks to support recovery from major emergencies. Three phases of recovery are defined including Departments' responsibilities. It provides an initial recovery checklist and describes Disaster Application Center (DAC), State and Federal recovery programs, and hazard mitigation.

Chapter 9. Training and Response Exercise Program. Establishes training requirements and protocols to insure all elements of the plan work in a cohesive manner.

Chapter 10. Plan Administration. Describes the composition and functional responsibilities of the EOP Task Force, distribution scheme, and procedures for revision.

Annex A. Threat Assessments. Outlines 10 key threats to life and property in the City and County of San Francisco.

Annex B. Hazard–Specific Plans. This annex contains an overview of City and County of San Francisco Radiological Defense Plan.

Annex C. Emergency Operations Center Checklists. Marked by colored tabs consistent with EOC vest colors, this annex provides operational checklists for EOC staff.

Annex D. Operational Areas Satellite Information System (OASIS) Report Forms. Contains the 29 separate reports required by the State of the EOC during emergency.

Annex E. Emergency Operations Center Maps. Contains newly devised maps of CCSF detailing EOC locations, staging areas, Fire Battalions and stations, Police Stations, Neighborhood Emergency Response Training ("NERT") staging areas, hospitals, first aid centers, Red Cross shelters, sirens, helicopter landing zones, casualty collection points, etc. These maps are under continual revision and represent the first attempt of its kind to marshal all such key information on a map of the City and County of San Francisco.

State/Regional and Local Law Enforcement

State troopers, highway patrols, sheriff deputies, and police officers are all first responders charged with public security and emergency operations. These functions range from regular patrol and enforcement, to assistance with evacuation and crowd control, to full-scale counter terrorism intelligence and response. The following is from the website of the Los Angeles Police Department's Critical Incident Management Bureau, which is a premiere example of a metropolitan law enforcement agency's emergency response efforts.

Critical Incident Management Bureau is comprised of Anti-Terrorist Division (ATD) and Emergency Services Division (ESD). Anti-Terrorist Division is now comprised of Criminal Conspiracy, Criminal Investigations, Intelligence Investigations, Surveillance, and Liaison Sections. Emergency Services Division (ESD) is comprised of Field and Community Support, Emergency Planning, Operations, and Hazardous Devices Sections. In short, Counter- Terrorism Bureau is responsible for planning, response and intelligence.

Counter-Terrorism Bureau (CTB), under the command of Police Administrator III John Miller reports directly to the Chief of Police.

- Anti-Terrorist Division
  - Criminal Conspiracy Section
  - Criminal Investigations Section
  - Intelligence Investigations Section
  - Liaison Sections.
  - Surveillance Section
- Emergency Services Division
  - Emergency Planning Section
  - Emergency Operations Section
  - Field and Community Support Section
  - Hazardous Devices Sections.
    - Bomb Squad Unit
    - Hazardous Materials Unit
  - Operations Section

Fire Services

Every municipality in North America has some form of public fire protection. Most cities employ dedicated fire departments. More remote outlying areas will have regional or countywide fire protection districts and states and provinces often have broad firefighter responsibilities such as forestry departments charged with combating large wildfires.

The following text, taken from the city of Ottawa's website, lists a very typical overview of a large city's responsibilities and their role as emergency first responders.

Fire Suppression[16]	**Disaster Support**
Structural	Planning
Non-structural	Response
Rural fires	Shelters
Industrial and special-hazard fires	EOC
Wild land fires	Information
Airport fires	Supply points
Marine fires	
Hazardous materials	**Public Assistance**
NBC* threats	Water delivery (rural)
Carbon monoxide calls	Lock out
	Heavy Lift
Prevention & Public Education	Wires down
Rescue/EMS Services	Controlled burns
Tiered Response to Medical Calls	
Motor vehicle/equipment accidents	
Confined space/high angle	
Ice and Water Rescue	
Trench	
Wilderness SAR+	
Urban SAR	

Urban Search and Rescue (USAR)[17]

In the early 1980s, the Fairfax County Fire & Rescue and Metro-Dade County Fire Department created elite search-and-rescue (US&R) teams trained for rescue operations in collapsed buildings. Working with the United States State Department and Office of Foreign Disaster Aid, these teams provided vital search-and-rescue support for catastrophic earthquakes in Mexico City, the Philippines and Armenia.

In 1991, the Federal Emergency Management Agency (FEMA) incorporated this concept into the Federal Response Plan, sponsoring 25 national urban search-and-rescue task forces. Today there are 28 national task forces staffed and equipped to conduct round-the-clock search-and-rescue operations following earthquakes, tornadoes, floods, hurricanes, aircraft accidents, hazardous materials spills and catastrophic structure collapses.

Courtesy of AP/Wide World Photos.

If a disaster event warrants national US&R support, FEMA will deploy the three closest task forces within six hours of notification, and additional teams as necessary. The role of these task forces is to support state and local emergency responders' efforts to locate victims and manage recovery operations.

Each task force consists of two 31-person teams, four canines, and a comprehensive equipment cache. US&R task force members work in four areas of specialization: search, to find victims trapped after a disaster; rescue, which includes safely digging victims out of tons of collapsed concrete and metal; technical, made up of structural specialists who make rescues safe for the rescuers; and medical, which cares for the victims before and after a rescue.

In addition to search-and-rescue support, FEMA provides hands-on training in search-and-rescue techniques and equipment, technical assistance to local communities, and in some cases federal grants to help communities better prepare for urban search-and-rescue operations.

The bottom line in urban search-and-rescue—someday lives may be saved because of the skills these rescuers gain. These first responders consistently go to the front lines when America needs them most. We should be proud to have them as a part of our community.

Not only are these first responders a national resource that can be deployed to a major disaster or structural collapse anywhere in the country. They are also the local firefighters and paramedics who answer when you call 911 at home in your local community.

Events such as the 1995 bombing of the Alfred P. Murrah building in Oklahoma City, the Northridge earthquake, the Kansas grain elevator explosion in 1998 and earthquakes in Turkey and Greece in 1999 underscore the need for highly skilled teams to rescue trapped victims.

Emergency Medical Services (EMS)

The function of emergency medical services is to provide first aid, trauma care, on-scene stabilization and transportation of victims at a critical incident. The following job description from the U.S. Department of Labor provides an excellent oversight of Emergency Medical Technicians first responder responsibilities.

Emergency Medical Technicians and Paramedics[18]

People's lives often depend on the quick reaction and competent care of emergency medical technicians (EMTs) and paramedics—EMTs with additional advanced training to perform more difficult prehospital medical procedures. Incidents as varied as automobile accidents, heart attacks, drownings, childbirth, and gunshot wounds all require immediate medical attention. EMTs and paramedics provide this vital attention as they care for and transport the sick or injured to a medical facility.

In an emergency, EMTs and paramedics typically are dispatched to the scene by a 911 operator, and often work with police and fire department personnel. (Police and detectives and firefighting occupations are discussed elsewhere in the Handbook.) Once they arrive, they determine the nature and extent of the patient's condition while trying to ascertain whether the patient has preexisting medical problems. Following strict rules and guidelines, they give appropriate emergency care and, when necessary, transport the patient. Some paramedics are trained to treat patients with minor injuries on the scene of an accident or at their home without transporting them to a medical facility. Emergency treatment for more complicated problems is carried out under the direction of medical doctors by radio preceding or during transport.

EMTs and paramedics may use special equipment, such as backboards, to immobilize patients before placing them on stretchers and securing them in the ambulance for transport to a medical facility. Usually, one EMT or paramedic drives while the other monitors the patient's vital signs and gives additional care as needed. Some EMTs work as part of the flight crew of helicopters that transport critically ill or injured patients to hospital trauma centers.

At the medical facility, EMTs and paramedics help transfer patients to the emergency department, report their observations and actions to emergency room staff, and may provide additional emergency treatment. After each run, EMTs and paramedics replace used supplies and check equipment. If a transported patient had a contagious disease, EMTs and paramedics decontaminate the interior of the ambulance and report cases to the proper authorities.

Beyond these general duties, the specific responsibilities of EMTs and paramedics depend on their level of qualification and training. To determine this, the National Registry of Emergency Medical Technicians (NREMT) registers emergency medical service (EMS) providers at four levels: First Responder, EMT-Basic, EMT-Intermediate, and EMT-Paramedic. Some States, however, do their own certification and use numeric ratings from 1 to 4 to distinguish levels of proficiency.

The lowest-level workers—First Responders—are trained to provide basic emergency medical care because they tend to be the first persons to arrive at the scene of an incident. Many firefighters, police officers, and other emergency workers have this level of training. The EMT-Basic, also known as EMT-1, represents the first component of the emergency medical technician system. An EMT-1 is trained to care for patients at the scene of an accident and while transporting patients by ambulance to the hospital under medical direction. The EMT-1 has the emergency skills to assess a patient's condition and manage respiratory, cardiac, and trauma emergencies.

The EMT-Intermediate (EMT-2 and EMT-3) has more advanced training that allows the administration of intravenous fluids, the use of manual defibrillators to give lifesaving shocks to a stopped heart, and the application of advanced airway techniques and equipment to assist patients experiencing respiratory emergencies. EMT-Paramedics (EMT-4) provide the most extensive prehospital care. In addition to carrying out the procedures already described, paramedics may administer drugs orally and intravenously, interpret electrocardiograms (EKGs), perform endotracheal intubations, and use monitors and other complex equipment.

Community Emergency Response Teams (CERT)[19]

The Community Emergency Response Team (CERT) program trains citizens to prepare for and respond to emergencies in their local communities.

CERTs are groups of neighborhood and community-based volunteers that undergo an intensive, 25-hour training program in basic disaster response skills, such as fire safety, light search and rescue, and medical operations.

Courtesy of Port St. Lucia Police Department

As a rule, emergency services personnel are the best-trained and equipped to respond to emergencies. However, following a catastrophic disaster, some neighborhoods may be on their own for a period of time because of the size of the area affected, lost communications, and impassable roads. CERT teams are self-deploying response groups that can begin initial response actions to save lives and protect property.

During non-emergency situations, CERT teams engage in the important work of disaster preparedness. Activities include educating neighbors and community business owners about the many hazards they may face and appropriate disaster preparedness steps to take.

CERT is one of four programs in the Department of Homeland Security's Citizen Corps initiative.

CERT History

The Community Emergency Response Team (CERT) concept was developed and implemented by the City of Los Angeles Fire Department (LAFD) in 1985. The LAFD recognized that citizens would very likely be on their own during the early stages of a catastrophic disaster. Accordingly, LAFD decided that some basic training in disaster survival and rescue skills would improve the ability of citizens to survive until responders or other assistance could arrive. The Whittier Narrows earthquake in 1987 underscored the area-wide threat of a major disaster in California. Further, it confirmed the need for training civilians to meet immediate post-disaster needs.

The training program the LAFD initiated proved to be so beneficial that the Federal Emergency Management Agency (FEMA) felt that the concept and the program should be made available to communities nationwide. In 1994, the Emergency Management Institute (EMI), in cooperation with the LAFD, expanded the CERT materials to make them applicable to all hazards.

In 2003, the Citizen Corps program was created to spearheaded the effort to harness the power of every individual through education, training, and volunteer service to make communities safer, stronger, and better prepared to respond to the threats of terrorism, crime, public health issues, and disasters of all kinds. CERT was selected as one of the primary programs offered to the American public to meet this challenge.

To date, communities in 28 States and Puerto Rico have conducted CERT training.

Corporate/private Emergency Response Teams (ERT)

Today, many private and corporate entities operate emergency response teams which range from volunteers trained on basics such as CPR and first aid and fire extinguisher use, to professional, full-time corporate responders trained in full hazardous material (HAZMAT) incident containment and fire suppression. The level of training and equipping of ERT's is usually commensurate with the nature of the facility. Administrative corporate offices or example might have teams consisting of company employees volunteering as floor wardens and first aid providers. An oil refinery, on the other hand, may have a full time private fire department on site.

Corporate ERT's often work either in conjunction with the security staff, are an element of security, or vice versa. Since security specialists typically have emergency medical and response training they typically are heavily involved in the ERT program. ERT members are a valuable resource in emergencies affecting their facility as they have specific training and knowledge of their location and business.

9-1-1 Communication Centers[20]

Most people living in North America are familiar with 9-1-1. The 9-1-1 call center is the hub of most city and/or county public safety response capabilities and is typically the trigger point that activates the emergency response mechanism. The following is from Rural/Metro Fire Department's Maricopa Regional Communications Center in Arizona, which encapsulates the functions of a major 9-1-1 call center.

Rural/Metro Fire Department's Maricopa Regional Communications Center is located within the company's Maricopa Operations Center, in Scottsdale, Arizona. The Center provides state-of-the-art Emergency Telecommunications services to Rural/Metro's Fire Suppression and Emergency Medical Services operations, as well as Medical Alarm monitoring services through Rural/Metro's Protection Services division.

The Center is a 9-1-1 Public Service Answering Point for both Fire Suppression and Emergency Medical Services, serving the areas of Scottsdale, Cave Creek, Carefree, Rio Verde, Fountain Hills, Paradise Valley, Queen Creek, Litchfield Park, Anthem, Gila Bend, Harquahala, and most of the unincorporated areas of both eastern and western Maricopa, and northern Pinal Counties. Each community we serve, whether urban, farming or resort communities, has its own special needs and we cater our services to those needs.

The Center handles more than 30,000 calls annually for both Fire/EMS emergency and non-emergency requests for service. Each 9-1-1 call initially is answered by the law enforcement responsible for that jurisdiction who then transfers the call to Rural/Metro as appropriate. For every incoming call received, approximately two outbound calls are made ranging from alerting law enforcement to notifying hospitals or other ancillary service agencies.

The Center is staffed 24 hours a day with highly skilled Emergency Telecommunication Specialists, trained not only in Radio and Telecommunications Systems and Emergency Call Taking, but also in Emergency Medical Dispatch. They are capable of providing Pre-Hospital/Pre-Arrival Instructions to callers experiencing medical and/or fire emergencies. This means we are able to begin lifesaving procedures as soon as the call is answered while emergency units are simultaneously being dispatched to the scene.

When a call is received, the Call Taker obtains the location of the emergency, the nature of the emergency and the caller's telephone number. As soon as these three pieces of information are placed into the computer the information is "shipped" to the Radio Operator for deployment of the closest most appropriate resources. The Radio Operator dispatches units simultaneously while the caller is still on the telephone with the Call Taker.

The Call Taker then obtains more detailed information from the caller such as information regarding the patient or the emergency incident. In the event of a medical call, the Call Taker would provide specific Pre-Hospital/Pre-Arrival Instructions to aid the patient until paramedics arrive. Or in the event of a fire emergency, the Call Taker would ensure the safety of the caller; instruct the caller to initiate evacuation, determine exactly what is burning, ascertain any hazardous material situation, etc.

The number of on-duty staff at any one time within the Center is based upon previous historical call volume and range from six to four personnel depending on the time of day. We also incorporate on-call personnel, available to respond to the Center through alphanumeric pager notification in the event of a major occurrence such as monsoon storms or major fires. Leadership is provided to staff personnel on all shifts with the presence of Communication Supervisors, Lead Dispatchers, and/or operational Chief Officer(s).

Chapter 3 Endnotes

[3] All job descriptions—U.S. Bureau of Labor Statistics, http://stats.bls.gov, March 21, 2004

[4] http://www.dhs/gov

[5] http://home.nyc.gov/html/oem

[6] http://www.fema.gov/

[7] http://www.dmort.org/

[8] http://oep.osophs.dhhs.gov/dmat/about/ndms.html#ndms

[9] Ibid

[10] http://www.ntsb.gov/Abt_NTSB/history.htm

[11] http://www.nrc.uscg.mil/nrsinfo.html

[12] www.doeal.gov/opa/Emergency/Public/20Information/NEST_Final

[13] http://www.redcross.org/

[14] http://www.ci.sf.ca.us

[15] http://lapdonline.org/

[16] http://city.ottawa.on.ca/city_services/fire

* Nuclear, Biological, Chemical

+ Search and Rescue

[17] http://www.fema.gov/usr/nusrs.shtm

[18] http://stats.bls.gov

[19] http://www.ci.nyc.ny.us/html/oem/html/programs/cert.html#basics

[20] http://www.ruralmetrofire.com/911comcenter.html

Discussion Questions

1) Which of the following is not a responsibility of first responders?

   a. Establishing response priorities

   b. Answering all media inquires without delay

   c. Evacuating persons still in harm's way

   d. Treating and transporting the injured

2) Which of the following is not an example of first responder profession?

   a. Firefighter

   b. Security Specialist

   c. Paramedic

   d. Medical Office Manager

3) Title 29 of the Code of Federal Regulations addresses, among other things:

   a. The rights of illegal immigrants

   b. Defines the roles of first responders in homeland security

   c. Hazard communications

   d. The charter mission of OSHA

4) Federal Homeland Security Mutual Aid Agreement provides for:

   a. Support for first responders outside major metropolitan areas

   b. Coordinating with the United Nations for international response operations

   c. Better sharing of information between the CIA and FBI

   d. Better sharing of information between the FBI and local law enforcement

5) Which of the following is not a major category of information typically found in an MSDS?

    a. Identification and content of the substance and manufacturer's contact information

    b. Date of expiration

    c. Toxicological (poisonous nature) information

    d. Disposal considerations

6) Scene size up includes which of the following:

    a. Body substance isolation

    b. Requesting additional resources

    c. Assessing other hazards

    d. All of the above

7) First responders must be compensated professionals, not volunteers.

    True   False

8) The Federal Emergency Management Agency (FEMA) is an agency within the Department of Homeland Security.

    True   False

9) According to DMORT, a mass fatality is generally defined as any event exceeding local mortuary capabilities.

    True   False

10) Since it is not a government agency, the American Red Cross cannot participate in critical emergency responses.

    True   False

Answers

1) B
2) D
3) C
4) A
5) B
6) D
7) False
8) True
9) True
10) False

4

Preparing for Disaster: Contingency and Business Continuity Planning

Overview:

This chapter will introduce you to the key concepts and principles of contingency and business continuity planning. The foundation of disaster readiness is the development of in-depth plans, which will outline actions, logistics and response actions required to conduct a thorough and effective emergency response. We will look at the history and need for contingency planning and the various elements involved in effectively preparing for disasters.

Contingency plans should outline what steps need to be taken in terms of assessing risks, structure the organization's policy towards operational continuity, and be shared with employee and general populations in order to educate and prepare business and public communities for disaster readiness.

Chapter Objections:

- *Identify the historical and legal requirements for contingency planning*
- *List the common types of disasters/disruptions public and private organizations must prepare for*
- *State the three major goals and four principles of contingency/business continuity planning (C/BCP)*
- *Explain the importance of disaster preparation for*
- *Explain the importance of public relations in C/BCP*

Although the Foreign Corrupt Practices Act (FCPA) of 1977 was originally designed to combat bribery and other forms of corruption in corporate dealings, it also had an unanticipated consequence of elevating contingency planning as a serious question of corporate liability.

The FCPA included a "standard of care" section that outlined the need for corporations to exercise prudence and care in controlling their assets. The act also went one step further by holding management personally responsible for the care of such assets and levied fines for negligence.

With such standards now a matter of major liability, workplace contingency planning emerged as an important discipline and business consideration.

Increasingly since the Seventies, the need for security and business continuity planning in the private and government sectors has become a reality. Whereas, the function was once a distant after-thought, many organizations now have dedicated business continuity planners on staff, spend hundreds of thousands of dollars on worksite risk assessments and hire outside consultants to help develop contingency plans to continue operations in the event of a disaster. Similarly, many government agencies are now mandated to develop plans that will detail how they will remain operational and transfer authority following a substantial disruption. Following the attacks of September 11th, 2001 the media reported that the U.S. Federal Government had enacted a "shadow government" of about 75 people to begin paralleling critical government functions from secure locations should another massive terrorist attack strike the Washington, DC area. A groundbreaking government continuity planning measure was just achieved in April of 2004 with the U.S. House of Representatives passing legislation that would require that body to hold mandatory emergency elections within 45 days of the House speaker confirming that any event any catastrophic event has left at least 100 of the 435 seats vacant.

To begin the discussion, let us look at some commonly accepted definitions of Contingency and Business Continuity Planning (C/BCP). As with many areas of security and emergency planning, the professional community often draws certain distinctions between physical and electronic (or information technology) systems. For the purposes of this discussion we will be focusing on physical contingency planning, but it is important to remember that many principles cross over to both disciplines.

The three major goals of any C/BCP program are:

1. Preservation of Life
2. Preventing/Mitigating Damage to Property and the Environment
3. Resumption of Operations

Contingencies include any foreseen or unforeseen events that could pose a threat to life and safety, damage property and the environment, and disrupt normal activities.

Some of the most common contingencies facing businesses and other organizations include:

- Fire
- Workplace violence
- Earthquake
- Tornado
- Hurricane or severe storm
- Flood
- Civil unrest
- Hazardous materials spill or release
- Terrorism
- Explosions
- Power failure
- Structural collapse
- Information attack/denial of service
- Corporate governance/integrity scandal
- WMD Use

Courtesy of PhotoEdit.

When conducting a worksite assessment in order to develop a contingency plan, one should generally focus on the following key considerations:

1. Does the organization have an official C/BCP policy? If not, this must be the first step. The policy will define how the organization will prioritize recovery operations and should have executive sponsorship from the highest levels.

2. Assessing risk versus probability. Determine the impact of various risks to key organizational functions and processes and then determine the allocation of counter-measures and recovery priorities based on the likelihood of those risks developing into actual contingencies.

3. What will be the structure of your emergency organization, what organizations and departments will play key roles and who will have executive decision making authority?

4. Identify needs and specifications backup facilities and emergency locations.

5. Establish transfer protocols for movement to back locations.

6. Establish transfer protocols for executive decision making authority if key decision makers suddenly became unavailable.

7. Identify and create a list of required emergency logistics which could include (but won't necessarily require): uninterrupted power supplies, first aid and health supplies; food, water and hygiene products; portable computers or other digital data-transfer equipment; independent light sources; wireless/satellite communications gear; cash reserves; maps

of facilities; emergency transportation capabilities; battery powered radios and/or televisions; foul-weather gear; de-watering equipment; toolkits; extra lumber; wall braces; emergency contact lists; etc.

8. Mutual aid agreements with other organizations and agencies

9. Procedures for evacuation, facility shut down and ramp-up

The following is an in-depth examination of C/BCP for a large government institution. This overview will begin an in depth exploration of the questions and considerations required of a comprehensive contingency plan.

"Contingency Planning" Defined[1]

"Any condition that prevents you from performing your critical business functions in an acceptable period of time."

What is Contained in a Business Recovery Plan?

Names and Telephone Numbers

Defined roles and responsibilities

Escalation procedures

Relocation Information

Vital records and data location

Critical Vendor Information

Media Information

Contingency Planning Outline

[This example is meant to convey the typical content of a detailed contingency plan. The format will likely vary for each organization. Components may be combined in lists, matrices or charts. Not all components will apply to all organizations.]

I. Initiation

Work group or team membership and objective

Roles and responsibilities for planning, plan approval, and quality assurance

List of services confirmed as vital

Strategy and schedule for planning

Contingency planning processes and protocols

1. Progress reporting

2. Plan review

3. Plan approval

4. Issue resolution process

5. Communication and coordination strategy with relevant intra and inter-agency organizations (including local government and community organizations)

Affirmation of executive support
Assessment of current disaster recovery or emergency preparedness plans (If none exist the Y2K Contingency Plan should drive the creation effort)

II. Business Impact Analysis (Risks)

Minimum Acceptable Levels of Service
1. List (or matrix) of service dependencies

2. List of service interfaces

3. Commitments to other organizations (specific services and service levels)

4. Minimum acceptable levels of service and/or output which could be tolerated under extraneous circumstances

5. List (or matrix) of components critical to support minimum levels of service

6. Executive approval for minimum acceptable service levels

Failure scenarios (potential risks)
1. Window of vulnerability (time period during which the service may be at risk)

2. Assessment of internal remediation effort status and likelihood to be complete on time

3. Assessment of reliance on, and condition of external services, suppliers and dependencies (confidence in continued availability of resource)

4. Potential failure scenarios with likelihood of occurrence

Impact of each failure scenario on vital business services with likelihood of occurrence
1. List or matrix of impact of each scenario on vital business services with likelihood of occurrence

Services for which contingency plans will be developed
1. List of services and the scope of contingency required (specific components or systems supporting the service that require contingencies)

2. Executive approval of contingency scope

III. Contingency Planning

Relevant contingency efforts of local and/or regional partners
Contingency strategies

1. List of services, components (if applicable), considered contingencies which support them and the benefit of the contingency

2. Considered contingencies and required resources

3. Assessment of considered contingencies

   a. How well the contingency mitigates risks of disruption to service?

   b. Assessment of time required acquiring, testing and implementing the contingency

   c. Sustainability of contingency within resource constraints

4. Executive approval for contingency strategies

Detailed contingency plans (for each contingency)

1. Contingency objective and scope

2. Contingency triggers

3. Schedule for preparation and deployment of contingency

4. Monitoring strategies to ensure identification of triggering events

5. Roles and responsibilities for contingency preparation and deployment (including updated contacts, contact mechanism and numbers)

6. Status reporting processes and protocols

7. Instructions to carry out contingency

8. Coordination strategy with local and regional organizations (if applicable)

9. Required resources and estimated costs

10. Agreements and assumptions with suppliers on whom each contingency is dependent

11. Communications strategy

12. Business resumption strategy

    a. Criteria for business resumption

    b. Priorities, processes and resources for business resumption

       1. Roles and responsibilities

       2. When to resume

       3. What to resume

       4. How to resume

13. Validation/testing strategy for contingencies and business resumption

    a. Which components will be tested?

    b. Members of test team(s)

14. Validation/testing plans

    a. Objectives

    b. Approach

    c. Required equipment and resources

    d. Necessary personnel

    e. Schedules and locations

    f. Procedures

    g. Expected results

    h. Acceptance criteria

15. Validation/testing results (Assessment of capability of contingencies and business resumption)

    a. Adequacy to support vital service

    b. Capacity to manage, record and track contingency activities

    c. Adequacy of controls

    d. Adequacy of resource availability to implement and sustain contingencies

    e. Adequacy of business resumption activities

The Principles of Contingency and Business Continuity Planning (C/BCP)

Preparing for a major disaster or disruption, especially at the community wide level, involves tremendous pre-planning and coordination. When a far-reaching disaster strikes, that is not the time to begin considering what steps need to be taken, what agencies need to address which functions, what logistics are required, and who will be in charge of operations. The four principles of emergency management are:

1. Mitigation—preparation and planning to prevent an emergency from occurring or to lessen the impact if one does

2. Preparedness—the development of plans, arrangement of logistics, identification of responders and staging areas, and education, training and drilling designed to ready response operations for a disaster

3. Response—the immediate, effective and coordinated effort made by trained personnel to contain and control and emergency situation

4. Recovery—blunting losses, begin salvage and initiating the rapid resumption of normal operations.

C/BCP frequently requires a worksite assessment in which the planning team identifies and prioritizes the most critical business functions. Many times business continuity planning creates "tiers" in which to group various operation functions from highest priority to lowest.

Courtesy of Liason/Getty Images, Inc.

The first major step in C/BCP is to identify those functions that, if disrupted, would completely halt all operations resulting in critical human capital and financial losses. These are Tier One priorities. Their loss means that all operations are suspended, fundamental business and organizational goals are not being met, and that the survivability of the organization is almost entirely dependent on getting these functions back up and running as quickly as possible. The goal for Tier One is zero or minimal downtime.

For a business or public organization, Tier One functions might include things like:

- Manufacturing/output
- Environmental health and safety (industrial hygiene, HAZMAT containment, fire and life safety)
- Power and electricity (Uninterrupted Power Supply—UPS)
- Plant security
- Primary networking and information technology systems (e-mail, internet, main servers and routers, sensitive data-bases, emergency phones and hotlines)
- Finance (petty cash-on-hand, emergency funds)
- Executive communications
- Executive decision-making
- Communications with/accounting for on-duty personnel
- Outreach and controlling communications

The second tier, Tier Two operations, are those functions for which the resumption of operations is a high priority; however, some time may be allowed to elapse before more serious organizational damage is done. For instance, Tier Two functions may include:

- Shipping and receiving
- Marketing and public relations

- Customer outreach
- Human resources
- Finance (payroll, accounts payable/receivable)
- Secondary networking and information technology (intranet, data archives, inter-office phones and telecomm)
- Heating, ventilating and air conditioning
- Communicating with off-duty personnel

Courtesy of United Features Syndicate.

In some cases, organizations may identify a Tier Three for non-essential functions where there is a much longer permissible window(possibly even indefinite)for downtime. Examples of Tier Three functions may include:

- Backlogged data entry
- Employee "perks" and team-building activities
- New construction projects
- System upgrade projects
- Re-tooling
- Non-essential communications ("touch-base" calls, regular reminders, electronic bulletin boards)

Y2K and C/BCP

In recent years there have been many events they have called attention to the urgent need for organizational contingency planning. The dreaded "Y2K Bug," predicated the since-disproved notion that computer-based systems all over the world might suddenly fail when the date changed from December 31, 1999 and January 1, 2000. Realizing that most computer processing systems were programmed to only change the last two digits of the year, the concern for many was that at 12:00:00 AM on January 1, 2000, systems programmed to read the year as 19__ would suddenly think it was January 1, 1900, sending the world's computerized infrastructure into total chaos.

Although this fear never manifested into an actual crisis, the months leading up to the year 2000 (or "Y2K") transition prompted a great deal of interest and investment into business continuity and contingency planning. Many organizations were either mandated or voluntarily participated in technical refreshes with Y2K compliant technology,; while, at the same time, they examined their existing structure to determine how they might be impacted if there was a sudden, massive, worldwide computer crash and the whole planet was thrown back into the dark ages.

Suddenly many private and public enterprises had contingency plans and logistics in place. Governments hired volunteer teams and/or dedicated professionals and companies to assess business continuity needs, develop plans and prepare facilities and information technology systems. After the Y2K threat failed to materialize, many of these plans and upgrades remained in place. Ironically, some of the planning that was done for Y2K actually proved quite useful during subsequent crises such as 9/11 and the Great Blackout of 2003, affecting a large part of the northeastern U.S. and southeastern Canada.

A perfect study of this unexpected benefit of Y2K planning is the story of the Toronto Police Services during the 2003 blackout. On August 14, 2003 over 50 million people in and around the metropolitan areas of Boston, New York, Cleveland, Detroit and Toronto were without power for more than a day. In the face of the total and mass loss of power, the Toronto Police Services initiated its heretofore unused Y2K contingency plan. Many were simple measures, such as: holding over several hundred dayshift officers into the evening; uninterrupted power supplies activating automatically to preserve communications infrastructure; and, having volunteers from the Salvation Army come to cook hamburgers on grills to feed police personnel.

By implementing these measures and having the plan ready to roll-out, the Toronto Police Services were able to keep operating smoothly and fulfilling their fundamental mission to protect and serve the citizenry of one of Canada's largest communities.

From the Toronto Police Services[2]:

On Friday, August 15, 2003 Toronto police Chief Julian Fantino held a press conference at police headquarters to address the city's policing issues during the province-wide blackout that prompted Premier Ernie Eves to issue a "state of emergency."

Yesterday at approximately 4:11 p.m. Ontario, along with parts of northeastern United States was in the dark, shutting down thousands of businesses and grounding flights at six major North American airports, including Pearson International Airport.

"This is a time for us to look after one another," said Chief Fantino. He urged the public to be mindful of the elderly, young children, and other loved ones needing assistance while without power. Temperatures expected to reach up to 31C today. Chief Fantino assured that all police services are fully operational and running smoothly.

Members of the public were reminded to avoid using 9-1-1 services unless it is an absolute emergency. Occurrences such as lost and found property, and minor thefts can be reported once full power is returned to the city.

Over 400 dayshift officers remained on duty and continued to work throughout the night to keep any criminal activity under control. There were 38 arrests and 114 occurrences directly attributed to the power outage. "The major arrests have been crimes of opportunity by the lowest form of criminal element," said Chief Fantino.

The Chief thanked the many Toronto citizens for their co-operation in helping to maintain order and safety in the city, as well as to the members of the Auxiliary Police Service for their added assistance. "We continue to ask people for their co-operation and patience," said Chief Fantino. "We are all in this together."

Reprinted from http://www.torontopolice.on.ca/modules, Toronto Police Service.

As with most cities affected by the massive 2003 blackout, the small community of Rochester Hills, Michigan issued a press release detailing the impact of the disruption of power. The account from Rochester Hills demonstrates how a smaller community without some of the same contingency planning options seemed much harder hit by the blackout.

AUGUST 2003 BLACKOUT[3]

PRESS RELEASE
At approximately 4:15 p.m. on August 14, 2003, the City of Rochester Hills along with Southeast Michigan and adjoining states experienced a catastrophic loss of electrical power. At 4:36 p.m. the Rochester Hills Fire Department activated the Emergency Operations Center and all personnel were called to duty.

Approximately 12 hours into this incident (approximately 4:00 a.m. August 15th), the City of Rochester Hills experienced total failure of our telephone system with exception of the 9-1-1 telephone lines. This occurred as a result of a failure of the service provider and was beyond the control of the City of Rochester Hills. This further resulted in the failure of our alpha paging system, however, the radio controlled paging system of the fire department remained operational throughout the duration of the incident.

By 8:00 a.m. on August 15th cell phones began to fail, again, as a result of the service provider not having power and their battery back-up systems being expended. Also, due to a lack of power, cable television was in large part inoperative. It was for these reasons that residents were unable to contact the city offices or the fire department on normal business telephone lines.

However, we stress that the 9-1-1 emergency telephone lines remained operative through the duration of this incident.

Due to the failure of cable television, it was difficult for city officials to communicate with the public, as this is our primary means of doing so.

From the start of this incident at approximately 4:15 on August 14th, until 7:00 a.m. on Saturday, August 16th, the fire department responded to 73 calls for assistance.

Electrical power was first restored to the City of Rochester Hills at approximately 5:00 p.m. on August 15th with the southeast corner of the city being restored. Power was gradually restored through the evening, with most areas being back on-line by 10:00 p.m. with a few remaining areas being restored the following evening.

Many areas experienced a decrease in water pressure ranging from a slight decrease to a near total loss of water. This was also a result of the loss of electrical power to the many pumping stations in the City of Detroit water system.

Finally, review the following document from the United States Food and Drug Administration. The first part of this two-section presentation outlines the need for Y2K planning. The second section presents the FDA's contingency plan, including: policies; logistics; identification of locations; and, "decision trees," which graphically demonstrate how executive contingency decisions will be made during a crisis.

The following FDA plans provide an excellent example of how an organization with enormous public health and safety responsibilities performed an internal assessment and then developed a thorough business continuity plan.

Business Continuity and Contingency Planning

June 14, 1999

> *"This risk of failure is not limited to the organization's internal information systems. Many federal agencies also depend on information and data provided by their business partners—including other federal agencies, hundreds of state and local agencies, international organizations, and private sector entities. Finally, every organization also depends on services provided by the public infrastructure—including power, water, transportation, and voice and data communications. One weak link in the chain of critical dependencies and even the most successful year 2000 program will fail to protect against major disruption of business operations."*
>
> *—From GAO's report, "Year 2000 Computing Crisis: Business Continuity and Contingency Planning," August 1988.*

This note is intended to provide you with guidance on reviewing and evaluating agency business continuity and contingency plans (BCCPs). By way of background, OMB issued Memorandum 99-16, "Business Continuity and Contingency Planning for the Year 2000," on May 13, 1999 to both large, small, and independent agencies. This memo directed agencies to submit their high-level business continuity and contingency plans (BCCPs) to OMB no later than June 15, 1999. It also identifies certain risk areas for which agencies should make common assumptions, while also identifying risk areas that will be unique to each agency.

The most important aspect of a BCCP is whether it takes a common sense approach to ensuring that the agency's most critical business functions will be sustained. Our job at OMB is to make sure that the agencies have identified their priority business functions and, within them, priority systems. Generally, because there is no one-size-fits-all solution, the plan should demonstrate that:

The plan has executive support.

The agency has assessed the overall effect on Y2K on the agency's business processes and has prioritized them.

The agency has prioritized its work on systems. ¨ The agency has developed reasonable assumptions about its risk areas and adopted appropriate responses, both managerial and technical.

The agency has in place a solid process for identifying problems, correcting them where possible, and implementing contingency plans where necessary.

The agency has tested its plan.

The agency has updated its disaster recovery plans and procedures. (Disaster recovery plans and procedures are usually addressed in an agency's Continuity of Operations Plan (COOP). The BCCP should not attempt to replicate the work of the COOP, but should be coordinated.)

> *See also the GAO Guide's phases of Initiation, Business Impact Analysis, Contingency Planning and Testing.*

In addition, the GAO guide describes a number of processes that may help you evaluate a BCCP. However, because agencies are providing only their high-level report, it may be difficult to discern some of these elements. Also, mall agencies or those with especially decentralized operations may have slightly different processes in place. Again, the test is whether the agency has developed a common-sense approach to mitigating risk and responding to system failures.

1. Has the agency formed a team of senior management officials, across the agency, who have identified core business processes, have identified the supporting automated systems and critical inputs, and have determined the appropriate priority level for each? This priority should be based both on risk of failure and on the impact on the agency's mission especially service to the customer.

2. Has the agency provided a master schedule and key milestones for development and testing of the BCCP? Is this schedule reasonable?

3. Has the agency identified its time horizon to impact? For example, will the most critical problems occur at the new fiscal year, at the new calendar year, or even into 2000?

4. Has the agency established a plan for coordinating its BCCP on all levels of the organization? For example, how will overseas offices operates? How will regional offices and field offices participate in the BCCP? Are these offices developing local plans? How will they communicate wit headquarters.

5. Has the agency developed scenarios that could occur and tested the BCCP against them? Especially, is there a plan to ensure that services to the public will continue at the local office level in the event of unavailability of automated systems?

6. Has the agency defined the events or dates that would implement (invoke) a BCCP? (TRIGGERS)

7. Has the agency prepared an outreach plan in anticipation of public anxiety or confusion about what services are available?

8. Is the agency arranging for key personnel to be available during the month of December and the roll-over weekend?

9. Has the agency arranged for training of staff in backup procedures, such as taking information on paper?

10. Is the agency planning for special "rollover weekend activities," including checking the facility, checking systems, running tests, backing up some data and holding it over for post-rollover testing, alerting or starting up back-up systems, and otherwise taking final steps to prepare for the date change?

Department of Health and Human Services
Food and Drug Administration
Public Infrastructure

Year 2000
Business Continuity and Contingency Plan

December 17, 1999

PREFACE

This Business Continuity and Contingency Plan (BCCP) was prepared by TRW, Inc., for the Food and Drug Administration (FDA) under the direction of the Office of Information Resources Management (OIRM). The plan describes the strategic contingencies recommended for the Agency's emergency business processes, as well as the specific contingency actions to be taken by FDA personnel should an extensive, Year 2000-related utility outage arise.

This BCCP should be updated by FDA should any changes occur in emergency business processes, mission critical systems, or contingency actions prior to January 1, 2000. It is also recommended that all personnel involved in the Agency's emergency business processes be made aware of this plan including the contingency actions and supporting materials they will be required to use should an extended infrastructure problem arise.

TABLE OF CONTENTS

1. INTRODUCTION

1.1. Overview

The US Office of Management and Budget (OMB) has required that all Federal Agencies perform business continuity contingency planning (BCCP) to prepare for the potential failure of systems as we cross into the Year 2000. Throughout this planning process, the FDA has considered how the Agency would operate without its mission critical systems, assessing the total situation and developing plans for the most likely contingencies. By conducting this business continuity contingency planning for each core business process, the Agency has ensured that it will successfully accomplish its mission into the Year 2000 in the event of mission critical system failures.

However, in addition to the questions regarding access to its critical data, there are many other factors that can affect the Agency's ability to continue with its critical business of safeguarding public health. The BCCPs for the Agency's core processes are based on risk assessments associated with potential system failures. These plans assume that FDA facilities will be open for business on Monday, January 3, 2000 and will be ready for a full range of business transactions. However, the plans do not address extended outages of the public infrastructure, which could be potentially devastating to Agency operations. Even if all of the FDA's internal systems work properly, there is a risk that other external factors will hinder the Agency's operations. These factors could include Year 2000 failures on the part of external power, water, or telecommunications suppliers, as well as failures in FDA partners—industry or government—upon whom FDA relies in order to conduct its mission.

This Public Infrastructure Business Continuity and Contingency plan will address how the Agency will continue to conduct its most important business processes in the event of a catastrophic failure of the public infrastructure.

1.2. Objective
The objective of this plan is to ensure that the Agency's most critical ("emergency") business processes can continue in the event of an extended outage of any element of the public infrastructure. To support this objective, this plan describes the risk of such an outage, identifies the Agency's emergency business processes, and presents contingency actions that can be used by FDA personnel to conduct its emergency business processes.

1.3. Scope
This public infrastructure contingency plan addresses business processes across the Agency. It provides detailed contingency information for the Agency's most critical processes—the emergency processes that must be continued even in light of extended, widespread utility outages. It provides more general guidance for all processes performed within the Agency.

1.4. Approach
Successful completion of FDA's business processes depends on a number of factors. Automated systems must be operational. The technical infrastructure must provide FDA users access to the automated systems, as well as to email, internet, and other electronic media used in the business processes. Building systems are also important. These systems, including security, fire detection and alarm, elevators, etc., must be available to allow personnel access to their offices and to ensure safe work environments. The public infrastructure is even more far-reaching, in that electricity, water, sewer, telephones, etc., are required in order for the buildings to open. A public infrastructure failure could therefore have devastating effects on the Agency's ability to fulfill its mission.

A disruption of essential public infrastructure services could result in FDA facilities closing for extended periods of time. In the event of an extended power outage, the entire eastern seaboard would most likely be affected as national power grids generally operate or fail as units. Public utilities such as telecommunications and water services require electricity for extended operations. Thus, in the event of electrical power outages, it is reasonable to assume that neither telecommunications nor water and sewer services would be continuously available. With no utilities, buildings would be closed, and traffic control systems/signals would not operate properly. Our entire region could be in a state of emergency, with the government urging people to stay home and off the roads as much as possible. However, even if electrical power is available, a failure of other utilities could result in FDA facilities being closed for extended periods of time, since

OSHA regulations require buildings to close when utilities are not operational. For many FDA processes, an extended shut-down of their facilities could be tolerated, given the seriousness of the nation's overall circumstances. However, a few of the Agency's processes must continue, in spite of, or even because of, such widespread infrastructure outages.

To assess the impact of public infrastructure failure on the FDA, we asked each FDA Center/Office to identify the critical business processes that absolutely must continue in the event of public infrastructure failures. CDER, CBER, OC, and ORA identified several processes that are critical to ensuring the safety of public health. These emergency processes are identified in Section 3 of this document.

1.5. How to Use This Plan

This plan should be referred to in the event of any failure of the public infrastructure, and should be referred to by the owner of every business process within the Agency. The plan identifies different types of business processes, as follows:

- Emergency processes—those few processes that absolutely must continue regardless of the type of emergency the Agency faces
- Core processes—the Agency's most important processes, as identified in the BCCPs
- Other processes—all of the other business processes conducted all across the Agency

The Y2K Outage Decision Tree shown at Figure 1-1 provides FDA's senior staff with various decision points to determine whether to implement emergency processes as a result of public infrastructure failures or to implement manual processes detailed in the BCCPs as a result of automated system failures. The decision tree shows the relationship between the emergency business processes in this plan, the core business processes in the BCCP's, and the other business processes performed across the Agency. For each of the Agency's business processes, managers can use the decision tree to assess their situation and obtain guidance on how to proceed. In following the decision tree, managers assess whether utilities, building systems, technical infrastructure, and automated systems are available. If needed services are not available, managers will assess whether they will be restored before the trigger point* for that particular process is met. Options are provided for numerous potential situations, assisting managers in their decision-making processes. In all cases, however, managers should use the decision tree as a tool—and not as a directive—in determining their best course of action. Further detail on using the decision tree follows the figure.

> * The trigger point is the point in time at which managers must take action, in order to assure their processes are completed successfully. For instance, if a process' trigger point is two hours, the process owner and staff may do nothing for up to two hours without impacting their ability to complete their process. After two hours, however, they must take action of some sort.

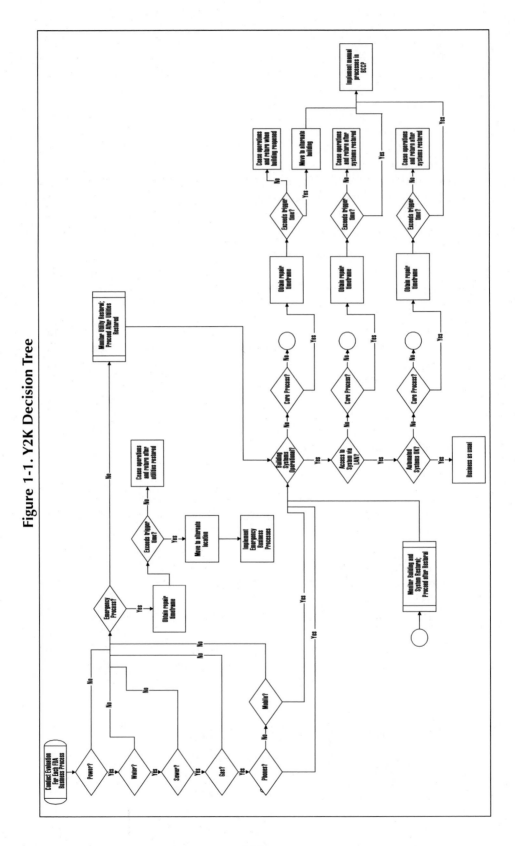

Figure 1-1. Y2K Decision Tree

1.5.1. Stepping through the Decision Tree

The decision tree at Figure 1-1 is for use by every process owner in the event of any sort of Y2K-related disruption. As such, it reflects a total view of FDA's contingency actions for its three types of business processes: emergency, core and other processes. For the sake of simplicity, Appendix A includes separate decision trees for use by owners of emergency processes, core processes, and other processes. Users may find these individual versions easier to follow. The next few paragraphs step through the decision tree in some detail. The decision tree addresses the actions associated with outages of utilities, building systems, and automated systems. The latter is further separated into local area networks and other aspects of the technical infrastructure, and the specific automated systems that support the process. This first section is followed by several specific examples that may be helpful.

1.5.1.1. Utilities

The process owner begins at the top, left-hand corner of the figure, in the box marked "Conduct Evaluations For Each FDA Business Process." The first (left-most column) set of decision points ask the manager whether any utilities are operational. Since an outage of any utility will close the facility, a "No" response brings the manager across the figure to the right. Please note that a telephone outage will not cause a facility to close if mobile/wireless telephone service is available (some sort of telephone service is required so that fire or other emergency services may be called by building occupants). If all utilities are operational, the manager follows the figure down, and then across, to the next section of the figure.

Once the manager has determined that a utility outage exists, he/she must determine whether the process under consideration is a FDA Emergency process, as described in Section 3 of this plan. If the process is not an emergency process, the manager, following the figure across to the right, sees that no further action is necessary until all utilities have been restored. If the process under consideration is an emergency process, the manager contacts the building manager to obtain the repair time for all outages, and then compares that repair time to the trigger time for the process. If the estimated repair time exceeds the trigger time, personnel should relocate as necessary and implement the emergency business processes described in this plan. (Note: most emergency processes in the FDA headquarters area will relocate to the Emergency Operations Center, or EOC.) If the estimated utility repair time does not exceed the trigger time for this process, the manager may cease operations and return after utilities have been restored. It is recommended that managers periodically confirm and update repair time estimates, comparing the updated times to the process's trigger time.

1.5.1.2. Internal Building Systems

Once utilities have been restored (or if no utility outages are experienced), the manager moves on to assess whether the building's internal systems, local area networks, and process-specific automated systems are operating properly. If all of these systems are operational, the manager follows the figure down, answering "Yes" to each decision point. If all of these systems are operational, then the business process under consideration may continue as normal. However, if the internal building systems, local area networks, and/or process-specific automated systems are not operational, the manager must determine whether the process under consideration is a FDA core business process, as described in Section 3 of this plan. If the process is not a core process, the manager, following the figure to connector circle "A," sees that no further action is necessary until all systems have been restored. If the process under consideration is a core process, the manager follows the appropriate "Yes" arrow on the figure.

If internal building systems are not operational, the building will be closed. In this case, the manager contacts the building manager to obtain the repair time for all outages, and then compares that repair time to the trigger time for the process. If the estimated repair time exceeds the trigger time, personnel should move to an alternate building and implement the manual processes described in the BCCP. If the estimated repair time does not exceed the trigger time for this process, the manager may cease operations and return after internal building systems have been restored.

1.5.1.3. Automated systems

Once the manager confirms that the building may be occupied, he/she must determine whether required systems are operational. If local area network systems are not operational, the manager contacts the Help Desk to obtain the repair time and compares that repair time to the trigger time for the process. If the estimated repair time exceeds the trigger time, personnel should implement the manual processes described in the BCCP. If the estimated repair time does not exceed the trigger time for this process, the manager may cease operations and return after the technical infrastructure has been restored.

Once the manager has confirmed that the technical infrastructure is operational, he/she must determine whether the process-specific automated systems (if any) are functioning properly. If the required systems are not operational, the manager contacts the Help Desk to obtain the repair time for system outages, and then compares that repair time to the trigger time for the process. If the estimated repair time exceeds the trigger time, personnel should implement the manual processes described in the BCCP. If the estimated repair time does not exceed the trigger time for this process, the manager may cease operations and return after systems have been restored. In all cases, it is recommended that managers periodically confirm and update repair time estimates, comparing the updated times to the process's trigger time.

1.5.2. Example—Emergency Process/Short Trigger Time

A manager responsible for an emergency process steps through the figure and discovers that there is a utility outage that closes the facility. He/She determines that the process is an emergency process and learns that the utilities should be restored within three days. He/She compares that to the trigger point for the process, sees that the trigger time is less than three days, and moves to relocate and implement the emergency processes.

1.5.3. Example—Emergency Process/Long Trigger Time

Another manager responsible for an emergency process steps through the figure and discovers that there is a utility outage that closes the facility. He/She determines that the process is an emergency process and learns that the utilities should be restored within three days. He/She compares that to the trigger point for the process and sees that the trigger time is fourteen days. Since the utilities will be restored before emergency actions are necessary, the manager sees that no further action is immediately required. He/She ceases operations and monitors the situation.

1.5.4. Example—Non-Emergency Processes

A manager responsible for a core or other process steps through the figure and discovers that there is a utility outage that closes the facility. He/She determines that the process is not an emergency process; therefore, no further action is immediately required. He/She ceases operations, monitors the situation, and proceeds once utilities have been restored.

Another manager responsible for a core process steps through the figure and discovers that all utilities are operational, but that a failure in building systems has closed the facility. He/She determines that the process is a core process, and learns that the building systems should be restored within four days. He/She compares that to the trigger point for the process, sees that the trigger point for this particular process is two days, takes action to relocate to an alternate site and implement the manual processes described in the BCCP.

1.6. Document Overview

This document is organized into four sections and a set of Attachments.

Section 2 discusses risks assessments completed for FDA facilities. Section 3 outlines core and emergency business processes. Table 3-1 describes the core business processes by program area. The FDA's emergency business processes are described in Table 3-2. Section 4 outlines the contingency actions for each emergency business process described in Table 3-2. Finally, Section 5 recommends actions for all facilities used by FDA.

Attachment 1 identifies all of the facilities which house the Agency's core business processes. Attachments 2 and 3 present the risk assessment data for all FDA facilities. Attachment 4 provides the Y2K Readiness Disclosure Statements for all utility providers for FDA facilities.

1.7. Related Plans
The following plans are referenced in this plan:

- FDA Strategic Plan
- BCCPs for FDA's core business processes
- ORA Rapid Response Plan
- FDA Facilities Day One Y2K Plan

2. RISK TO FDA FACILITIES

In order to conduct their business, Agency personnel must have access to a suitable facility. Facilities may be deemed unavailable for a number of different reasons. Internal building systems must be functional in order for facilities to be open. Section 2.1 addresses risk from internal building systems that directly support facilities which house the Agency's core processes. Public utilities must also be available in order for buildings to be open. Sections 2.2 and 2.3 discuss risk deriving from the public infrastructure.

Although risk is a concern for every FDA facility, special attention has been paid to the facilities where core processes are performed. These facilities, which house the Agency's core business processes, are identified at Attachment 1.

2.1. Risk from Internal Building Systems
Every FDA facility contains a number of internal building systems that are necessary to the operation of the facility. These internal building systems include such things as fire alarms, elevators and escalators, heating and ventilation systems, and so on. The Y2K status of these systems has been assessed by building managers and reported through GSA to OFACS. This status is indicated on the risk assessment report at Attachment 1 under the heading "Facility Y2K Status."

Of the Agency's more than 300 facilities, 71 of them house FDA core processes. At the time of this writing, the Y2K status of three facilities (4%) is "Unknown". This "Unknown" status reflects the fact that a Y2K review of these facilities is currently being conducted and completion is expected by mid-December. Table 2.1 identifies these facilities and their points of contact. These points of contact should be contacted regarding facility status and contingency plans.

Per OFACS, all of the critical buildings in Montgomery County, MD and the Washington, DC area are Compliant.

2.2. Risk from Public Infrastructure
As mentioned earlier, any extended utility outage will force the FDA to close the affected facilities. Therefore, for every facility used by FDA, the

Table 2-1. Facilities Whose Y2K Compliance Status is Unknown

Facility	FDA Point of Contact	Facility Status Point of Contact	Facility Contingency Plan?
New England District Office (ORA) One Montvale Avenue Stoneham, MA	Linda Muccioli (781) 279-1739	Sandy Steinberg Archon Group (972) 368-2561	Under Review, per Archon Group
Bensenville Resident Post (ORA) 1000 Tower Lane Bldg	Glory Franklin (312) 353-5863, ext. 130	Pat Sobieski Hamilton Partners (630) 250-4915	Unknown
Bensenville, IL Import Office (ORA) 300 Pearl Street Buffalo, NY 14202	Cindy Maciejewski (716) 551-4461, ext. 3102	George Wallenfels Acquest Holdings (716) 856-5100	Yes

utility providers were identified, and the utilities'-reported Y2K status was collected. Based on their reported status, an assessment was made of the risk of an extended outage. The following guidelines were used in making this risk assessment:

- *Compliant*—Provider has remediated and fully tested all mission critical systems, and has contingency plans in place in case of unanticipated failure.
- *Noncompliant—Low Risk*—Provider has remediated and fully tested all mission critical systems but does not have contingency plans in place in case of unanticipated failure.
- *Noncompliant—Medium Risk*—Provider has remediated mission critical systems but has not conducted thorough Y2K testing.
- *Noncompliant—High Risk*—Provider reports system Noncompliance, or Provider has not remediated and tested all mission critical systems.

2.3. Risk Assessment Results

The results of these risk assessments are shown in the attachments to this plan. At the time of this writing, based on their reports, all power, gas, sewer, telephone, and water providers for facilities housing core processes are assessed as "Compliant" or "Noncompliant—Low Risk." In addition, all wireless providers that were identified by ORA are also assessed as "Compliant" or "Noncompliant—Low Risk."

Attachment 2 shows the risk assessment for all facilities sorted by city and state. Attachment 3 shows the risk assessment sorted by overall criticality of the facilities. Attachment 4 includes a copy of each provider's Y2K Readiness Disclosure Statement. Please note that Attachment 4 consists of several separate binders, which are to be maintained in the OFACS office.

3. CORE AND EMERGENCY BUSINESS PROCESSES

The Agency's core business processes are defined as the most important functions performed by the Agency. Contingency plans for these core business processes are identified in the BCCPs, which assumed that facilities would generally be accessible. Specifically, it was assumed the primary Y2K problems would be failures of the Agency's automated systems. These core business processes are described in Section 3.1.

However, if there are widespread, extended outages of the public infrastructure and FDA facilities are closed, the Agency will not even be able to perform their core business processes. In this event, the Agency has identified a very small number of its most critical business processes, referred to as "emergency" processes. These are the processes that absolutely must continue in order to safeguard the public health. These emergency processes are described in Section 3.2.

3.1. Core Processes

Table 3-1 identifies the Agency's core business processes.

3.2. Emergency Processes

The processes identified in Table 3-2 comprise the small set of business functions that FDA must continue in case of an emergency.

4. CONTINGENCY PLANS FOR EMERGENCY BUSINESS PROCESSES

4.1. Summary of Contingencies

The actual contingency actions that will be undertaken by FDA personnel in the event of a public infrastructure failure are summarized in Table 4-1. For each of the Agency's five emergency processes, the table identifies the facilities in which the processes are normally conducted and the risk of a Y2K-related infrastructure outage. It then indicates the trigger point at which the contingency action would be implemented, the alternate location, and a summary of the contingency actions themselves.

The EOC, or Emergency Operations Center, is a principal component of FDA's Y2K contingency plan. This Center, constructed and managed by ORA's Emergency Operations Group, has been established to be fully self-sufficient in the event of any type of infrastructure outage. The EOC is located in the Twinbrook Building, and has been equipped with generator power, water, sanitation facilities, satellite telephones, and other requirements needed for a core staff to perform emergency operations. It will be fully staffed from December 30 to January 4, ready to react to any type of Y2K-related emergency that could affect the public health. ORA has also

Table 3.1

Program Area	Process	Description
BIOLOGICS: Center for Biologics Evaluation and Research (CBER)	Review and approve investigational biologics	Review Investigational New Drug (IND) applications to approve the use of investigational biologics in human clinical trials
	Review and approve biologics for market	Review and approve Biologic License Applications (BLAs) for new biologic therapeutics to enter the market
HUMAN DRUGS: Center for Drug Evaluation and Research (CDER)	Review and approve human drugs for market	Review Investigational New Drug (IND) applications, New Drug Applications (NDAs), Abbreviated NDAs (ANDAs), and Over the Counter (OTC) submissions to approve investigational drug use in human clinical trials and the entrance of new drugs, generic drugs, and over the counter drugs into the market
	Perform post-market surveillance and compliance with monitoring of human drugs	Conduct post-market surveillance and adverse event reporting and investigate, inspect, and analyze regulated products and establishments for compliance FDA regulations
	Perform financial management	Provide CDER-level financial control, expenditure tracking, and report generation
MEDICAL DEVICES MEDICAL DEVICES AND RADIOLOGICAL HEALTH: Center for Devices and Radiological Health (CDRH)	Monitor Mammography quality	Review and certify all facilities performing mammography for legal operation

FOOD SAFETY: Center for Food Safety and Nutrition (CFSAN)	Perform pre-market clearance for food products	Review and approve petitions for food ingredients and color additives in foods, drugs, cosmetics, and some devices
ANIMAL DRUGS AND FEEDS:	Review and approve animal drugs for market;	Review and approve investigational and market applications for new animal drugs
Center for Veterinary Medicine (CVM)	Perform post-market surveillance and drug animals. experience reporting on animal drugs	Perform post-approval activities associated with drugs administered to animals.
NATIONAL CENTER FOR TOXICOLOGICAL RESEARCH (NCTR)	Perform Multi-Generational studies	Maintain a breeding colony that will ensure the phenotypic variety, quantity, and quality of animals needed for large studies.
OFFICE OF REGULATORY AFFAIRS **(ORA)**	Perform Domestic Compliance and Surveillance	Inspect, investigate, and analyze domestic regulated products, pharmaceutical establishments, and drug development procedures for compliance with FDA regulations.
	Provide Import Surveillance	Approve for release into U.S. commerce all regulated products imported into the United States.
MISSION SUPPORT: Office of the Commissioner (OC)	Central Accounting Services	Provide Agency-wide budget formulation and execution, accounting, payment processing, financial reporting, foreign and domestic travel, employee relocation, payroll liaison and financial systems
	Timekeeping and Personnel Administration Support	Track timekeeping for FDA civilian personnel in support of payroll processing
	Security Access and ID System	Manage the physical security of all FDA facilities

Table 3.2

Program Area	Process	Description
Drugs	Adverse Event Reporting	Monitor adverse events related to approved human drugs using the MedWatch System
Regulatory Affairs, with Drugs and Biologics	Emergency Operations	Coordinate FDA responses to public health emergencies. This includes such events as drug shortages and one-time, emergency usage of Investigational New Drugs (IND).
Regulatory Affairs	Foods Import Surveillance	Monitor the safety of food being imported into the United States.
Mission Support	Time Reporting for Payroll	Process employee time and attendance, ensuring that FDA employees are paid correctly and on time.
	Building Security	Provide Physical security to all FDA facilities across the country.

Table 4–1. Summary of Contingency Actions

Emergency Process	Critical Facilities	Risk of Y2K Utility Outage	Trigger Point	Alternate Site	Contingency Actions
Adverse Event Reporting (CDER)	Parklawn	Low	Jan 1, 2000	EOC	Relocate MedWatch fax to EOC
Emergency Operations (ORA, CDER, & CBER)	Parklawn and Woodmont	Low	Jan 1, 2000	EOC	Duty officer receives calls, coordinates with FDA personnel
Food Import Surveillance (ORA)	District & Regional Offices, large Residence Posts (RP)	Low	Jan 1, 2000	EOC	If port closed, divert shipments. Otherwise, relocate to nearby RP or Customs office.

Emergency Process	Critical Facilities	Risk of Y2K Utility Outage	Trigger Point	Alternate Site	Contingency Actions
Time Reporting for Payroll (OC)	Parklawn	Low	Jan 14, 2000	EOC	Perform manual process
Building Security (OFACS)	All FDA Facilities	Low	Jan 1, 2000	N/A	Physically lock all doors, limit access to one door, manually check badges

provided space within the EOC for other FDA Centers in the event that their own facilities are unavailable for emergency processes. More information on the EOC may be found in ORA's Rapid Response Plan.

4.2. Description of Emergency Contingency Actions

4.2.1. Adverse Event Reporting (CDER)

In the event of an emergency, CDER will continue a scaled-back version of its current MedWatch program. Under the direction of Roger Goetsch, (301) 770-9299, and in coordination with ORA's Emergency Operations staff, a small team of personnel will meet to review incoming reports. The team will perform triage on the reports, searching for and acting on those reports related to newly released drugs and vaccines (those items most likely to encounter serious adverse events). The fax on which MedWatch reports are submitted will be relocated to the EOC for the period December 30 to January 4.

4.2.2. Emergency Operations

All FDA Emergency Operations will be handled according to existing procedures, with the only difference being the location of the Emergency Operations staff. As stated earlier, all Emergency Operations will be at the EOC from December 30 to January 4. For example, all Treatment INDs will be handled according to the existing after-hours procedure. Physicians requesting approval for emergency uses of INDs will contact the ORA duty officer, as usual. The DEIO duty officer will then contact the appropriate CDER/CBER representative for approval. The duty officer normally maintains a listing of CDER/CBER representatives and their contact information, including home telephone and cellular telephone numbers and pager information. A log of all Treatment IND activity will be maintained, and will be input into the appropriate system upon restoration of normal operations.

4.2.3. Food Import Surveillance (ORA)

In the event of a widespread regional or national emergency, ensuring the safety of the food supply will be critical. If a particular port is closed due to outages of electricity or other infrastructure elements, U.S. Customs Service port officials may take action to divert shipments to ports that are open. These diverted shipments could result in higher workloads for FDA agents at ports that are operational. If a port is open but the OASIS system is not operational, field agents will use the manual processes documented in the BCCP to process the shipments. In addition, ORA will, if necessary, divert inspectors from other areas to assist with processing incoming shipments. They may also, as necessary, request assistance from local state and USDA inspectors. All inspection results will be maintained manually, and then input into the appropriate system upon restoration of normal operations.

4.2.4. Time Reporting for Payroll (OC)

As long as the electricity is functional on January 14th, a team of four OC personnel will gather the necessary materials from their Parklawn office and relocate to the EOC. Under the direction of Mike Fullem, Director Financial Systems (OFM), (301) 827-2788, they will perform the manual process described in the BCCP. The time and attendance data will then be delivered to the Department of Health and Human Services (HHS), so that the payroll may be run. However, if the electric utilities are not operating, banks cannot perform electronic funds transfers. In this event, OC will delay their time and attendance processing until power has been restored. OC will maintain a log of all activity, and will input all data into the appropriate system upon restoration of normal operations.

4.2.5. Building Security (OFACS)

Because physical security is vital, OFACS will ensure that security personnel are on-site at every FDA facility. If security systems fail, guards will manually check badges of visitors. If facilities have been closed, guards will allow key personnel into the facility for brief visits. More detailed information concerning physical security may be found in the FDA Facilities Y2K Day One Plan, available from Ms. Katherine Busch, (301) 827-7063.

APPENDIX A—SIMPLIFIED DECISION TREES

Figure A-1. Decision Tree for Emergency Processes

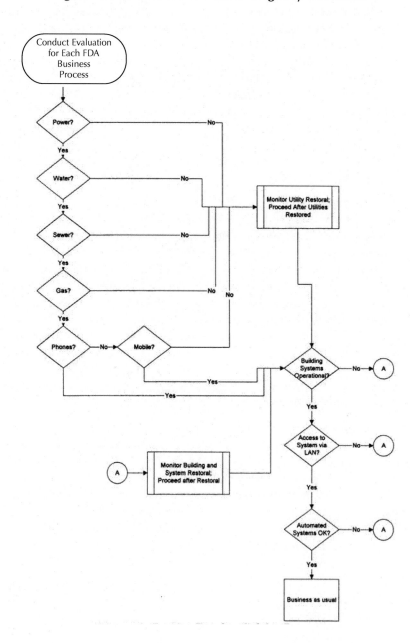

Figure A-2. Decision Tree for Core Processes

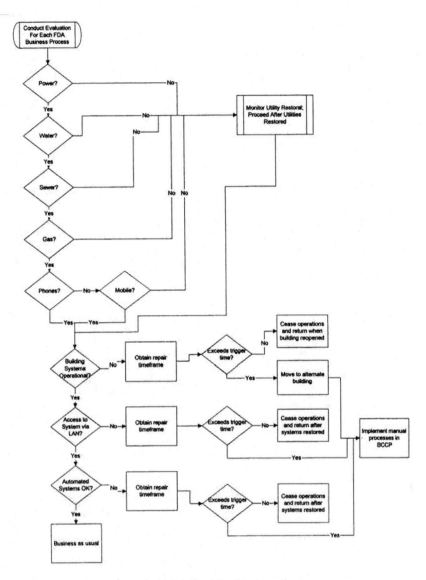

Figure A-2. Decision Tree for Core Processes

Figure A-3. Decision Tree for All Other Processes

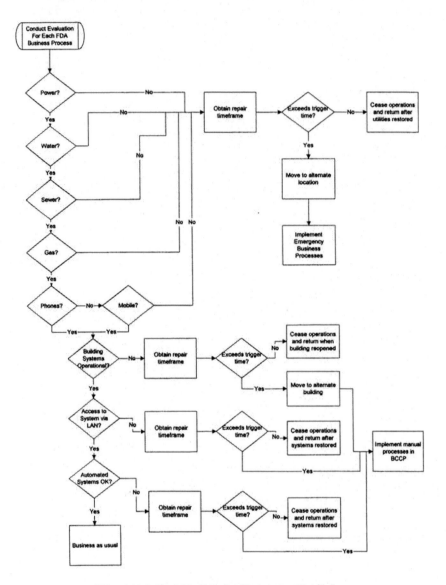

Figure A-1. Decision Tree for Emergency Processes

ATTACHMENT 1. FACILITIES THAT SUPPORT CRITICAL PROCESSES

The following facilities house one or more of the Agency's core business processes. Facilities are listed alphabetically by Center/Office, then by state, and then by city. The Facility Y2K Status was reported by GSA or building managers to OFACS, and is included here for convenience.

Center/ Office	Facility Address	Affected Business Process	Facility Y2K Status
CBER	Woodmont Place 1401 Rockville Pike WOC 1 Rockville, MD 20852-1420	Review and approve investigational biologics	Compliant
CBER	Rockwall II Building 5515 Security Blvd Rockville, MD 20852-1420	Review and approve biologics for market	Compliant
CDER	Parklawn Office Bldg. 5600 Fishers Lane Rockville, MD 20857	Review and approve human drugs for market; Perform post-market surveillance and compliance monitoring of human drugs; Perform financial management	Compliant
CDER	1225 Wilkins Avenue Rockville, MD 20857	Maintain the Document Control Room	Compliant
CDRH	Suite 400 1350 Piccard Rockville, MD 20850-4314	Monitor Mammography quality	Compliant
CFSAN	1110 Vermont Ave., NW Washington, DC 20005-3500	Perform pre-market clearance for food products	Compliant
CVM	Metro Park II 7500 Standish Place Rockville, MD 20850-2773	Review and approve animal drugs for market; Perform post-market surveillance and drug experience reporting on animal drugs	Compliant
CVM	Phillips Building 7520 Standish Place Rockville, MD20855-2733	Review and approve animal drugs for market; Perform post-market	Compliant

		surveillance and drug experience reporting on animal drugs	
NCTR	3900 NCTR RD NCTR 005 Jefferson, AR 72079-9501	Perform Multi-Generational Studies	Compliant
NCTR	3900 NCTR RD NCTR 005A Jefferson, AR 72079-9501	Perform Multi-Generational Studies	Compliant
NCTR	3900 NCTR RD NCTR 005B Jefferson, AR 72079-9501	Perform Multi-Generational Studies	Compliant
NCTR	3900 NCTR RD NCTR 005C Jefferson, AR 72079-9501	Perform Multi-Generational Studies	Compliant
NCTR	3900 NCTR RD NCTR 006 Jefferson, AR 72079-9501	Perform Multi-Generational Studies	Compliant
OC	Parklawn Office Bldg. 5600 Fishers Lane Rockville, MD 20857	Perform central accounting services; Provide timekeeping and administration support	Compliant
OC	5630 Fishers Lane Rockville, MD 20857	Manage physical security	Compliant
ORA	BS Truck Compound Intl Boundary Line Nogales, AZ 85621	Perform domestic/import compliance and surveillance	Compliant
ORA	Parkway Centre 1431 Harbor Bay Pkwy Alameda, CA 94502-7070	Perform domestic/import compliance and surveillance	Compliant
ORA	Newport Gateway, Suite 300 19900 MacArthur Blvd. Irvine, CA 92715-2445	Perform domestic/import compliance and surveillance	Compliant
ORA	Pacific Place, Suite 700 222 West 6th Street Import Operations Section Long Beach, CA 90731-3354	Perform domestic/import compliance and surveillance	Compliant
ORA	Los Angeles District Laboratory 1521-33 West Pico Blvd.	Perform domestic/import compliance and surveillance	Compliant

	Los Angeles, CA 90015-2486		
ORA	Oakland Federal Building, Suite 260 South 1301 Clay Street Oakland, CA 94512-5217	Perform domestic/ import compliance and surveillance	Compliant
ORA	New Commercial FAC Via De La Amistad; Otay San Diego, CA 92173	Perform domestic/ import compliance and surveillance	Compliant
ORA	DFC Bldg. 20 W. 6th Avenue & Kipling Street P.O. Box 25087 Lakewood, CO 80225-0087	Perform domestic/ import compliance and surveillance	Compliant
ORA	South Point Pkwy Ctr, Suite 502 6800 South Point Pkwy Jacksonville, FL 32202	Perform domestic/ import compliance and surveillance	Compliant
ORA	Suite 200 555 Winderley Place Maitland, FL 32751	Perform domestic/ import compliance and surveillance	Compliant
ORA	Custom Clearance Ctr Miami Resident Post 6700 NW 25th Street Miami, FL 33122	Perform domestic/ import compliance and surveillance	Compliant
ORA	Atrium Office Park 865 SW 78th Avenue Plantation, FL 33324	Perform domestic/ import compliance and surveillance	Compliant
ORA	Buschwood III, Room 170 3350 West Buschwood Park Drive Tampa, FL 33618	Perform domestic/ import compliance and surveillance	Compliant
ORA	Peachtree Summit FB 401 W. Peachtree Street Atlanta, GA 30309	Perform domestic/ import compliance and surveillance	Compliant
ORA	Crawford & Annex 60 Eighth Street, NE Atlanta, GA 30309	Perform domestic/ import compliance and surveillance	Compliant
ORA	Annex 11 Lab Facility 70 Eighth Street Atlanta, GA 30309	Perform domestic/ import compliance and surveillance	Compliant

ORA	J. Gordon Low Bldg. A 120 Barnard Street Savannah, GA 31401	Perform domestic/ import compliance and surveillance	Compliant
ORA	O'Hare R.P., Import Office 1000 Tower Lane Bensenville, IL 60106	Perform domestic/ import compliance and surveillance	Unknown
ORA	Burrell Building, Rm 510 20 North Michigan Avenue Chicago, IL 60602	Perform domestic/ import compliance and surveillance	Compliant
ORA	Chicago District Office Gateway IV (Suite 550-South) 300 South Riverside Plaza Chicago, IL 60606	Perform domestic/ import compliance and surveillance	Compliant
ORA	901 Warrenville Road, Suite 360 Lisle, IL 60532	Perform domestic/ import compliance and surveillance	Compliant
ORA	Moffett Tech Center 6502 S. Archer Road Summit-Argo, IL 60501- 1948	Perform domestic/ import compliance and surveillance	Compliant
ORA	Annex 11630 West 80th Street P.O. Box 15905 Lenexa, KS 66214-3338	Perform domestic/ import compliance and surveillance	Compliant
ORA	Textron Marine Sys P 6600 Plaza Drive New Orleans, LA 70127	Perform domestic/ import compliance and surveillance	Compliant
ORA	New England District Office One Montvale Avenue 4th Floor Stoneham, MA 02180	Perform domestic/ import compliance and surveillance	Unknown
ORA	Winchester Engineering & Analytical Center 109 Holton Street Winchester, MA 01890	Perform domestic/ import compliance and surveillance	Compliant
ORA	Dundalk Import Ops. Dundalk Marine Terminal 2700 Broening Hwy., Shed 8, 2nd Fl Baltimore, MD 21222-4107	Perform domestic/ import compliance and surveillance	Compliant
ORA	FDA Building 900 Madison Ave. Baltimore District Office Baltimore, MD 21201	Perform domestic/ import compliance and surveillance	Compliant

ORA	Calverton Off Park 7 11750 Beltsville Drive Beltsville, MD 20705-4044	Perform domestic/ import compliance and surveillance	Compliant
ORA	Parklawn Office Bldg. 5600 Fishers Lane Rockville, MD 20857	Perform domestic/ import compliance and surveillance	Compliant
ORA	Food & Drug 1560 East Jefferson Ave. Detroit, MI 48207-3179	Perform domestic/ import compliance and surveillance	Compliant
ORA	Bridge Cargo Inspect 2828 Howard Street Detroit, MI 48216-2016	Perform domestic/ import compliance and surveillance	Compliant
ORA	Food & Drug Adm. Bldg. 240 Hennepin Ave Minneapolis, MN 55401	Perform domestic/ import compliance and surveillance	Compliant
ORA	U.S. CT and Customhouse 1114 Market Street St Louis, MO 63101-2045	Perform domestic/ import compliance and surveillance	Compliant
ORA	Suites 122 & 123 12 Sunnen Drive St. Louis Branch (STL-BR) St Louis, MO 63143-3800	Perform domestic/ import compliance and surveillance	Compliant
ORA	1201 Corbin Street Elizabeth, NJ 07201	Perform domestic/ import compliance and surveillance	Compliant
ORA	Waterview Corporate Center, 3rd Floor 10 Waterview Plaza New Jersey District Office Parsippany, NJ 07054	Perform domestic/ import compliance and surveillance	Compliant
ORA	New York District, F.B. No. 2 29 & 3rd Avenue 850 3rd Avenue Brooklyn, NY 11232	Perform domestic/ import compliance and surveillance	Compliant
ORA	Buffalo District 300 Pearl St. Olympic Towers, Suite 100 Buffalo, NY 14202	Perform domestic/ import compliance and surveillance	Unknown
ORA	1 Peace Bridge Plaza Buffalo, NY 14213-2493	Perform domestic/ import compliance and surveillance	Compliant

ORA	Administration Bldg. 198 W. Service Rd IS Route 87 North Champlain, NY 12919-4440	Perform domestic/ import compliance and surveillance	Compliant
ORA	Halmar Cargo Building, JFK-RP Bldg. 75 JFK Airport New York-Queens Jamaica, NY 11434-4221	Perform domestic/ import compliance and surveillance	Compliant
ORA	Customs Immigration Bldg Lewiston, NY 14092	Perform domestic/ import compliance and surveillance	Compliant
ORA	250 Clinton Bldg., Suite 120 Syracuse, NY 13202	Perform domestic/ import compliance and surveillance	Compliant
ORA	Cincinnati District 6751 Steger Drive Cincinnati, OH 45237	Perform domestic/ import compliance and surveillance	Compliant
ORA	U.S. Customhouse, Rm 900 2nd & Chestnut Sts. Philadelphia, PA 19106	Perform domestic/ import compliance and surveillance	Compliant
ORA	Mercantile Plaza Bldg., Office 710 Ponce de Leon & Munoz Road Hato Rey, San Juan, PR 00918	Perform domestic/ import compliance and surveillance	Compliant
ORA	San Juan District P.O. Box 5719 Puerta de Tierra Station San Juan, PR 00901-3102	Perform domestic/ import compliance and surveillance	Compliant
ORA	L. Mendel Rivers FB, Rm 505 334 Meeting Street Charleston, SC 29403-6417	Perform domestic/ import compliance and surveillance	Compliant
ORA	Memphis R.P. Rm 2087, Eaglecrest Bldg. 225 N. Humphreys Blvd. Memphis, TN 38120-2149	Perform domestic/ import compliance and surveillance	Compliant
ORA	295 Building 295 Plus Park Blvd Nashville, TN 37217 Bldg. 2, Suite 250, Echelon II	Perform domestic/ import compliance and surveillance	Compliant

	9430 Research Road Austin, TX 78759		
ORA	3310 Live Oak Street Dallas District Office Dallas, TX 75204	Perform domestic/ import compliance and surveillance	Compliant
ORA	Dallas District 3032 Bryan Street Dallas, TX 75204	Perform domestic/ import compliance and surveillance	Compliant
ORA	Suite 102 7920 Elmbrook Drive Dallas SW Regional Office Dallas, TX 75247-4982	Perform domestic/ import compliance and surveillance	Compliant
ORA	USBB BR of the Amers Bldg. D, Room 101 3600 E. Paisano Drive El Paso, TX 79905	Perform domestic/ import compliance and surveillance	Compliant
ORA	Federal Building, Rm 821 200 Granby Mall Norfolk, VA 23510	Perform domestic/ import compliance and surveillance	Compliant
ORA	Station Bldg. No. 2 9901A Pacific Hwy Border St Blaine, WA 98230-9242	Perform domestic/ import compliance and surveillance	Compliant
ORA	Seattle District Office (FDA Bldg.) 22201—23rd Drive S.E. P.O. Box 3012 Bothell, WA 98041-3012	Perform domestic/ import compliance and surveillance	Compliant
ORA	Puget Sound RP Suite 2400 1000 2nd Avenue Seattle, WA 98101-1041	Perform domestic/ import compliance and surveillance	Compliant

Crisis Communication Plan

Public Health Preparedness and Response to Bioterrorism Grant

Focus Area F: Risk Communication and Health Information Dissemination
(Public Information and Communication)

Updated December 22, 2003

Table of Contents

MEMORANDUM

TO: Whom It May Concern

DATE: December 22, 2003

FROM: Gregory A. Wilson, M.D.
State Health Commissioner

RE: Crisis Communication Plan

I hereby endorse this updated *Crisis Communication Plan* for the delivery of risk communication and public health information to the public in the event of a bioterrorism, nuclear, or chemical event or other public health emergency.

I recognize that this is an evolving plan, as more information about crisis and emergency risk communication becomes available and as our response plans for Indiana are completed.

Plan Overview

Purpose:

During a bioterrorism event, the Indiana State Department of Health (ISDH) Office of Public Affairs (OPA) will coordinate and deliver risk communication and public health information to the public through every available channel, including

- the media (through a Joint Information Center [JIC], if activated),
- the ISDH Web site,
- the ISDH phone bank,
- community meetings,
- distributed flyers, and
- through partners/stakeholders.

These operations will be accomplished in close coordination with the Governor's Press Office, the State Emergency Management Agency (SEMA) public information officer (PIO), other appropriate State agency public information officers, and local health (department) officers or administrators, in accordance with federal, state, and local emergency plans.

Overall Objectives:

To gain public confidence by providing information that is:

- timely,
- empathetic,
- caring,
- accurate,
- credible, and
- pertinent;

To keep the public calm, by:

- acknowledging uncertainty;
- recognizing people's fears;
- taking care not to over-reassure;
- explaining the process in place to find answers;
- expressing wishes ("I wish I had answers....");
- giving people specific things to do; and
- asking more of people (to share the risk).

To direct public action as determined by the State Health Commissioner;

To meet the needs of the news media;

To meet the needs of partners/stakeholders; and

To coordinate with other federal, state, and local agencies involved in responding and providing information to the public.

PRINCIPLES OF RISK COMMUNICATION IN A CRISIS
Be first. Be right. Be credible.

In a crisis, people make decisions differently. They simplify, and cling to current beliefs.

They remember what they see or have previously experienced, which means that first messages carry more weight. So in a crisis, we initially communicate:

- Simply
- Timely
- Accurately
- Repeatedly
- Credibly
- Consistently

We can build trust and credibility by expressing:

- Empathy and caring
- Competence and expertise
- Honesty and openness
- Commitment and dedication

Be careful with risk comparisons. Peter Sandman, Ph.D. says the true risk and the perceived risk can be quite different. The source of the risk can be as troubling as the degree of risk. Be careful not to compare a high outrage, low hazard risk to a low outrage, high hazard risk. Bioterrorism is, for most people, high outrage and low hazard. It can't be compared with a low outrage, high hazard risk like driving a car.

Here is a risk comparison that could work: "Research indicated that, in Hawaii, a person is 10 times more likely to be killed by brain damage from a falling coconut than to be killed by a shark." In this case, the risks are both natural in origin, fairly distributed, exotic, and outside the control of the individual.

Don't over-reassure. According to Sandman, a high estimate of harm modified downward is much more acceptable to the public than a low estimate of harm modified upward. Tell people how scary the situation is; even though the actual numbers are small, and watch them get calmer.

Put the good news in subordinate clauses. Sandman says one very good approach is to put the good news in subordinate clauses, with the more alarmist side of the ambivalence in the main clause. Example: "It's too soon to say we're out of the woods yet, even though we haven't seen a new anthrax case in X days."

Acknowledge uncertainty. Acknowledging uncertainty, Sandman says, is most effective when the communicator both shows his or her distress and acknowledges the audience's distress: "How I wish I could give you a definite answer on that."

Stop trying to allay panic. According to Sandman, bad news doesn't cause panic. Panic comes from conflicting message from those in authority.

Recognize the difference in your audiences. The person who's removed from the real danger but is anticipating the high risk is much more likely to respond inappropriately than the person in the heat of the battle who is primed to act on the information and doesn't have time to mull it over, Sandman says. The vicarious rehearsal can be overwhelming in an emergency

Acknowledge people's fears. Sandman says that when people are afraid, the worst thing to do is pretend they're not. The second worst is to tell them they shouldn't be afraid. Allow people the right to feel fear.

Give people things to do. Anxiety is reduced by action and a restored sense of control.

There are three types of actions:

- Symbolic behaviors, like going to a candlelight vigil
- Preparatory behaviors, like buying water and batteries
- Contingent "if, then" behaviors, like creating an emergency family communication plan)

Ask more of people, to share the risk. Recommend a three-part action plan:

- You must do X
- You should do Y
- You can do Z

Crafting the initial message. Go forward as quickly as possible with what you do know.

Explain the process of discovering what you don't know. Use these tips:

- Be short
- Be relevant
- Give positive action steps
- Be repetitive
- Avoid all jargon
- Don't be judgmental
- Don't make promises that can't be kept
- Don't use humor

Dealing with rumors. Rebut a rumor without really repeating it. Limit the rebuttal to the places where the rumor exists.

Prepare to answer these questions:

- Are my family and I safe?
- What can I do to protect myself and my family?
- Who is in charge here?
- What can we expect?
- Why did this happen?
- Were you forewarned?
- Why wasn't this prevented?

- What else can go wrong?
- When did you begin working on this?
- What does this information mean?

As a spokesman:

- Know your organization's policies
- Stay within the scope of responsibilities
- Tell the truth.
- Embody your agency's identity.
- Stay on message:
- "What's important is to remember…"
- "I can't answer that question, but I can tell you…"
- Before I forget, I want to tell your viewers…"
- "Let me put that in perspective…"

LINE AND STAFF RESPONSIBILITIES FOR OFFICE OF PUBLIC AFFAIRS

Command and control—The director of the Office of Public Affairs, or in her absence, the marketing director and then the bioterrorism media director, will assume these responsibilities:

- Direct the work related to the release of information to the media, public, and partners;
- Activate the plan based on careful assessment of the situation and the expected demands for information by media, partners, and the public;
- Coordinate with horizontal communication partners as outlined in the plan to ensure that messages are consistent and within the scope of ISDH's responsibility;
- Provide updates to the State Health Commissioner, the Director of Emergency Preparedness, EOC command and Governor's Office, as determined in the plan;
- Advise the State Health Commissioner, the Governor's Office, and the chain of command regarding information to be released, based on the ISDH role in the response;
- Ensure that risk communication principles are employed in all contact with the media, public, and partner information release efforts;
- Be familiar with incident-specific policy, science, and situation;
- Review and approve materials for release to media, public, and partners;
- Obtain required clearance of materials for release to media on all information not previously cleared;
- Determine the operational hours/days, and reassess these throughout the emergency response; and
- Ensure that resources are available (people, equipment, and supplies).

Direct media—The director of the Office of Public Affairs and the marketing director or the bioterrorism media relations director, will jointly assume these responsibilities, as directed by the available person in charge of OPA or the State Health Commissioner or his designee:

- Assess media needs and organize mechanisms to fulfill those needs during the crisis;
- Triage the response to media requests and inquiries;
- Ensure that media inquiries are addressed as appropriate;
- Support spokespersons;
- Develop and maintain media contact lists and call logs;
- Produce and distribute media advisories and news releases;
- Produce and distribute materials, like fact sheets, audio releases, and video releases;
- Oversee media monitoring system and reports (analyzing news clips and video clips to determine needed messages, to discover which information needs to be corrected, and to identify concerns, interests, and needs arising from the crisis and the response);
- Ensure that risk communication principles to build trust and credibility are incorporated into all public messages delivered through the media; and
- Serve as a liaison from ISDH and act as a member of the JIC or field site team for media relations.

Direct public information—The marketing director and the bioterrorism media relations director, or in the absence of one of them, the Focus Area F coordinator, will jointly assume these responsibilities, as directed by the available person in charge of OPA or the State Health Commissioner or his designee:

- Manage the mechanisms to respond to the public who request information directly from the organization by telephone, in writing, or by e-mail;
- Activate and supervise the emergency telephone bank;
- Manage the e-mail inquiries coming in over the Web site;
- Assist, as requested, in the public correspondence response system; and
- Organize and manage, with the Webmaster, the emergency response Web site and Web pages, including establishing links to other emergency response Web sites.

Direct partner/stakeholder information—If assigned by the State Health

Commissioner or his designee, the director of OPA or the marketing director or the bioterrorism media relations director will assist the director of Emergency Preparedness, the director of the Office of Policy, the director of the Office of Legislative Affairs, the director of the Local Liaison Office, and other executive staff in carrying out these duties:

- Establish communication protocols based on prearranged agreements with identified partners and stakeholders;
- Arrange regular partner briefings and updates;

- Solicit feedback and respond to partner information requests and inquiries;
- Oversee partner/stakeholder monitoring systems and reports (analyzing environment and trends to determine needed messages, to discover which information needs to be corrected, and to identify concerns, interests, and needs arising from the crisis and the response);
- Help organize and facilitate official meetings to provide information and to receive input from partners or stakeholders;
- Develop and maintain lists and call logs of legislators and special interest groups;
- Respond to requests and inquiries from legislators and special interest groups.

Content and material for public health emergencies—The marketing director and the bioterrorism media relations director, or in the absence of one of them, the Focus Area F coordinator, will jointly assume these responsibilities, as requested by the director of OPA or the director of Emergency Preparedness or the State Health Commissioner or his designee:

- Develop and establish mechanisms to rapidly receive information from the EOC regarding the public health emergency;
- Translate EOC situation reports and meeting notes into information appropriate for public and partner needs;
- Work with subject matter experts to create situation-specific fact sheets, Q/A sheets, and updates;
- Compile information on possible public health emergency topics for release when needed;
- In consultation with appropriate staff, test messages and materials for cultural and language requirements of special populations;
- Receive input from other communication team members regarding content and message needs;
- Use analysis from media, public, and partner monitoring systems to adopt messages; and
- Identify additional content requirements and material development.

INTERNAL INFORMATION VERIFICATION AND APPROVAL PROCEDURES

Three people should officially clear a document before it is released from ISDH:

1. The State Health Commissioner or his designee

2. The director of the Office of Public Affairs or, in her absence, the marketing director or the bioterrorism media relations director

3. The subject matter expert (usually the State Epidemiologist)

This clearance should take place simultaneously and in person, whenever possible.

Some releases, especially those that deal with Administration policy, should be cleared by the Governor's Office or by the counter-terrorism director.

Have as much information as possible on a topic pre-developed and pre-cleared. But make sure that this prepared information is sensitive to a crisis situation. When people are sick and dying, the words you choose will naturally have to be more careful, so choose them that way from the start.

DESIGNATED SPOKESPERSONS
For ISDH:
- State Health Commissioner
- Director of OPA
- Marketing director
- Bioterrorism media relations director

For Bioterrorism Planning:
- State Health Commissioner
- Assistant Commissioner, Information Services and Policy
- Director of Emergency Preparedness

For Bioterrorist Agents:
- State Health Commissioner
- State Epidemiologist
- Veterinary Epidemiologist
- Director of Surveillance Investigation
- Appropriate subject matter experts

IDENTIFIED VEHICLES OF CRISIS INFORMATION DISSEMINATION
The OPA will use the following vehicles to provide risk communication and to inform and instruct the media, citizens, and partners/stakeholders about health and medical factors involved in the emergency:

- Telephone, with calls made to media and partners/stakeholders and received on our phone bank from citizens;
- E-mail, using prepared media, LHD, and partner/stakeholder lists and listserves;
- Fax, using pre-programmed broadcast fax lists on a fax computer and a separate (redundant) fax machine;
- Partner newsletters and fax and/or e-mail distribution lists;
- Mail and Airborne Express to send video news releases and other bulky items;
- Face-to-face, including media briefings and community meetings;
- ISDH Web site, partner/stakeholder Web sites, and media Web sites;
- Media, including print, radio, and television;
- Printed materials, including Quick Facts sheets (available on the Web) and other specially prepared leaflets.

A diagram of a community meeting poster session, an example of how to use risk communication to facilitate discussion and deal with people's anxiety during a public meeting.

STRATEGIC NATIONAL STOCKPILE PROGRAM

The health communications plan, materials, and messages should contain the following information about the SNS Program:

> The agent and its threat to the public. The particulars of the event will affect how many people seek treatment at dispensing sites and treatment centers. This information will determine how much SNS materiel and information about the SNS that you will need to provide those locations. The information should answer these questions:
>
> - Is the agent contagious?
> - Who should be concerned about exposure?
> - Who should seek preventive treatment at dispensing sites and who should seek symptomatic treatment at treatment centers?

Directions to and information about dispensing and treatment locations. This information will affect the use of specific locations and the amount of SNS materiel and the number of deliveries of that materiel that you make to specific locations. The information should answer these questions:

For State:
- What is the dispensing process?
- What forms of identification are needed?
- What information is needed to pick up medications for other family members?
- Children: weight, age, health information, drug allergies, current medications
- Adults: health information, drug allergies, current medications.

For Local:
- When will the dispensing operation start and what hours will it be open?
- Where is the nearest dispensing site?
- What is the best street access to each dispensing site?
- Where should the public park at each dispensing site if it drives?
- What is the best way to get to the dispensing site (walk, use public transportation, drive)?

Information about the drugs the public will receive. The information should include the following:

- Reasons for using specific drugs or changing drug regimens. The cultural and ethnic sensitivity with which you provide the latter information is important to ensure that neighborhoods do not think others are getting favorable treatment when they receive different drugs. This information will affect the amount of specific drugs that you have to provide to dispensing and treatment locations. It will also affect the public's acceptance of those drugs.

- Importance of taking medication. This information must stress the importance of taking all of a prescribed regimen (e.g., 60 days of doxycycline for anthrax). This information affects the demand for SNS materiel and minimizes the likelihood of more people becoming symptomatic. Adherence is a well-known problem and will be especially challenging during an emergency if the treatment regimen is long, the prescribed drugs cause unpleasant side effects, and disease outbreaks stop before the public finishes its regimen.

- Danger of overmedicating. This information focuses on dispelling the notion that if two doses per day are good, four or six must be better. Its goal is to reduce the demand for SNS materiel by discouraging individuals from picking up drugs from multiple dispensing sites. A secondary goal is to minimize the possibility that some individuals will take more of a regimen than is safe.

LOCAL HEALTH DEPARTMENT COMMUNICATION PLAN

Detailed communication plans must be in place before a public health emergency occurs.

External Communication

There will be communication to other agencies that will respond to the emergency situation accompanying public health threats. A designated person and a back up should arrange to coordinate all communication to the other agency partners. If advance warning of an emergency occurrence is possible, the lines of communication should be activated and frequent reports and updates should be made. Once an emergency is declared, the communication patterns may be altered depending on which agency assumes the lead role. In large-scale events, an "Incident Command" structure will be the likely organizational structure. Among the staff will be a Public Information Officer (PIO) and all communications should be routed through the PIO to assure coordinated responses by the different agencies. It will also be necessary for the LHD to be in constant touch with ISDH, both to report local situations and to receive helpful information. Frequent reports should be coming into the LHD from any enhanced local surveillance network activated during the emergency. At the same time, health alerts should be going out of the LHD to local medical facilities or emergency medical services. ISDH will be generating updated health alerts to LHDs and to selected medical providers, but LHDs are responsible for guaranteeing that all health care personnel in their own jurisdiction are receiving these updates.

Internal Communication

Vertical communication will also be occurring within the Local Health Department (LHD) (as well as within the other responding agencies) so that field personnel reports are quickly received and passed up the lines of authority in the agency. Likewise, decisions made by those in charge must be quickly and efficiently passed to those who will carry out the directives.

Methods of Communication

Use of phone, radio equipment, faxes, e-mail and other efficient devices must be tested before there is a need to assure that the equipment and technology are fully functional. Depending on the nature of the emergency, some information may need to be sent or received through secure channels. If the LHD or other government agency maintains a hotline (e.g. a line for public complaints or public information), the number(s) for this line could be released for use during an emergency. Advance planning should include developing "surge capacity" for the phone line including expanded hours and back up staffing. Likewise, if the LHD has a web site, Frequently Asked Questions (FAQs) can be posted there for public information.

Public Affairs

During and after a public health emergency, the need for public information is critical. Heightened public fear and misinformation can thwart efforts to reach affected populations and provide adequate control measures. Armed with factual information, the public can be a powerful ally in combating a public health emergency. Coordination between the local health department (LHD) and the ISDH is extremely important, particularly in multi-county situations. The LHD has more knowledge and trust of the population within its jurisdiction. ISDH has current information on a wide range of public health emergency issues that is readily available to LHDs. A consistent message must be provided to maintain smooth operations and credibility.

The ISDH Office of Public Affairs (OPA) is available at any time to assist the LHD with media issues. The ISDH media relations staff can be contacted 24/7 at one of these numbers:

Margaret Joseph, 317-233-7315 Pager 317-381-3906

Jennifer Dunlap, 317-233-7090 Pager 317-393-0954

If the crisis involves multiple counties, the OPA will issue news releases and handle print and electronic media inquiries. OPA staff may be dispatched to a central location in the affected area to assist, and is equipped to issue news releases in the field. If the crisis occurs in one county, the LHD may elect to issue news releases and take media inquiries or may request that the ISDH cover that responsibility. If the LHD elects to handle media issues itself, it should send copies of releases to the OPA (FAX: 317-233-7873) prior to sending them to the media. The LHD should evaluate alternative media avenues that might effectively reach potentially high-risk populations, hearing impaired, vision impaired, and shut-ins. It's important to prepare extra staff to handle the large number of phone calls that will result after the news release is issued.

Establishing good communication with local media can be accomplished in advance. Relationships with local reporters can be developed through routine announcements or "stories" of public interest generated by the LHD. Once an emergency is underway, reporters will know the spokesperson. This individual should be readily available to take advantage of the opportunity to provide high quality information, particularly if misinformation or rumors are fueling public concern. The LHD can inform reporters about when the next updates will be available and can proactively schedule press conferences. Lack of cooperation by officials will not prevent the story from being covered. Reporters may turn to other less reliable sources, especially if they do not receive information from official sources. Statements of what is being done to address the situation help reassure the public. In instances where the LHD is not the lead agency it is sometimes helpful to hold joint press conferences with the lead agency so that public health information is integrated into other announcements.

The ISDH *Protocol for Mass Prophylaxis* contains a sample community alert for use in the event of a public health emergency. The ISDH also has information for each county regarding languages spoken other than English and levels of English proficiency for those individuals whose primary language is not English. The ISDH can provide translation of typical public health alert announcements in several different languages. Other strategies to acquire translation services include contacting local colleges and universities, as well as cultural centers. Even after the crisis, local print and electronic media will usually want updates of any further cases of illness and control measures implemented. The ISDH will generally handle these calls. If the LHD elects to take these calls, the LHD should inform the ISDH of the information released.

Addressing Public Concerns
With respect to the media during an outbreak of disease, it is essential that there is accurate and timely information in a manner that addresses the nature of the outbreak in question and outlines how those exposed are being handled and the steps being taken to minimize the threat to the community. Demand for treatment or prophylaxis may outstrip available resources, especially if the "worried well" self report to facilities where these operations are underway. Useful information about who may be at risk and who is not at risk can help focus resources on those most in need.

Preparation for communication to all potential recipients of LHD information should include generalized fact sheets, health alerts, mass prophylaxis arrangements, and press releases that can be customized to the particulars of the emergency. Be aware of possible disease agents and maintain files with information for quick reference. These files help answer questions from law enforcement, fire departments, medical personnel, the public, and the media. Know where to seek additional information from ISDH, medical experts, or other reliable sources.

Messages provided need to be tailored to the audiences in a way that makes the messages easy to understand and relevant to them. Effective strategies to reach culturally diverse populations include:

- identifying respected leaders or healers within the population
- identifying bilingual programs to craft and translate public health information

- developing lists of locations where culturally diverse groups gather (e.g., churches, restaurants, markets)
- linking with school nurses in schools that serve students who speak languages other than English.

Recent experience with public concerns about potential exposure to spores of Bacillus anthracis has highlighted the need for effective communication. Recommendations for helpful messages include statements that:

1. Recognize and empathize with public concerns

2. Acknowledge that reports from the media may be confusing

3. Avoid comparing the present risk to other risks that are not part of the present fears

4. Provide frequent updates of information based on medical and scientific data

5. Give the public suggestions for actions that will help safeguard health

6. Assure the public that the LHD is also working actively to minimize health risks

These same types of messages can be adopted for interactions with individuals who may be phoning or making visits to the LHD staff.

Figure 2 illustrates how a LHD would interact with partners/stakeholders with a Joint Information Center (JIC) during a public health emergency.

Figure 2 Official Communication During a Public Health Emergency

Local Health Department (LHD) as Lead Agency	ISDH
Local Health Department as Part of Emergency Operations Center (EOC)	Elected Officials Other Officials & Professionals as needed
Emergency Management Agency (EMA)	Health Care Facilities
Emergency Medical Services (EMS)	
General Public	

First Responders: Mentally Preparing for a Disaster

Establish a proper mindset—"Expect the best, but plan for the worst" is perhaps the best summation for the first responder's mindset. Conduct your daily activities with optimism and professionalism, but always mentally prepare to adjust your mindset to a disaster recovery mode. Training and education are the best tools for being able to make this mental adjustment. Time and time again, first responders who have performed effectively under the stress of an actual critical incident relate during debriefings that they simply "fell back on their training." The more you plan and train on how you will react, the better your chances are that you will be able to respond and carry out your responsibilities automatically, without having to think too much about it.

The more realistic your training is the more it will help as well. Some of the best training for professional first responders will be hands-on simulations where emphasis is placed on realism. A mass casualty exercise, for example, in which role players simulate victims may provide highly realistic training and will help first responders mentally prepare. Some mass casualty exercises include visual and auditory effects such as smoke machines, mock explosion or gunshot sounds, apply fake blood and make-up that simulates wounds on victim role-players; have the "victims" scream and groan for help. As elaborate as these measures sound, they will go a long way to helping a first responder instantly adjust and cope with carrying out their duties in a real incident.

Establishing a game plan and educating employees, community. Security specialists and first responders alone cannot address all the contingency planning and security needs of a populace. The contingency/business continuity plan must be shared with the general community, with all persons understanding their roles and responsibilities. Realistically though, most of the general public will not be overly interested in, or take time to understand their roles in such planning. Have you ever been aboard a commercial airline and noticed during the pre-flight safety briefing given by the flight attendants that the vast majority of the passengers aren't paying attention? Although the flight attendants are trying to tell the passengers how to save their own lives during an emergency, most people don't want to listen. Even in the post 9/11 world most people still have a strong degree of denial regarding the need to prepare for an emergency.

Contingency plans must be broadcast and shared with the employee or community population, but realistically, the information shared should be concise, to the point and easy for the general public to follow. Regular employee briefings, posters and promotional activities, intranet or broadcasts with easy to follow instructions can be helpful means of sharing the requirements of a contingency/business continuity planning.

Understanding the IIPP-Most modern business and organizations are required by law to have written injury and illness prevention plans (IIPPs). Many modern security requirements will stem from IIPPs, often including specific measures for addressing and mitigating workplace violence and spelling out evacuation standards. IIPPs are also required to communicate the following key information:

- Communicating with employees on matters concerning safety and health;
- Identifying, evaluating and reducing workplace hazards;
- Implementing procedures for injury/illness investigation;
- Mitigating hazards in the workplace;
- Training employees; and
- Maintaining records.

g. Study: Prior to 9/11 there was substantial reason to believe U.S. Civil Aviation, the World Trade Center in New York, and federal facilities in Washington, DC were at great risk for such an attack. How could those threats have been better acted upon and what contingency planning could have been done to better prepare the effected facilities, corporate assets and populations?

Discussion Questions:

1) The congressional law which, when passed in 1977 helped highlight the need for contingency planning, is known as the
   _____ _____ _____ _____.

2) Which of the following is not a major goal of a contingency/business continuity plan?

   a. Preservation of life
   b. Preservation of job site analysis
   c. Preventing/mitigating damage to property and the environment
   d. Resumption of operations

3) Contingencies include any foreseen or unforeseen events which could pose a threat to life and safety; damage property and the environment; and _____ _____ _____.

4) Mitigation—_____ and _____ to prevent an emergency from occurring or to lessen the impact if one does.

5. Response—the _____, _____ and _____ effort made by trained personnel to contain and control and emergency situation.

6. Recovery—blunting losses, begin salvage and initiating the _____ _____ of normal operations.

---

7) Tier One functions are those processes and systems that if disrupted, would completely halt all operations resulting in critical human capital and financial losses.

   True   False

8) Tier two operations are non-essential functions that allow for a longer possibly even indefinite period of downtime.

   True   False

9) Although not needed on January 1, 2000, many organizations that had planned for Y2K found that they were able to continue operations during subsequent crisis such as 9/11 and the 2003 blackout by implementing Y2K contingency plans.

   True   False

10) Realistic drills and training are generally not overly useful to first responders preparing for disaster.

   True   False

Answers:

1) Foreign Corrupt Practices Act

2) B

3) Disrupt normal activities

4) Preparation and planning

5) Immediate, effective, coordinated

6) Rapid resumption

7) True

8) False

9) True

10) True

5 Incident Command Systems and the Roles

Overview:

In chapter five we will begin discussing the realities of incident command. As we have examined in previous chapters, many agencies in the U.S. and Canada operate independently, within smaller self-governing states, provinces and municipalities. These distinctions, although important for governance, do create certain complications when responding to large-scale emergencies and threats.

Establishing command, control and communications over an incident, coordinating multi-agency responses and integrating logistics and equipment have all given rise to the need for structured incident command systems.

Chapter Objectives:

- *Explain the historical events which drove the need for coordinated incident command systems such as ICS and SEMS*
- *State the basic principles of SEMS and ICS*
- *Define the different roles and responsibilities with the Incident Command System*

Standardized Emergency Management System (SEMS)

As a result of the 1991 East Bay Hills Fire in Oakland, Senate Bill 1841 was passed by the legislature and made effective January 1, 1993. The law is found in Section 8607 of the Government Code. The intent of this law, is to improve the coordination of state and local emergency response in California. The statute directed the Governor's Office of Emergency Services (OES), in coordination with other state agencies and interested local emergency management agencies, to establish by regulation the Standardized Emergency Management System (SEMS). The SEMS Regulations took effect in September of 1994.

Purpose and Scope of the SEMS Law

The basic framework of SEMS incorporates the use of the Incident Command System (ICS) (developed under the Fire Fighting Resources of California Organized for Potential Emergencies (FIRESCOPE) Program,) multi-agency or inter-agency coordination, the State's master mutual aid agreement and mutual aid program, the operational area concept and the Operational Area Satellite Information System (OASIS).

SEMS provides for a five level emergency response organization, activated as needed, to provide an effective response to multi-agency and multijurisdiction emergencies.

The use of SEMS facilitates:

- The flow of emergency information and resources within and between involved agencies at all SEMS organizational levels.
- The process of coordination between responding agencies.
- The rapid mobilization, deployment, use, and tracking of resources.

SEMS is designed to be flexible and adaptable to the varied emergencies that can occur in California, and to meet the emergency management needs of all responders.

By law, state agencies must use SEMS when responding to emergencies involving multiple jurisdictions or multiple agencies.

Local governments are strongly encouraged to use SEMS, and they must use SEMS in order to be eligible for state funding of response related personnel costs. While local governments are not required to take the State Approved Courses of Instruction on SEMS, they will be required to maintain minimum training competencies in SEMS.

SEMS is a management system. It is based on a proven system that has been in use for over twenty years. SEMS provides an organizational framework and guidance for operations at each level of the state's emergency management system. It provides the umbrella under which all response agencies may function in an integrated fashion.

Review of Common SEMS Terms and Definitions

In order to gain a better understanding of SEMS, and to allow you to more effectively use the system, it is important to be able to describe the following terms and know their relationships in SEMS.

Emergency A condition of disaster or extreme peril to the safety of persons or property. Emergencies can be small or large.

Emergency response agency Any organization responding to an emergency or providing mutual aid support to such an organization whether in the field, at the scene of an incident, or to an operations center.

SEMS Introductory Course (Should this be here?)

Student Reference Manual, page (Should this be here?)

response personnel Personnel involved with an agency's response to an emergency.

Incident Command System (ICS) A nationally used standardized on-scene emergency management system.

Multi-agency or inter-agency coordination Agencies working together at any SEMS level to facilitate decisions.

Mutual Aid Voluntary provision of services and facilities when existing resources prove to be inadequate. California mutual aid is based upon the State's Master Mutual Aid Agreement. There are several mutual aid systems included in the mutual aid program.

Operational Area An intermediate level of the state emergency services organization consisting of a county and all political subdivisions within the county area.

Emergency Operations Center A location from which centralized emergency management can be performed. EOC facilities are found at local governments, operational areas, regions and state.

Need for SEMS Training

Training is essential to the effective use of SEMS at all levels. The State has developed and provided an approved Course of Instruction that can be used at each of the five levels in SEMS. Agencies at all SEMS levels may use the Approved Course of Instruction developed by the State, or use an internal training program to meet required training competencies. Training competencies are described at each level of the State's training curriculum as performance objectives.

There are four courses within the SEMS Training Program:

1. **Introductory** (this course) A self-study or instructor based course with four modules.

2. **Field Level** Nineteen modules of instruction are available for the Field Response Level. The modules are clustered into four sub-tier courses: ICS Orientation, Basic, Intermediate, and Advanced. Each sub-tier should be taken at different stages of career development. Together they provide over 75 hours of instruction.

3. **Module A2** Introduction to SEMS Components and Features

A. Module Description

Module A2 provides the student with a basic understanding of the four elements of the SEMS law, the five SEMS levels, the five functions of SEMS, and the basic concepts of SEMS.

B. Module Content

1. Five basic components of SEMS—SEMS will integrate several of the state's primary emergency response programs. The primary components which comprise SEMS are:

   • The Incident Command System as developed by FIRESCOPE*

   • Multi-Agency Coordination System (MACS) developed by FIRESCOPE*

   • The Master Mutual Aid agreement

   • Use of Operational Areas

   • The Operational Area Satellite Information System (OASIS)
     *FIRESCOPE (Firefighting Resources of California Organized for Potential Emergencies) is a cooperative interagency program established by the fire services. Each of the components is briefly discussed to provide you with a better understanding of their role and importance in SEMS.

The Incident Command System (ICS)

The ICS was developed as a part of the FIRESCOPE program during the 1970's by an interagency working group representing local, state and federal fire services in California. After field tests, ICS was adopted by the fire services in California as the standard all hazards response system. ICS also has been adopted nationally by the federal land management agencies as the standard for response to all wildland fires. A national generic version of ICS has been developed by a multi discipline working group. This system will be used in the State's Field Response Level Approved Course of Instruction. A module on Mutual Aid and a module on EOC, Operational Area and ICS Coordination have been added to that curriculum.

Multi-agency Coordination

Multi-agency or inter-agency coordination as it applies to SEMS, means the participation of agencies and disciplines involved at any level of the SEMS organization working together in a coordinated effort to facilitate decisions for overall emergency response activities, including the sharing of critical resources and the prioritization of incidents. Multi-agency coordination is generally that which takes place among agencies within a jurisdiction. For example, between police, fire, and public works departments working together at an EOC. Inter-agency coordination is generally that which takes place between agencies in different jurisdictions or between agencies at different levels. For example, a county sheriff, municipal police and national guard. SEMS Guidance and the Approved Courses of Instruction all describe how multi-agency or inter-agency coordination takes place at the various SEMS levels.

The Master Mutual Aid Agreement

A Master Mutual Aid Agreement in California was originally signed in 1950. Under this agreement, cities, counties and the State joined together to provide for a comprehensive program of voluntarily providing services, resources and facilities to jurisdictions when local resources prove to be inadequate to cope with a given situation. A copy of the California Master Mutual Aid Agreement is attached to the Student Reference Manual. Written mutual aid plans and operating procedures have been developed for several discipline specific mutual aid systems that function on a statewide basis within the Master Mutual Aid Agreement. The fire and rescue and law enforcement systems are examples which we hear the most about. Emergency Medical, Coroner and Search and Rescue systems also exist. Public works and building officials mutual aid systems are under development.

The mutual aid systems, current and planned, form essential links in SEMS. A comprehensive discussion of mutual aid is contained in SEMS guidance, and one module of the Field Level Course of Instruction is devoted to the subject of Mutual Aid.

Operational Areas

An Operational Area is one of the five organizational levels in SEMS. An Operational Area consists of a county, and all political subdivisions within the county area. The governing bodies of each county and of the political subdivisions in the county may organize and structure their operational area. The county will be the lead agency for the operational area unless another arrangement is established by agreement. The operational area is used by the county and the political subdivisions within the operational area for the coordination of resources and information, and to serve as a link in the system of communications and coordination between the state's emergency operation centers and the operation centers of the political subdivisions within the operational area.

OASIS—Operational Area Satellite Information System

The Operational Area Satellite Information System (OASIS) is a satellite based communications system with a high frequency radio backup. OASIS provides the capability to rapidly transfer a wide variety of information reports between OASIS user agencies. In SEMS, OASIS can be viewed as both a communications network and information dissemination system linking three of the five SEMS organizational levels. The communications components to the system include a satellite system in each operational area linked to selected state, federal and local agencies. The information processing component of OASIS contains fifteen forms which provide a rapid and accurate means of transferring information between locations on the OASIS network.

Organizational/response levels and activation requirements.

SEMS regulations describe five organizational response levels. The levels are:
- Field
- Local Government
- Operational Area
- Region
- State

The following is a brief description of each level:

a. **Field Response Level** The field response level is the level where emergency response personnel and resources carry out tactical decisions and activities under the command of an appropriate authority in direct response to an incident or threat. SEMS regulations require the use of ICS at the field response level of an incident. The Field Response level is described in Part I—B of the SEMS Guidelines, and in the Field Level Approved Course of Instruction.

b. **Local Government Level** Local governments include cities, counties, and special districts. Local governments manage and coordinate the overall emergency response and recovery activities within their jurisdiction. In SEMS, the local government emergency management organization and its relationship and connections to the Field Response level may vary depending upon factors related to SEMS Introductory geographical size, population, function, or complexity. The local government level is described further in Part I-C of the SEMS Guidelines.

c. **Operational Area** Under SEMS, the operational area means an intermediate level of the state's emergency services organization which encompasses the county and all political subdivisions located within the county. The operational area manages and/or coordinates information, resources, and priorities among local governments within the operational area, and serves as the coordination and communication link between the local government level and the regional level.

It is important to note, that while an operational area always encompasses the entire county area, it does not necessarily mean that the county government itself manages and coordinates the response and recovery activities within the county. In most cases, the county EOC will function as both the Operational Area EOC and the EOC for the county. The decision on organization and structure within the Operational Area is made by the governing bodies of the county and the political subdivisions within the county. The operational area level is described more fully in Part I–D of the SEMS Guidelines.

d. **Regional** Because of its size and geography, the state has been divided into six Mutual Aid Regions. The purpose of a mutual aid region, is to provide for the more effective application and coordination of mutual aid and other emergency related activities. The Office of Emergency Services (OES) provides administrative oversight over the mutual aid regions through three Administrative Regional Offices. The map shows the relationship between mutual aid regions and OES regional offices. In SEMS, the regional level manages and coordinates information and resources among operational areas within the mutual aid region, and also between the operational areas and the state level. The regional level also coordinates overall state agency support for emergency response activities within the region. The regional level is described further in Part I–E of the SEMS Guidelines.

e. **State** The state level of SEMS manages state resources in response to the emergency needs of the other levels, and coordinates mutual aid among the mutual aid regions and between the regional level and state level. The state level also serves as the initial coordination and communication link between the state and the federal disaster response system. After initial contact at the state level, those federal response elements deemed necessary by the REOC Director will be directed to SEMS co-locate with state counterparts at the REOC. The state level is described further in part

Basic features used at each SEMS level

SEMS has several features based on the Incident Command System (ICS). The field response level uses functions, principles, and components of ICS as required in SEMS regulations. Many of these field response level features are also applicable at local government, operational area, regional and state levels. In addition, there are other ICS features that have application to all SEMS levels. Described below are the features of ICS which are applicable to all SEMS levels. These features are covered in more detail in appropriate parts of the Guidance, and the approved training courses. Essential Management Functions SEMS is based on the Incident Command System (ICS). ICS has five primary functions applicable to any emergency. These are: command, operations, planning/intelligence, logistics and finance/administration. These functions are required for use at all SEMS levels. To avoid confusion, and to stress the role of the EOC, the term management is used rather than command at all EOC levels.

Management by Objectives

The Management by Objectives feature of ICS as applied to SEMS, means that each SEMS level should identify measurable and attainable objectives to be achieved. The time frame necessary to accomplish these objectives is known as the Operational Period.

Action Planning

Action planning should be used at all SEMS levels. The use of action plans provides designated personnel with knowledge of the objectives to be achieved and the steps required for achievement. Once objectives are determined, the operational period action plan provides a framework for establishing the necessary organization, making assignments and allocating resources to accomplish the objectives. At the incident, action plans are known as Incident Action Plans.

Organizational Flexibility—Modular Organization

At each SEMS level, only those parts of the planned organization that are necessary to meet current objectives need to be activated, and the organization can be arranged in various ways within or under the five SEMS functions. The tasks assigned to non-activated parts of the organization will be the responsibility of the next highest level in the organization.

Organizational Unity and Hierarchy of Command or Management

Organizational Unity means that every individual within an organization has designated supervision. Hierarchy of command/management means that all parts of the organization within each activated SEMS level are linked together to form a single overall organization within appropriate span-of-control limits.

Span of Control

Maintaining a reasonable span of control is the responsibility of every supervisor at all SEMS levels. ICS development established a one to seven ratio as the maximum span of control under emergency response conditions. One to five ratio was established as an optimum. This means that in an emergency response organization, one supervisor should have direct supervisory authority of no more than five positions if they are performing separate functions..

Personnel Accountability

Personnel accountability is accomplished through the Organizational Unity and Hierarchy of Command/management feature along with the use of check-in forms, position logs and various status keeping systems.

Common Terminology

Common terminology is applied to organizational elements, position titles, facility designations and resources in order to rapidly enable multi-agency, multijurisdiction organizations, disciplines and resources to work together effectively.

Resources Management

At all SEMS levels, there is a responsibility related to managing resources. This will vary from level to level in terms of tactical directing and controlling, to coordination, to resource inventorying or strategic planning.

Integrated Communications

At the field response level, integrated communications is used on any emergency involving multiple agencies. At all EOC levels, and between all SEMS levels there must be a dedicated effort to ensure that communications systems, planning, and information flow are being accomplished in an effective manner.

Titles and Roles for the five SEMS functions at the Field and EOC levels.

The primary functions found in ICS are:

- Incident Command

- Operations

- Planning/Intelligence

- Logistics

- Finance/Administration

These same functions with some minor variation in titles and associated activity are the key functional activities found at all SEMS EOC levels. The table below provides a brief summary of the titles and definitions of activities associated with these functions.

Primary SEMS Function Field Response Level EOCS at Other SEMS Levels

Command/ Management Command is responsible for the directing, ordering, and/or controlling of resources. Management is responsible for overall emergency policy and coordination.

Operations The coordinated tactical response of all field operations in accordance with the Incident Action Plan. The coordinating all jurisdictional operations in support of the response to the emergency.

Planning/Intelligence The collection, evaluation, documentation, and use of information related to the incident. Collecting, evaluating, and disseminating information and maintaining documentation.

Logistics Providing facilities, services, personnel, equipment, and materials in support of the incident. Providing facilities, services, personnel, equipment, and materials.

Finance/Administration Financial and cost analysis and administrative aspects not handled by the other functions. Financial activities and administrative aspects not assigned to the other functions.

SEMS concept of teamwork, coordination and effectiveness

SEMS as a management system provides for a fully integrated and coordinated multiple level response to multi-agency, multi jurisdictional emergencies. The bringing together of the Incident Command System, multi-agency or inter-agency coordination, mutual aid systems the operational area concept and OASIS into a single standardized management system is a major step forward in increasing the effectiveness of California's response to emergencies.

SEMS Implementation

The SEMS Statute requires all state agencies to implement and use SEMS in responding to multi-agency or multiple jurisdiction emergencies. Local agencies are encouraged to implement SEMS, but are not required to do so under law. Use of SEMS by local government agencies is required to obtain state reimbursement for response related personnel costs. The following material has been developed by an inter-agency working group to assist state and local agencies in implementing and maintaining SEMS.

1. SEMS Statute—Government Code Section 8607, January 1993

2. SEMS Regulations—California Code of Regulations Title 19. Division 2, Sections 2400-2450.

3. SEMS Guidelines—in three parts

4. SEMS Training Curriculum

Module A3—SEMS Operating Requirements and Individual Responsibilities

A. Module Description

Module A3 provides the student with an understanding of the basic operating requirements needed to individually work within, and support, a Standardized Emergency Management System (SEMS) field response and Emergency Operations Center (EOC) organization.

The following topics will be covered:
- Roles and Functions for Personnel in SEMS organizations at all levels
- SEMS pre-assignment responsibilities
- SEMS Check-in Process
- Reporting to supervisors within SEMS
- Incoming briefings in SEMS
- General operating requirements for SEMS
- General demobilization/release requirements for SEMS
- Where to go for additional field or EOC SEMS training

B. Module Content

1. Roles and Functions for Personnel in SEMS organizations at all levels

Field Level   At the field level, emergency response personnel may assume a variety of roles within the Incident Command System. Agency policy will often dictate what personnel will fill what roles. A concept here is to use the most qualified individuals regardless of rank or position. The determination of what role they will perform will be a function of:

- The kind and size of the emergency
- Disciplines involved
- Personnel background and experience
- Training
- Qualifications and certifications
- Agency policy

ICS provides an emergency management structure which allows for the most qualified personnel to be used at any position.

Incident Commanders may at the onset of the emergency be relatively low ranking personnel. ICS provides a mechanism for the transfer of command if the emergency requires more qualified personnel. EOC Level The five major functions required within the organization at the EOC level may require personnel from a variety of agencies within a municipality, operational area, region or state, depending upon the level being activated. Shown below, are two examples. One for local government and operational areas, and the other for region and State.

Local Government or Operational Area EOC Function Staffing Considerations

Management Administrative personnel, special district managers, emergency management, fire, law enforcement are recommended for use in initial EOC activations.

Operations Key department. managers and public safety personnel will generally coordinate these activities within the EOC during initial activations.

Planning/Intelligence Emergency Management, CAO, fire, law enforcement, planning depts., utilities and other departments can contribute personnel depending upon the nature of the emergency.

Logistics Departments of General Services, Public Works and utilities are good candidates to provide personnel for this EOC function. Other departments may also have the background to manage or assist in this function.

Finance/Administration City/County CAO, Finance Departments are candidates for managing this function within an EOC

Region/State EOC Function Staffing Considerations

Management SOC Director—OES Director, Chief Deputy Director, Deputy Directors. REOC Director—Regional Administrators

Operations To fill Section/Branch Positions: OES, CDF, Fire Marshal, CALEPA, DHS, DFG, CHP, State Police, CNG, EMSA, Mental Health, DSS, ARC, OSHPD, PUC etc.

Planning/Intelligence OES Staff, CDF, CNG, DFG, CALTRANS plus Technical Advisors as necessary from CDMG, DHS etc.

Logistics To fill Section/Branch Positions: General Services, OES, CDF, DFG, CNG, DPA, EDDP

Finance/Administration OES, Department. of Finance

2. SEMS pre-assignment responsibilities

The activation of any SEMS level (field or EOC) may require personnel to be temporarily relocated for an indefinite time. While most activation's will generally be of short duration (one day to a few days), there may be situations in which personnel will be absent from their normal workplace and homes for extended periods many days or even weeks. The following are general guidelines to take before departing for those situations which will require an extended stay or out-of-jurisdiction travel:

- Assemble or update a travel kit containing any special technical information, e.g., maps, manuals, contact lists, and other reference materials that you may need.

- Prepare personal items that you will need for your estimated length of stay.

- Review your emergency assignment. Know to whom you will report and what your responsibility will be.

- Have a clear understanding of the decision-making authority you hold for your agency while at an incident or at an EOC. Determine this as soon as you realize you may be assigned to an incident or to your own or another EOC.

- Determine what communications procedures should be followed so you can contact your headquarters or home office if necessary.

- Ensure that family members know your destination and how to contact you in the event of a family emergency.

- Familiarize yourself with travel and pick-up arrangements that have been established for you.

- Determine what your return mode of transportation will be if possible.

SEMS Check-in Process

Field Response Level All personnel assigned to an incident which is using ICS must check-in upon arrival. The check-in function at an incident ensures that there is complete and continuous accountability over all assigned personnel. There are various specified locations at an incident where personnel and resources check-in can be accomplished. These will be covered in the field level course.

EOC Levels To ensure accountability of personnel, it is essential that a check-in function be established at all EOC levels. Currently, this is done through the use of sign-in sheets, rosters etc. An adaptation of the ICS check-in form and procedure for EOCs may be useful for the EOC level check-in function.

Reporting to supervisors within SEMS

Under the unity of command or management feature of SEMS, all personnel operating within a field response ICS organization, or at an EOC level must have a supervisory reporting link established.

Incoming briefings in SEMS

All incoming personnel, whether to an ICS organization at the Field Response level, or reporting to an EOC, should be provided with a briefing, prior to their assuming their assigned position. Briefings should include:

- Current situation assessment.
- Identification of specific job responsibilities expected of you.
- Identification of co-workers within your job function and/or geographical assignment.
- Availability of communications.
- Location of work area.
- Identification of eating and sleeping arrangements as appropriate.
- Procedural instructions for obtaining additional supplies, services and personnel.
- Identification of operational period work shifts.
- After receiving your briefing and activating your assignment, give a similar briefing to any personnel assigned to you.

General operating requirements for SEMS

Following are several important requirements related to the use of SEMS at any level: SEMS requires emergency response agencies to use basic principles and components of emergency management including ICS, and multi-agency or inter-agency coordination. The five primary functions of Command or Management, Operations, Planning/Intelligence and Administration/Finance must be provided for in all organizations at any SEMS level. Personnel in a SEMS organization at any of the five levels must be assigned to a designated function within the organization, and at all times have designated supervision. Personnel assigned within a SEMS organization will safely carry out their assignment for an operational period or until relieved, and will brief their relief as required by agency standard operating procedures.

General demobilization/release requirements for SEMS

Agency requirements for demobilization at incidents at the Field Response or at EOC levels will vary considerably. Large incidents and/or EOCs within larger jurisdictions may require the establishment of a Demobilization Unit within the Planning/Intelligence Section to help facilitate the demobilization process.

General demobilization considerations for all personnel at either the Field Response or EOC levels are to:
  * Complete all work assignments.
  * Brief subordinates regarding demobilization.
  * Complete and file required forms and reports.
  * Follow agency check-out procedures.
  * Evaluate performance of subordinates prior to release.
  * Return any communications equipment or other non-expendable supplies.
  * Report to assigned departure points on time or slightly ahead of schedule.

Where to go for additional field or EOC SEMS training

An inter-agency group has developed four approved courses of instruction in SEMS.
  * Introduction to SEMS
  * SEMS for Field Response
  * SEMS for EOC's
  * Executive SEMS Course

The Field Response SEMS course has been adapted from a generic National ICS training curriculum, and is divided into four sub-courses. Information on all SEMS courses is available through: OES Headquarters OES Regions California Specialized Training Institute (CSTI)

INCIDENT COMMAND SYSTEM
Position Manual
STAGING AREA MANAGER—HIGH RISE INCIDENT

ICS-HR-222-5
January 28, 1999

This document contains information relative to the Incident Command System (ICS) component of the National Interagency Incident Management System (NIIMS). This is the same Incident Command System developed by FIRESCOPE.

Additional information and documentation can be obtained from the following sources:

OES—FIRESCOPE—OCC
Document Control
2524 Mulberry Street
Riverside, CA 92501-2200
(909) 782-4174
Fax (909) 782-4239

CONTENTS

CHAPTER I CHECKLIST

1.1 CHECKLIST USE
The checklist presented below should be considered as a minimum requirement for the position. Users of this manual should feel free to augment these lists as necessary. Note that some of the activities are one-time actions while others are ongoing for the duration of an incident.

1.2 HIGH RISE INCIDENT STAGING AREA MANAGER'S CHECKLIST
a. Obtain briefing from Operations Section Chief, or Incident Commander.

b. Proceed to selected floors and evaluate layout and suitability. Select Staging Area floor, and advise Operations and Logistics Sections Chiefs. Request necessary resources and personnel.

c. Establish Staging Area layout and identify/post each function area as appropriate to the incident size and expected duration—Crew Ready Area, Air Cylinder Exchange, Equipment Pool, Rehabilitation/Aid Area.

d. Determine, establish or request needed facility services—sanitation, drinking water, and lighting. Coordinate with Logistics Section or Systems Control Unit to maintain fresh air. Maintain Staging area in an orderly condition.

e. Establish a check-in function for arriving and departing crews.

f. Determine required resource levels from the Operations Section Chief.

g. Designate area(s) for Rapid Intervention Crew or Company (RIC) to standby in a state of readiness.

h. Maintain accounting of resources in Staging and periodically update Operations Section Chief and Resources Unit. Advise the Operations Section Chief when reserve levels reach pre-identified minimums.

i. As requested by Operations Section Chief or Incident Commander, direct crews and equipment to designated locations.

j. Secure operations and demobilize personnel as determined by the demobilization plan.

k. Maintain Unit Log (ICS Form 214).

CHAPTER 2 ORGANIZATION, PERSONNEL AND PROCEDURES

2. 1 ORGANIZATION

The High Rise Incident Staging Area Manager is responsible for the management of all functions at the in-building Staging Area, and reports to the Operations Section Chief. The High Rise Incident Staging Area Manager's organizational responsibilities vary somewhat from the standardized ICS position in that the area also provides a safe refuge/support function within the building. An air cylinder exchange and a rehabilitation/aid function are typically established as part of the area.

2.2 PERSONNEL

The number of personnel needed to perform the major responsibilities assigned to the unit will vary based upon the size and duration of the incident. The minimum number of personnel may be estimated from the information presented in 2.3, below.

2.3 MAJOR RESPONSIBILITIES AND PROCEDURES

The major responsibilities of the High Rise Incident Staging Area Manager are stated below. Following each activity are listed the procedures for implementing the activity.

a. Obtain briefing from Operations Section Chief or Incident Commander.

   1. Determine the estimated size and duration of incident.

   2. Identify current location, and existing assignments and commands relating to an already established Staging Area.

   3. Obtain assigned communications channels.

b. Proceed to selected floors and evaluate layouts and suitability. Select Staging Area floor, and advise Operations and Logistics Section Chiefs. Request necessary resources and personnel.

   1. Select a floor free of atmospheric contamination with adequate open spaces for the needed functions.

   2. Protect occupant furnishings, equipment and records from damage.

   3. Provide personnel for check-in/accounting, air cylinder exchange, communications, and support. Coordinate with Medical Unit for staffing of the Rehabilitation/Aid area.

c. Establish Staging Area layout and identify/post each function area as appropriate to the incident size and expected duration—Crew Ready Area, Air Cylinder Exchange, Equipment Pool, Rehabilitation/Aid Area.

   1. Locate Crew Ready Area and Rehabilitation/Aid areas away from stairwell doors. Locate Air Cylinder Exchange adjacent to the stairwell door or doors.

   2. Post or write directions to Staging Area on stairwell walls, advise Lobby Control and Operations of location. Post clear directional signs to Staging Area functional areas.

d. Determine, establish or request needed facility services—sanitation, drinking water, and lighting. Coordinate with Logistics Section or Systems Control Unit to maintain fresh air. Maintain Staging area in an orderly condition.

   1. Check the operation of building systems. Order alternative water supplies if not functioning.

   2. Order back-up power and lighting sources in anticipation of building power failure.

   3. Maintain workable spaces and passageways. Coordinate with Ground Support for empty air cylinder rotation.

e. Establish a check-in function for arriving and departing crews.

   1. Record crews or personnel assigned to report to Staging in an available status. Record crews or personnel departing to assignments or locations out of Staging.

f. Determine required resource levels from the Operations Section Chief.

   1. Maintain ongoing communication regarding appropriate personnel levels and readiness.

2. Brief Staging Area Check-In/Accounting personnel regarding target levels.

g. Designate area(s) for Rapid Intervention Crew or Company (RIC) to standby in a state of readiness.

h. Maintain accounting of resources in Staging and periodically update Operations Section Chief and Resources Unit. Advise the Operations Section Chief when reserve resource levels reach pre-identified minimums.

1. Track individual personnel or crew designation as appropriate.

2. Track assembled equipment resources. Coordinate with Ground Support Unit to provide air cylinder rotation. Coordinate with Logistics Section Chief or Base Manager, as appropriate, for needed equipment.

i. As requested by Operations Section Chief or Incident Commander, direct crews and equipment to designated locations.

1. Obtain necessary information regarding selected stairwells, use of elevators, reporting locations, and organizational elements. Confirm required accompanying resources and equipment.

j. Secure operations and demobilize personnel as determined by the demobilization plan.

1. Based upon the demobilization plan, transfer control and responsibility for any building or facility used to appropriate property management.

2. Coordinate with Ground Support Unit for the return of all equipment to Base.

k. Maintain Unit Log (ICS Form 214).

Rapid Incident Command System (RICS)[2]

Incident Commander

The command function is directed by the Incident Commander, who is the person in charge at the incident, and who must be fully qualified to manage the response. Major responsibilities for the Incident Commander include:

- Performing command activities, such as establishing command and establishing the ICP
- Protecting life and property
- Controlling personnel and equipment resources
- Maintaining accountability for responder and public safety, as well as for task accomplishment
- Establishing and maintaining an effective liaison with outside agencies and organizations, including the EOC, when it is activated
- Establishing command

- Ensuring responder safety
- Assessing incident priorities
- Determining operational objectives
- Developing and implementing the Incident Action Plan (Incident Action Plan)
- Developing an appropriate organizational structure
- Maintaining a manageable span of control
- Managing incident resources
- Coordinating overall emergency activities
- Coordinating the activities of outside agencies
- Authorizing the release of information to the media
- Keeping track of costs

An effective Incident Commander must be assertive, decisive, objective, calm, and a quick thinker. To handle all of the responsibilities of this role, the Incident Commander also needs to be adaptable, flexible, and realistic about his or her limitations. The Incident Commander also needs to have the capability to delegate positions appropriately as needed for an incident. Initially, the Incident Commander will be the senior first-responder to arrive at the scene. As additional responders arrive, command will transfer on the basis of who has primary authority for overall control of the incident. As incidents grow in size or become more complex, the responsible jurisdiction or agency may assign a more highly qualified Incident Commander. At transfer of command, the outgoing Incident Commander must give the incoming Incident Commander a full briefing and notify all staff of the change in command.

As incidents grow, the Incident Commander may delegate authority for performing certain activities to others, as required. When expansion is required, the Incident Commander will establish other Command Staff positions: Information Officer, Safety Officer, Liaison Officer.

- The Information Officer handles all media inquiries and coordinates the release of information to the media with the Public Affairs Officer at the EOC
- The Safety Officer monitors safety conditions and develops measures for ensuring the safety of all assigned personnel
- The Liaison Officer is the on-scene contact for other agencies assigned to the incident

The Incident Commander will base the decision to expand (or contract) the ICS organization on three major incident priorities:

- **Life safety.** The Incident Commander's first priority is always the life safety of the emergency responders and the public.
- **Incident stability.** The Incident Commander is responsible for determining the strategy that will:

Minimize the effect that the incident may have on the surrounding area. Maximize the response effort while using resources efficiently. The size and complexity of the command system that the Incident Commander develops should be in keeping with the complexity (i.e., level of difficulty in the response) of the incident, not the size (which is based on geographic area or number of resources).

- Property conservation. The Incident Commander is responsible for minimizing damage to property while achieving the incident objectives. As incidents become more involved, the Incident Commander can activate additional General Staff sections (that is, Planning, Operations, Logistics, and/or Finance/Administration), as necessary.

Often the ICS system requires two independent specialist positions that report to and directly work with the Incident Commander. One is the safety officer and the other is the public information officer.

Safety Officer
The safety officer monitors safety conditions and develops measures for ensuring the safety of all assigned personnel. The safety officer is the only positions empowered to override and IC's decision if that decision is believed to be needlessly dangerous- such as sending an operations team into a confined space without sufficient protective equipment.

Public Information Officer
The PIO handles all media inquiries and coordinates the release of information to the media with the Public Affairs Officer at the Emergency Operations Center. Whenever a first responder is approached by a member of the media, the responder should refer the reporter to the PIO.

Planning
In smaller events, the Incident Commander is responsible for planning, but when the incident is of larger scale, the Incident Commander establishes the Planning Section. The Planning Section's function includes the collection, evaluation, dissemination, and use of information about the development of the incident and status of resources. This section's responsibilities can also include creation of the Incident Action Plan (Incident Action Plan), which defines the response activities and resource utilization for a specified time period.

Logistics
The Logistics Section is responsible for providing facilities, services, and materials, including personnel to operate the requested equipment for the incident. This section takes on great significance in long-term or extended operations. It is important to note that the Logistics Section functions are geared to support the incident responders. For example, the Medical Unit in the Logistics Section provides care for the incident responders not civilian victims.

Operations

The Operations Section Incident Command Finance/Administration Section Logistics Section Operations Section Planning Section The Operations Section is responsible for carrying out the response activities described in the Incident Action Plan. The Operations Section Chief coordinates Operations Section activities and has primary responsibility for receiving and implementing the Incident Action Plan. The Operations Section Chief reports to the Incident Commander and determines the required resources and organizational structure within the Operations Section. The Operations Section Chief's main responsibilities are to:

- Direct and coordinate all operations, ensuring the safety of Operations Section personnel
- Assist the Incident Commander in developing response goals and objectives for the incident
- Implement the Incident Action Plan
- Request (or release) resources through the Incident Commander
- Keep the Incident Commander informed of situation and resource status within operations
- Manage all technical specialists and convergent volunteers.
    1. Technical Specialists
        a. Firefighters
        b. HAZMAT Technicians
        c. Law Enforcement & Security
        d. Electricians
        e. Carpenters
        f. Communications Technicians
        g. Welders
        h. Structural Engineers
    2. Medical
        a. Registered Nurses
        b. Physicians and Physician's Assistants
        c. Medical Examiners
        d. Paramedics
        e. Emergency Medical Technicians
    3. Search & Rescue
        a. Canine Teams
        b. Urban Search & Rescue Specialists
    4. Convergent volunteers
        a. Sentries
        b. "Go-fers"

    c. Runners

    d. Additional searchers

Administration & Finance

Though sometimes overlooked, the Finance/Administration Section is critical for tracking incident costs and reimbursement accounting. Unless costs and financial operations are carefully recorded and justified, reimbursement of costs is difficult, if not impossible. The Finance/Administration Section is especially important when the incident is of a magnitude that may result in a Presidential Declaration. Each of these functional areas can be expanded into additional organizational units with further delegation of authority. They also may be contracted as the incident deescalates.

ICS Concepts and Principles

The adaptable ICS structure is composed of major components to ensure quick and effective resource commitment and to minimize disruption to the normal operating policies and procedures of responding organizations. Remember that ICS concepts and principles have been tested and proven over time-in business and industry and by response agencies at all governmental levels. ICS training is required to ensure that all who may become involved in an incident are familiar with ICS principles. In this section you will find how the application of these concepts and principles makes ICS work. An ICS structure should include:

- Common terminology (plain-English radio codes, area-wide standards for unit IDs)
- A modular organization
- Integrated communications (800 MHz radio, common frequencies, radio patch capability)
- Unity of command
- A unified command structure
- Consolidated Incident Action Plans
- A manageable span of control
- Designated incident facilities (alternate, mobile or consolidated communication centers)
- Comprehensive resource management

Common terminology is essential in any emergency management system, especially when diverse or other than first-response agencies are involved in the response. When agencies have slightly different meanings for terms, confusion and inefficiency can result. Do you know what a Staging Area is? Will all responders understand what a Staging Area is? In ICS, major organizational functions, facilities, and units are predesignated and given titles. ICS terminology is standard and consistent among all of the agencies involved. To prevent confusion when multiple incidents occur at the same time within the same For example, an incident that occurs at 14th and Flower might be called "Flower Street Command." One that occurs

Incident Command System

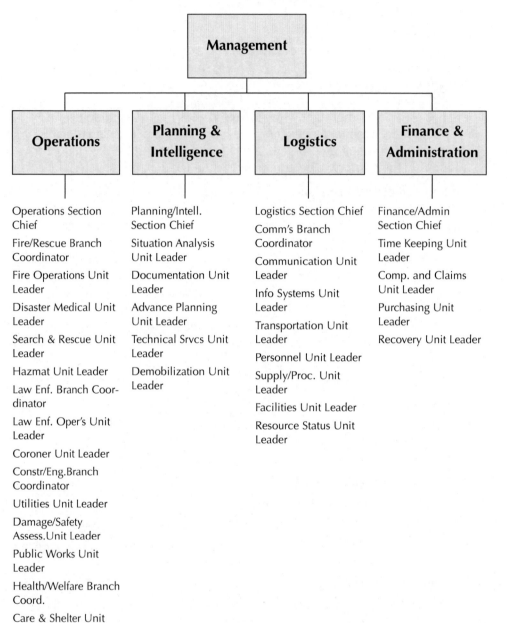

Management

Operations	**Planning & Intelligence**	**Logistics**	**Finance & Administration**
Operations Section Chief	Planning/Intell. Section Chief	Logistics Section Chief	Finance/Admin Section Chief
Fire/Rescue Branch Coordinator	Situation Analysis Unit Leader	Comm's Branch Coordinator	Time Keeping Unit Leader
Fire Operations Unit Leader	Documentation Unit Leader	Communication Unit Leader	Comp. and Claims Unit Leader
Disaster Medical Unit Leader	Advance Planning Unit Leader	Info Systems Unit Leader	Purchasing Unit Leader
Search & Rescue Unit Leader	Technical Srvcs Unit Leader	Transportation Unit Leader	Recovery Unit Leader
Hazmat Unit Leader	Demobilization Unit Leader	Personnel Unit Leader	
Law Enf. Branch Coordinator		Supply/Proc. Unit Leader	
Law Enf. Oper's Unit Leader		Facilities Unit Leader	
Coroner Unit Leader		Resource Status Unit Leader	
Constr/Eng.Branch Coordinator			
Utilities Unit Leader			
Damage/Safety Assess.Unit Leader			
Public Works Unit Leader			
Health/Welfare Branch Coord.			
Care & Shelter Unit Leader			
Public Health Unit Leader			

at 14th and Penn could be called "Penn Street Command." Other guidelines for establishing common terminology include:

- Response personnel should use common names for all personnel and equipment resources, as well as for all facilities in and around the incident area
- Radio transmissions should use clear text (that is, plain English, without "ten" codes or agency-specific codes)

All common terminology applies to all organizational elements, position titles, and resources. A modular organization develops from the top-down organizational structure at any incident. "Top-down" means that, at the very least, the Command function is established by the first-arriving officer who becomes the Incident Commander. As the incident warrants, the Incident Commander activates other functional areas (i.e., sections).

In approximately 95 percent of all incidents, the organizational structure for operations consists of command and single resources (e.g., one fire truck, an ambulance, or a tow truck). If needed, however, the ICS structure can consist of several layers. Integrated communications is a system that uses a common communications plan, standard operating procedures, clear text, common frequencies, and common terminology. Several communication networks may be established, depending on the size and complexity of the incident.

Unity of command is the concept by which each person within an organization reports to only one designated person. A unified command allows all agencies with responsibility for the incident, either geographic or functional, to manage an incident by establishing a common set of incident objectives and strategies. Unified command does not mean losing or giving up agency authority, responsibility, or accountability. The concept of unified command means that all involved agencies contribute to the command process by:

- Determining overall objectives
- Planning jointly for operational activities while conducting integrated operations
- Maximizing the use of all assigned resources

Under unified command, the following always apply:

- The incident functions under a single, coordinated Incident Action Plan
- One Operations Section Chief has responsibility for implementing the Incident Action Plan
- One ICP is established

Some examples of how unified command is applied are shown in the visual below. Consolidated Incident Action Plans describe response goals, operational objectives, and support activities. The decision to have a written

Incident Action Plan is made by the Incident Commander. ICS requires written plans whenever:

- Resources from multiple agencies are used
- Several jurisdictions are involved
- The incident is complex (e.g., changes in shifts of personnel or equipment are required)

Incident Action Plans should cover all objectives and support activities that are needed during the entire operational period. A written plan is preferable to an oral plan because it clearly demonstrates responsibility, helps protect the community from liability suits, and provides documentation when requesting State and Federal assistance. Incident Action Plans that include the measurable goals and objectives to be achieved are always prepared around a timeframe called an operational period. Operational periods can be of various lengths, but should be no longer than 24 hours. Twelve-hour operational periods are common for large-scale incidents. The Incident Commander determines the length of the operational period based on the complexity and size of the incident. A manageable span of control is defined as the number of individuals one supervisor can manage effectively. In ICS, the span of control for any supervisor falls within a range of three to seven resources, with five being the optimum. If those numbers increase or decrease, the Incident Commander should reexamine the organizational structure.

Designated incident facilities include:
- An ICP at which the Incident Commander, the Command Staff, and the General Staff oversee all incident operations.
- Staging Areas at which resources are kept while awaiting incident assignment. Other incident facilities may be designated for incidents that are geographically dispersed, require large numbers of resources, or require highly specialized resources.

Comprehensive resource management:
- Maximizes resource use
- Consolidates control of single resources
- Reduces the communications load
- Provides accountability
- Reduces freelancing
- Ensures personnel safety

All resources are assigned to a status condition.

- Assigned resources are performing active functions.
- Available resources are ready for assignment.

Out-of-service resources are not ready for assigned or available status. Any changes in resource location and status must be reported promptly to the Resource Unit by the person making the change. Personnel accountability is provided throughout all of ICS. All personnel must check in as soon as they arrive at an incident. Resource units, assignment lists, and unit logs are all ways for personnel to be accounted for. When personnel are no longer required for the response, they must check out so that they can be removed from the resource lists. The ICS principles can and should be used for all types of incidents, both small and large-from a warrant execution to a hostage situation or a search for a missing child. Because ICS can be used at virtually any type of incident of any size, it is important that all responders use the ICS approach.

Discussion Questions:

1) The Incident Command system was developed to coordinate multi-agency responses

   True   False

2) The ICS was developed as a part of the _____ program during the1970's by an interagency working group representing local, state and federal fire services in California

3) The _____ Section Chief assists the Incident Commander in developing response goals and objectives for the incident

4) Which of the following is not a function of the Incident Commander?

   a) Performing command activities, such as establishing command and establishing the ICP

   b) Establishing command

   c) Providing media briefings every fifteen minutes

   d) Managing incident resources

5) Which of the following is not a principle of the ICS system?

   a) Common terminology is to be used over two-way radios (plain-English radio codes, area-wide standards for unit IDs)

   b) Integrated communications (800 MHz radio, common frequencies, radio patch capability)

   c) Separate incident action plans

   d) Comprehensive resource management

6) The ICS requires written plans whenever:

   a) Resources from multiple agencies are used

   b) Several jurisdictions are involved

   c) The incident is complex (e.g., changes in shifts of personnel or equipment are required)

   d) All of the above

---

7) Common terminology is essential in any emergency management system, especially when diverse or other than first-response agencies are involved in the response.

True   False

8) The Safety Officer and Public Information Officer both function as direct members of the Incident Commander's staff.

True   False

9) The Safety Officer has limited authority to contradict the Incident Commander and must ultimately abdicate even if he disagrees with the IC's decision on safety grounds.

True   False

10) The Logistics Section is responsible for providing facilities, services, and materials, including personnel to operate the requested equipment for the incident.

True   False

Answers

1) True

2) FIRESCOPE

3) Operations

4) B

5) C

6) D

7) True

8) True

9) False

10) True

6 Disaster Scene Management

Overview:

Now that we have examined contingency planning and the ICS structure, we will begin looking at actual tactical principles and considerations for managing a disaster scene.

In particular, this chapter will focus on the principles of disaster management, Incident Command decisions, documentation and after-action reporting.

Chapter Objectives:

- *Explain the security specialists focuses for disaster management*
- *State the considerations of an incident commander in managing a disaster scene*
- *Define the elements of a proper de-briefing*
- *Explain the importance of de-brief and after-action reporting*

Security Specialist's focuses for disaster management:

1. Prevention—As we have discussed at great length, the most important responsibility of a security specialist is prevention. Being trained, educated, attuned and aware of any deviances in normal operating conditions, and ensuring an operational mindset of maintenance and surveillance are the best ways to prevent small discrepancies from becoming larger crisis.

2. Early detection and notification—If a break-down, discrepancy or completely unforeseen event does occur, the next line of action for disaster management for security specialists is to be alert and properly trained to activate notification procedures and ensure that the appropriate responders are alerted and en route.

3. C_3 (Contain, Control & Communicate)—Once there is an emergency scene, the role of the security specialist is to rely on his/ her training and experience to establish: containment—preventing the emergency from spreading and further degrading; control—restricting access to the emergency scene to trained responders only; and communication—facilitating the flow of useful information to the incident commander, and restricting the flow of gossip, speculation and counterproductive information to unauthorized sources.

4. After-action—The emergency is not over simply because the IC declares an "all-clear." In order to prevent further losses, exploitation of compromised facilities, and preserve evidence for investigation a disaster scene may have to be properly secured and controlled for hours, days, weeks, months of even years after a critical incident (Ground Zero in New York).

Incident Command Considerations

Establishing Command Post

The CP must always be upwind and uphill of an event so as not to be in the path of any toxins, smoke or hazardous materials.

The Operations chief will be responsible for managing convergent volunteers. As volunteers begin responding to the CP, the Ops chief will begin screening and assigning volunteers based on needs and priorities. Oftentimes volunteers may be used for simple but vital tasks such as running messages, serving as sentries, or just delivering food and coffee to responders.

Courtesy of AP/Wide World Photos.

The Public Information Officer will be responsible for establishing a central point for media communications liaison and briefings. The PIO must establish him/herself as the focal point of media relations and to communicate the briefing schedule to media contacts.

> *Coordinating with other agencies*—As additional resources and responding agencies arrive at the scene, the IC may appoint a liaison officer who will brief and coordinate with newly arrived agencies.
>
> *All clear*—When the IC determines a scene to be "all-clear", the immediate threat must be sufficiently contained, there must be a satisfactory sense that no further rescue operations are needed, and that the event is now ready to move in to an on-going investigative/ scene security phase.
>
> *De-briefing*—A de-briefing is mandatory. The IC will ensure that all equipment and responders are accounted for; that scene clean up is initiated; and that scene security has been arranged. During de-briefing an objective review is to be made regarding what went well and what could be improved upon in future operations. De-briefs are often fairly informal at the scene site, but are sometimes conducted in more formal and in-depth settings with documentation, analysis, overviews, formal presentations, and final reports with conclusions and recommendations regarding future operations.

Size-up

"Size up" is the quick assessment of a situation, which includes the initial decisions that must be made concerning how an emergency will be managed. A good "size-up" provides accurate situation information about hazards and necessities for a response scene.

Scene Security

The IC will designate personnel to control access to the scene and set a containment perimeter.

Command Post Security

A realistic concern for responders in the modern world is their own security. Terrorists often seek secondary attacks to take out first responders. For this reason, the IC must ensure that the CP is secured and that access is restricted to a controlled number of authorized personnel.

Evacuation

All personnel should be trained in advance regarding proper evacuation procedures. On September 11th, 2001 almost 25,000 people were evacuated from the World Trade Center towers before the buildings collapsed. The importance of ensuring personnel know how and when to evacuate cannot be understated.

One difficult decision that an IC may have to make is when to evacuate a building. The decision may not always be obvious, especially if there are business pressures such as economic and productivity losses posed by an evacuation. Even on 9/11, after an airliner struck the north tower, an initial evacuation of the south tower was tragically aborted by a PA announcement stating the danger had been confined to the north tower and that it would be safer to have south tower employees remain at their desks.

The IC must be ready to make difficult decisions regarding evacuation orders.

Triage

The classification of casualties to determine the priority of need and care. This is a difficult, but highly effective skill for mass-casualty events where the incident commander and medical team must determine the best allocation of treatment resources by victim needs and chances of survivability pending immediate care.

Determining Incident Command Staff

The IC must determine whom, among available responders is best qualified to assume the various key roles of the incident command system. Contingency plans will usually identify designated individuals and departments to fill these key roles. If for some reason these positions haven't already been filled or designated, or the primary and backup responders are unavailable, the IC must designate qualified persons on scene.

The IC must consider the technical qualifications of the responders. Medical education, HAZMAT qualifications, engineering experience, first responder training all are the types of things an IC should consider when designating IC staff. As with all positions in the IC structure, including the IC, replacement should always be considered if and when more qualified responders arrive.

Allocation and Deployment of Resources

The Operations, logistics and administration chiefs must keep the IC abreast of resource availability and costs. The IC must be regularly updated so that he/ she may be able to make the most informed decisions regarding resource allocation.

Situation Report: The following is an actual FEMA situation report issued by on scene responders at Oklahoma City Bombing in April 1995.

FEMA SITUATION REPORT 002(P)

April 20, 1995 @ Noon, EDT

OKLAHOMA CITY BOMBING

All times are Central Daylight Time unless otherwise stated.

Situation:

On April 19, 1995, at 9:05 am, in Oklahoma City, OK, one car bomb destroyed the Alfred Murrah Federal Building. The building normally housed approximately 500 people, and it is estimated that there were 250 visitors on the day of the bombing.

The following Federal agencies were located in the bombed building:

- Department of Defense
- Department of Transportation
- General Services Administration
- General Accounting Office
- Health and Human Services
- Housing and Urban Development
- Department of Justice
- Department of Labor
- Office of Personnel Management
- Department of Treasury
- U.S. Army, Air Force, and Marine Recruiting Stations
- U.S. Department of Agriculture
- Department of Veterans Affairs

Casualties:

As of 5:00 am EDT, April 20, the Public Health Service reports 29 confirmed dead, between 150 and 200 injured, and 140 missing.

Weather:

The National Weather Service forecasts clear to partly cloudy skies on April 20, with highs from the mid-60s to mid-70s. The extended forecast calls for a slight chance of showers and thunderstorms on April 22.

Status of Declaration:

President Clinton signed Emergency Declaration FEMA-3115-EM on April 19, 1995. The Incident Period is April 19, 1995. Emergency Assistance under Title V of the Stafford Act will be provided as deemed necessary by FEMA Director James Lee Witt, who arrived in Oklahoma City the evening of April 19. An emergency declaration under Title V of the Stafford Act permits the Federal Government to provide emergency assistance to save lives, protect property and public health and safety and to lessen or avert the threat of further damage. This declaration is specifically being declared under the authority of Section 501 (b), which Congress created to allow the President to provide immediate assistance for an "emergency involving Federal primary responsibility". It is based on the fact that the explosion occurred at a Federally owned facility.

Status of Federal Operations:

FEMA has activated a small Emergency Support Team to assist at FEMA Headquarters in Information and Planning and Urban Search and Rescue.

The Federal Coordinating Officer (FCO) is Dell Greer. The Regional Operating Center (ROC) was activated at 10:00 am, April 19. It is now in 24-hour operation and will continue until further notice.

Mobile Emergency Response System (MERS):

The MERS vehicle and support team from Denton, TX has arrived in Oklahoma City and is assisting the FBI in establishing additional communications capability on site.

Transportation:

Highways, airport, railroad, marine, transit: No impact.

Pipeline:

The Department of Transportation Research and Special Programs Administration Office of Pipeline Safety reports that Oklahoma Natural Gas Company has shut off service to the area around the explosion and will conduct leak tests once they are allowed access to the area. The pipeline company is tracking down leak complaints. Some small gas leaks have been reported. No secondary incidents related to gas leaks have occurred.

Information And Planning:

FEMA is collecting, processing, and disseminating information about the emergency at both the Regional Operations Center and FEMA Headquarters to facilitate the overall activities of the Federal Government in providing response assistance.

Mass Care:

A ten-block area around the explosion area was evacuated. The American Red Cross (ARC) is setting up a shelter for those from a large apartment complex of approximately 600 apartments. ARC is sending in two additional canteens to support local chapter operations.

The American Red Cross has activated their Disaster Health and Mental Health people to possibly deploy to Oklahoma City.

ARC has established a 48-hour moratorium on disaster inquiries.

Resource Support:

This part of the Federal Response Plan was activated at 1:00 am EDT, on April 20, 1995, at FEMA Headquarters to support the efforts in identifying, locating, and acquiring the necessary assets required to provide logistical/resource support.

Health And Medical:

The Department of Veterans Affairs has dispatched medical professionals to augment local hospital personnel and psychiatric crisis teams to work with both the injured and onlookers.

Urban Search And Rescue:

Two Urban Search and Rescue teams with specially trained personnel consisting of rescue, medical and search components have arrived in Oklahoma City. These teams are from Phoenix, AZ and Sacramento, CA. Teams from Virginia Beach, VA and New York City will arrive today at 2:30 pm. Two additional teams, from Montgomery County, MD and Los Angeles County, CA, have also been activated and are awaiting transportation.

Donations:

The American Red Cross has a national toll-free number to call to offer donations: 1-800-435-7669 (1-800-HELP-NOW).

The following is an on-going activity summary of the Oklahoma City bombing, showing the methods used for after-action reporting and de-briefs.

Detailed Summary of Daily Activity4
Daily Summary, Log Entries for April 26–May 23

Wednesday, April 26, 1995

- The one-week anniversary of the explosion is observed at the site as Governor and Mrs. Keating, Lt. Governor Fallin and Mayor and Mrs. Ron Norick lead the rescue workers in a one-minute moment of silence at exactly 9:02 a.m.

- Search and rescue efforts continue with emphasis concentrated on the "pit" area of the building (central-interior location), where debris is heavy and victims are believed to be located. Six US&R Task Forces remain on rotating duty as the New York City and Virginia Beach teams demobilize.

- Four firefighters from Midwest City and six from Tinker Air Force Base provide continuous decontamination support to the rescue workers.

- National Guardsmen, provided by the Oklahoma Military Department, initiate an evidentiary sifting mission through rubble transported to the Oklahoma County Sheriff's gun range. This mission is tasked at the request of the FBI.

- From previous donations coordinations meetings, a Donations Task Force is identified and an organizational meeting is held at the DFO. Represented at the meeting are Lt. Governor Fallin, the Federal Coordinating Officer, State Coordinating Officer, Oklahoma City officials, the Oklahoma Department of Human Services, FEMA's donations specialists, the FEMA Voluntary Agency Coordinator, the American Red Cross, the Salvation Army, Feed the Children, Adventist Community Services, the Oklahoma Restaurant Association and Americorps. The task force is presented with two separate issues to address: 1. Items needed by individuals and families affected by the blast, and the workers supporting them; and, 2. Items needed by individuals and organizations working within the blast area. It is emphasized that the task force is not challenged with meeting the long-term needs of victims nor the donated funds which have been arriving from around the world, since the explosion.

- Two bomb dog teams arrive in Oklahoma City to support the U.S. Marshal's Service in providing security at the federal courthouse.

- The FBI releases the Regency Tower from the crime scene. Inspection of the building is completed and it is found to be structurally sound. Approximately 400 people resided in 260 apartment units at the time of the blast. Oklahoma City Metro Transit provides transportation to the displaced residents, who are allowed to enter the building and pick-up any essential items or possessions. (The Regency Tower residents were allowed to move back in after repairs were made on October 26, 1995)

- President Clinton signs Major Disaster Declaration FEMA-1048-DR, providing individual assistance to eligible applicants in Oklahoma City. The national teleregistration number is activated and victims are encouraged to apply. The Federal and State Coordinating Officers brief Oklahoma's Congressional Delegation on this development at the DFO.

Thursday, April 27, 1995

- Rescue crews are temporarily removed from "the pit" area of the building as a concrete slab shift is detected. Engineers evaluate the situation and re-initiate the recovery operation. To date, only ten minor injuries have been sustained by rescue workers.

- Oklahoma City Public Works officials release their initial survey figures of the damaged area. Their assessment shows 312 structures sustaining some damage, 25 buildings with major structural damage and 10 buildings destroyed.

- The MACC is down-sized and relocated to the Oklahoma City Emergency Operations Center (EOC), 4600 Martin Luther King Boulevard. Emergency Support Function Three (ESF-3: Public Works and Engineering), ESF-9 (Urban Search and Rescue) and the Joint Information Center (JIC) move to the DFO. The remaining ESFs and ODCEM Forward Operations move to the Oklahoma City EOC.

- Americorps volunteers assist the Donations Coordination Team with warehouse inventory and goods reception at various sites.

- Through the aid of ODCEM and the Oklahoma Department of Central Services, FEMA and GSA locate a site to establish a Recovery Service Center (RSC), where applicants can visit one-on-one with representatives of various programs offering aid. The location is in Shepherd Mall, N.W. 23rd St. and Villa. Plans are made to open the RSC Saturday, April 29th, but GSA and SBA immediately relocate to handle administrative functions and assist with previously disbursed loan applications. The American Red Cross makes plans the move their service center to this location and the Oklahoma Baptists plan to establish a child-care facility to aid in the assistance process.

- By close of business, 250 individuals have applied for disaster assistance through FEMA's teleregistration service.

Friday, April 28, 1995

- The Menlo Park US&R Task Force completes securing overhead hazards (large concrete slabs) on the north and east sections of the building. Crews continue working in "the pit" area, where several more victims are believed to be located. Continued removal of debris, while necessary, is believed to weaken the remaining structure. Numerous breaks are taken for constant engineering evaluation and additional shoring efforts.

- FEMA Director Witt and his staff meet with Governor Keating and ODCEM Director Feuerborn before departing to Washington, D.C.

Saturday, April 29, 1995

- Several more victims are recovered from "the pit" area of the building. Additional debris is removed and hanging hazards secured. Cracks in two northern columns of the building are shored with steel banding and epoxy.

- The Orange County, California, US&R Task Force arrives in Oklahoma City as the Los Angeles County and Montgomery County teams are demobilized.

- Oklahoma City Fire Department disbands the Command Post at the Southwestern Bell Telephone Building.

- The RSC is fully operational at Shepherd Mall with personnel staffed to represent the following organizations/programs:

FEMA Disaster Housing	SBA
FEMA/State Individual and Family Grants	Federal Employees Education & Assistance Fund
ODCEM	
Oklahoma Employment Security Commission	Social Security Administration
American Red Cross	Veterans Administration
Oklahoma Department of Human Services/Aging	Internal Revenue Service
	Oklahoma County
Salvation Army	FEMA/State Public Affairs
Department of Area-wide Aging	Oklahoma State Insurance Commission

- A telephone bank is also provided for those who have yet to apply for assistance through the teleregistration service. A total of 23 media outlets visit the RSC during the first day of operation.

- Oklahoma Representatives J.C. Watts and Frank Lucas are briefed at the DFO and tour the Murrah Building.

- The owner, head coach and several members of the Dallas Cowboys football team visit the Myriad Convention Center, Family Assistance Center and area hospitals on a good will mission.

Sunday, April 30, 1995

- A crane and dump truck are involved in an accident at the site, but no injuries occur.

- The MACC is down-sized once again and relocated to the Oklahoma City Fire Department Technical Logistics Center at 225 N.W. 6th St., in a covered garage. All FEMA support to the MACC is transferred to the DFO or demobilized. ODCEM Forward Operations remain in the MACC.

- The U.S. Public Health Service's "Disaster Studies Health Group" begin collecting documentation concerning patients treated after the explosion.

- California Congressman Jerry Lewis is briefed at the DFO and bomb site, and visits Governor Keating and ODCEM Director Feuerborn.

Monday, May 1, 1995

- Operations at the site officially transition to a recovery mission. Work is continued by hand and with the limited use of heavy equipment, but is suspended several times due to inclement weather conditions.

- US&R Task Forces from Fairfax County and Metro Dade County are demobilized. Prior to leaving, the Metro Dade County Team presents the YMCA with $1,000 to replace damaged playground equipment.

Tuesday, May 2, 1995

- Recovery operations concentrate on the "bowl" area, as structural engineers monitor the situation closely for signs of shifting. Due to unpredictable spring weather, a growing concern for the safety of the workers and the newly emphasized recovery mission, operations for the day are limited to an 0600 - 1800 HRS time frame.

- US&R Task Forces from Menlo Park and Puget Sound are demobilized, leaving Orange County as the only team remaining. At 1800 HRS the decision is made to halt all US&R support, but to keep technical specialists on until May 6 to act in an advisory capacity to Oklahoma City Fire Department.

- All rescue/recovery efforts are expected to be completed by Friday, May 5, at which time the site will be turned over to the FBI and restricted to investigative personnel only.

- The 54th Quartermaster Graves Registration Unit is released.

  - All Mobile Emergency Response Support (MERS) personnel and equipment, except logistical support, are released by 2400 HRS.

Wednesday, May 3, 1995:

- All rescue/recovery operations at the site are being conducted by Oklahoma City Fire Department, as the US&R Task Force from Orange County demobilizes. Prior to departure, the Orange County Team presents an orange tree and plaque to Oklahoma City officials.

- The Oklahoma Military Department completes its sifting mission at the Oklahoma County Sheriff's gun range.

- Governor Keating requests the inclusion of Public Assistance (i.e., infrastructure damages) in Presidential Major Disaster Declaration FEMA-1048-DR-OK.

- By late afternoon, applications for disaster assistance total 968. Temporary Housing checks issued to date total $408,696 and the Small Business Administration has distributed 496 loan applications.

Thursday, May 4, 1995:

- Recovery work continues at the site, conducted totally by Oklahoma City Fire Department. The General Services Administration (GSA) requests engineering support to monitor the structure after the rescue/recovery mission is completed. Two structural engineers from the U.S. Army Corps of Engineers, Tulsa District, assume this mission and relieve engineers currently supporting the recovery operation.

- The American Red Cross Family Services, Health Services and Mental Health Divisions form a "compassion team", designed to contact families of the deceased and all others who were directly victimized by the disaster.

Friday, May 5, 1995:

- At 0005 HRS the Oklahoma City Fire Department officially halts all recovery operations at the site. It is believed that three bodies remain in the rubble, but due to their perceived location, structural engineers feel that the safety factor is too great to pursue their recovery until after the implosion of the building.

- Rescue/recovery workers gather at the site for a memorial service, closed to the media.

- The FEMA Disaster Mortuary Team (DMORT) completes its mission for the State Medical Examiner's Office and is deactivated.

- Responsibility of the Family Assistance Center, at First Christian Church, is transferred to the Oklahoma Department of Mental Health and Substance Abuse Services. The center, through federal funding efforts, becomes "Project Heartland", a program designed to meet the long-term needs of victims. ("Project Heartland" eventually relocates to 5500 N. Western Ave., where it remains at the date of this report.)

- President Clinton approves the inclusion of Public Assistance in Major Disaster Declaration FEMA-1048-DR-OK.

Saturday, May 6, 1995:

- Training and demobilization of the FEMA Donations Team continues, with emphasis placed on returning donated goods to the original donor.

- Operations of the Defense Coordinating Office are transferred to Ft. Sill, Oklahoma.

Sunday, May 7, 1995:

- Recovery activities continue.

Monday, May 8, 1995:

- All Emergency Support Function (ESF) operations are transferred from the Disaster Field Office (DFO) to FEMA Region VI, in Denton, Texas.

- A consortium of 15 religious organizations is established, known as "Interfaith Disaster Recovery of Greater Oklahoma City", to better meet the needs of disaster victims.

- The Recovery Service Center reports 889 visitors, to date. Individual Assistance registrations total 1,242 and SBA reports 715 loan applications issued. The American Red Cross and the Individual and Family Grant Program are working together to meet the funeral/medical expense needs of victims.

Tuesday, May 9, 1995:

- After conferring with state and local officials, the General Services Administration (GSA) determines the best way to raze the remains of the Murrah Building is by implosion. GSA proceeds to make arrangements, contracts and proposes a date for the pending event.

- A Federal Building Performance Team arrives in Oklahoma City to study the effects of the blast and make recommendations to mitigate damages from similar events. The team is comprised of representatives from FEMA, the U.S. Army Corps of Engineers, GSA, the American Society of Civil Engineers, the National Institute of Standards and Technology and support contractors. The team is briefed by GSA officials on the status of the structure, but access is prohibited, due to safety factors.

- The donations distribution site at the U.S. Post Office, northwest corner of N.W. 5th and Harvey Ave., is closed.

- A Public Assistance Applicants' Briefing is held at the Oklahoma Historical Society Auditorium to educate potential applicants on the intricacies of the federal-state program.

Wednesday, May 10, 1995:

- Recovery activities continue.

Thursday, May 11, 1995:

- The Recovery Service Center reports 1,368 registrations and 1,205 visitors, to date. SBA has issued loan applications to 542 individuals and 243 businesses.

Friday, May 12, 1995:

- GSA selects the bid of a Maryland-based demolition company to implode the Murrah Building. A date has yet to be announced.

- The FEMA Voluntary Agency Coordinator holds the first Unmet Needs Committee meeting with key members from the Voluntary Agencies Active in Disasters (VOAD) group. Within a few weeks the group of approximately 20 agencies and funds grows to more than 80. (The group is renamed the Oklahoma City Bombing Disaster Resource Coordination Committee and continues to meet weekly. The committee is continuing to develop a long-term recovery network, in cooperation with the National Association of Social Workers, Oklahoma Chapter, to constantly address victim, survivor, family and disaster workers' long-term needs. Additionally, FEMA, working in conjunction with the Department of Justice, U.S. Attorney's Office, is continuing the long-term recovery process by identifying issues that could be resolved by federal assistance.)

- The Recovery Service Center reports 655 Disaster Housing applications issued to verification inspectors with 594 of the inspections completed and processed. Disaster Housing payments, to date, total $547,951.

Saturday, May 13, 1995:

- Recovery activities continue.

Sunday, May 14, 1995:

- Recovery activities continue.

Monday, May 15, 1995:

- FEMA representatives and Feed the Children volunteers assist Regency Tower residents with the packing and moving of personal property so reconstruction of the building can begin.

- A meeting, coordinated by the United Way of Oklahoma City, is held for families who had children at the Murrah Building day-care center. Individuals are encouraged to talk with FEMA and voluntary agency representatives about their immediate and long-term needs.

Tuesday, May 16, 1995:

- It is determined that at the time of the explosion 260 units of the Regency Tower were occupied, 72 of which still need to be vacated prior to reconstruction. By close of business, only 15 units have items which have yet to be moved or are under contract to be moved.

- Due to decreased activity, representatives from the Oklahoma Department of Human Services, Oklahoma County and Feed the Children relocate from the Recovery Service Center to their appropriate headquarters. Arrangements are made with Feed the Children to provide transportation for Regency Tower victims from the Trade Winds and Central Plaza motels to the Recovery Service Center.

Wednesday, May 17, 1995:

• Recovery activities continue.

Thursday, May 18, 1995:

• A Public Assistance meeting is held between ODCEM, FEMA and the Oklahoma City YMCA. The meeting is designed to determine eligibility of the non-profit organization, however, the YMCA reports it has accepted an insurance settlement and additional assistance is unnecessary.

Friday, May 19, 1995:

• Disaster victims making application through FEMA's National Teleregistration Center are advised that, due to computer problems, no individual control numbers will be issued for three to five days. This creates a significant problem since voluntary agencies use the control number to identify duplication of benefits, etc. FEMA is working to correct the malfunction, but asks the voluntary agencies to proceed in their efforts without the control number.

• The Donations Management Team ceases operations at the DFO. Future inquiries/activities will be coordinated through United Way personnel, located at the Recovery Service Center.

Saturday, May 20, 1995:

• Recovery activities continue.

Sunday, May 21, 1995:

• Recovery activities continue.

Monday, May 22, 1995:

• Recovery activities continue.

Tuesday, May 23, 1995:

• At 0702 HRS the remains of the Alfred P. Murrah Building are imploded. In the next few days, the bodies of the three remaining victims are located, precisely where they were believed to be. This brings the final death count to 168, including the Oklahoma City nurse who responded to the incident and was mortally wounded when struck in the head by a piece of debris.

California's Task Force Three, centered on the Menlo Park Fire District is one of the nation's premiere Urban Search and Rescue teams in the country. After 9/11 the team was placed on Federal alert and was deployed to New York City. The following is their comprehensive after-action report submitted to FEMA. This report is an excellent example of the documentation required to de-brief and account for large scale disaster recovery after-action reporting.

FEDERAL EMERGENCY MANAGEMENT AGENCY

National Urban Search and Rescue Response System
World Trade Center Incident After Action Report

California Task Force 3
September 18—30, 2001
Revised March 15, 2002

WTC Response Table Of Contents

CA-TF3 WTC Response Executive Summary

On September 11, 2001, members of California Task Force 3's (CA-TF3) Urban Search and Rescue (US&R) Team were placed on Alert by the Federal Emergency Management Agency (FEMA), after two large Passenger Aircraft struck the World Trade Center (WTC) Complex in New York City, a third Passenger Aircraft struck the Pentagon in Washington D.C, and a fourth Passenger Aircraft crashed in Pennsylvania.

California Task Force 3 has a colorful and proud history of prior Federal, State, and local Task Force deployments, which have prepared and positioned the Task Force for response to catastrophic events. These deployments include:

- 1989 Loma Prieta Earthquake San Francisco Bay Area
- 1992 Hurricane Iniki Hawaiian Islands
- 1994 Northridge Earthquake Los Angeles
- 1995 Oklahoma City Bombing Oklahoma City
- 1997 California Flooding Northern California
- 1998 California Flooding Northern California
- 1999 Taiwan Earthquake Taiwan
- 2000 Y2K Celebrations San Francisco Bay Area

The success of Task Force 3 can be directly contributed to the involvement and investment of the Menlo Park Fire Protection District, the sponsor for the Team, and the contributions and dedication of our participating agencies and Civilian Professionals. These agencies include:

• Burlingame Fire Department
• CDF San Mateo County
• Half Moon Bay Fire District
• Redwood City Fire Department
• Milpitas Fire Department
• Mountain View Fire Department
• NASA Ames DART
• San Jose Fire Department
• San Mateo Fire Department
• Santa Clara Fire Department
• South San Francisco Fire Department

With thousands of people reportedly injured and/or dead in both Washington D.C and New York City, members of Task Force 3 mobilized themselves as the Nation prepared itself for an unknown future. Unlike other Americans, most Task Force members have stated that as part of the National Response System, it wasn't so much a matter of if they were going to go, but rather when, and where. CA-TF3 was activated for the New York City World Trade Center Event on September 18th,and began its mobilization and response in the early hours of September 19th. The Team arrived at the Jacob Javits Convention Center in New York in the early hours of April 20th and was assigned the unique responsibility of developing the first Rapid Response Task Force (RRTF) capability protecting the City of New York in case of any additional collapsed structure events. CA-TF3 was split into two separate Rapid Response Task Forces operating first out of Fort Totten in Queens, as well as later operating out of the Jacob Javits Convention center for approximately four days, or from September 21st– 25th. Its equipment was left in place to insure continuity of operations for other Task Forces assigned this mission. CA-TF3 was then re-assigned to work at the World Trade Center Plaza Area from September 25th– 29th where the Task Force worked closely with FDNY, NYPD and Port Authority Police in the active search and recovery of victims within the Plaza Zone of Operations. During this period of time, CA-TF3 actively worked with FDNY to search the sub-level areas of the complex, interface with existing debris removal operations involving Cranes and other more basic means, and worked to establish a very successful personnel accountability system for the Plaza Area. CA-TF3 was demobilized on the 29th of September and pre-positioned at McGuire Air Force Base where they were returned to California on September 30th.

Shortly after the teams return, the Task Force conducted several debriefing sessions, and hosted a picnic for team members and their families.

To date, the most significant affects of this mission have been related to health and wellness issues surrounding the deployment of Team members, many who have been ill.

On behalf of California Task Force 3, it was our extreme pleasure to serve our Country and the people of New York City in their hour of need, and to once again bring honor to ourselves, the agencies we represent, our Task Force, the great State of California and the National Urban Search and Rescue Response System.

Thank You!

Harold Schapelhouman, Captain Special Operations
Menlo Park Fire Protection District
California Urban Search and Rescue Task Force 3
Task Force Leader

Mission Introduction

On September 11, 2001, California Task Force 3 was placed on Alert based upon evolving significant collapse events in both New York and Washington D.C., as well the potential for additional attacks against the United States.

The Task Force was activated on September 18th for mobilization to the World Trade Center event in New York City and arrived at McGuire Air Force Base in New Jersey on September 19th, 2001, where the team was transported to the Jacob Javits Convention Center in Mid-Town Manhattan in New York City arriving on September 20th. During this mission, the Team was assigned two primary tasks while in New York City:

1. Development and Staffing of the Rapid Response Task Force Concept
2. Site work consisting of search and recovery operations specifically at the World Trade Center Plaza Area and all related sub-level areas under the Plaza

The Task Force's deployment time was for approximately 13 days, with each team member spending at least 56 hours, or four Operational Periods, at the World Trade Center Plaza.

Chronology Of Events

September 11, 2001

Two Aircraft Strike the World Trade Center Towers FEMA Places all Urban Search and Rescue Task Forces on Alert Task Force 3 members respond to Fire Station 77 Special Operations and begin preparations for the team's departure

September 12, 2001

Task Force 3 members continue cache work preparations

September 13, 2001

Task Force 3 members continue cache work preparations

September 14, 2001

With approval, the Cache is moved to Travis Air Force Base For load certification by the Military. A group of Logistics Support Team members accompany the Cache as well as two members of Oakland's Task Force 4.

September 15, 2001

Logistics Support Group members return from Travis AFB.

September 16, 2001

Task Force 3 members continue personnel equipment cache work

September 17, 2001

Task Force 3 members continue personnel equipment cache work

September 18, 2001

Task Force 3 is ACTIVATED by FEMA at 0800 hours. Official Notifications are sent out to all Team Members and Participating Agencies. Pre-medical screening and mask fit testing is done on all responding personnel.

September 19, 2001

All Team Members are assembled at 0300 hours for an early morning Departure for Travis Air Force Base. Individual Gear is assembled, a Team Briefing occurs and DNA swabs are taken from all Team Members.

0600

the buses arrive and the Team is loaded by position for transport to Travis AFB.

0800

the buses arrive at Travis AFB and are slightly delayed due to Extra security measures at the front Gate.

1100

the Logistics Group along with the Teams equipment cache is loaded onto a C-141 and leaves for McGuire Air Force Base in New Jersey.

1230

the rest of the team is loaded onto a C-5 and leaves for McGuire AFB in New Jersey.

2200

the entire Task Force is re-united at McGuire AFB in New Jersey. Arrangements have been made to transport the personnel and equipment to New York. The cache is loaded onto two Transports and the Team Loads onto two buses, which immediately leave for New York. Enroute, the Task Force Leaders are advised that they will be taking on the roll of the Rapid Response Task Force (RRTF).

September 20, 2001 0100

The Task Force Arrives at the Jacob Javits Convention Center in Mid-Town Manhattan. The Task Force Leaders receive their instructions and the team beds down in a remote section of the center.

0530

The Task Force Leaders attend the morning briefing and are given further details on the needs and issues surrounding the RRTF. Ray Lynch from the Mayors Office of Emergency Management (OEM) meets with the Task Force Leaders regarding this assignment and introduces them to his assistant Charlie Bianco.

0700

Task Force members eat breakfast and are shown where the team will be setting up its Base of Operations (BoO). Task Force members begin to bring in the pallets, unload the cache and organize the BoO.

1000

Members of the Management Team discuss the implementation and needs of the RRTF mission. Vehicles are ordered via OEM, Random House Publishing in New York and Menlo Park Fire in California where Fire Engineer Rob Dehoney uses his contacts in the Apparatus fleet world to order up two Rescue Companies.

Working back through the Incident Support Team's Logistics Branch, equipment is ordered for the RRTF mission. But the Emergency Support Function 9 Leader has difficulty with the team's use of the ICS ordering form, the need for cache items not owned by the Task Force, but on the Federal Equipment list, and non-traditional items needed to accomplish this very unique mission.

1700

Under special instructions by the Mayor of the City of New York, Ray Lynch with OEM advises the Task Force Leaders that it is imperative that they have a fully functional RRTF within 24 8 hours due to additional risks and threats against the City of New York.

September 21, 2002

0700

an empty Beer Truck from Heineken provided by Random House Publishing arrives.

0900

a Volunteer Fire Rescue Company Vehicle from Brookhaven New Jersey arrives empty and members of Task Force 3 begin the process of loading the vehicle with equipment.

1000

a Department of public works truck arrives.

1100

a bus to transport half the team to Fort Totten arrives. Team members are loaded onto the bus for a 45-minute trip to the Fort, which is located on the water in Queens.

1200

Team members arrive at Fort Totten and are briefed by FDNY personnel who use the facility as a Training Center. In the words of the Chief running this facility "Treat this place as you would your Firehouse". The team moves into the barracks at Fort Totten and establishes a Command Post.

1500

The Rescue Truck arrives from the Javits Convention Center and Team Members place the truck into service after going through the vehicle and checking the Truck. Additional equipment arrives on the Public Works Flatbed Truck.

1600

Team members at Fort Totten assemble a Western Shelter Tent for eating, another for equipment, and a small tent for personnel decontamination.

1600

A lumber load arrives at Fort Totten and is placed near a cutting station that has been established for large-scale lumber cutting. Work begins on cutting the lumber for shores and cribbing to outfit the Rapid Response Task Force. Work continues past dark but is halted once it is determined that it is unsafe.

1700

A Public Works Flat Bed Truck limps into Fort Totten and Team members work on the truck until dark. The Truck is later mistakenly reported stolen.

1700

The FDNY Chief at Fort Totten advises Fire Communications that the Rapid Response Task Force is in service.

September 22, 2001

0530

> Task Force Leader Ed Greene and Plans Officer Phil White attend the Morning Briefing.

0900

> A second Fire Rescue Vehicle arrives at the Javits Convention Center donated by Pierce Manufacturing. The Task Forces equipment is placed on this truck and the Second RRTF goes into service by that afternoon.

0900

> Lumber cutting continues at Fort Totten and the first truck is loaded and sent to Javits and becomes part of the second Rapid Response Task Force by noon. Another lumber load is ordered and arrives at Fort Totten and an identical cribbing shoring kit is put in place on a Public Works Truck by that evening.

September 23, 2002

0530

> Task Force Leaders Greene and Schapelhouman attend the morning briefing at the Javits Convention Center and report that both Rapid Response Task Forces are up and running.

0900

> Extensive Training is conducted at Fort Totten where members of the Rapid Response Task Force 2 conduct Rope Rescue, Pneumatic Shore, and Metal Cutting Training all day.

0900

> The Rapid Response Task Force at Javits reconfigures the Base of Operations and organizes the remainder of the cache.

September 24, 2002

0530

> Task Force Leader Greene and Plans Officer White attend the morning briefing at the Javits Convention Center.

0800

> Task Force Leader Schapelhouman and Plans Officer Kohlman meet with the FDNY commander at Fort Totten and advise him that they will be transitioning out with another team tomorrow, but leaving everything set up.

0900

Extensive Training is conducted again at Fort Totten where members of the Rapid Response Task Force 2 also perform a readiness exercise.

1500

RRTF 1 at Javits goes out on Patrol in the City and visits a FDNY Fire Station, Madison Square Gardens and the Empire State Building sites.

1500

Rapid Response Task Force 2 at Totten has another meeting with FDNY and begins to prepare a transition plan.

1730

Task Force Leaders Greene and Schapelhouman attend the evening briefing at the Javits Convention Center where they are advised of their new assignment at the World Trade Center.

2000

Task Force Leader Schapelhouman recons the WTC Site meeting IST members Fraone and Sargent. He leaves the site at 0300 on September 25th and returns to Fort Totten.

September 25, 2001

0800

CA-TF3, Team 1, is assigned to the WTC Plaza area where they interface with FDNY Command. They establish a personnel tracking system using the T-Card system and work closely with FDNY.

1000

CA-TF3, Team 2, begins the process of moving out of the barracks at Fort Totten. Team members welcome the Nebraska Task Force with a round of applause and say goodbye to the FDNY staff at Fort Totten.

1100

Team 2, leaves for the Javits Convention Center, the team immediately experiences difficulty when they loose their Police escort and they run into traffic gridlock as they find out that State Police are stopping all trucks coming over bridges or under tunnels into New York City. The team eventually acquires another police escort into New York and arrives at the Javits Convention Center around 1400 hours where they eat and try to rest the crew.

1900

CA-TF3 Team 2 leaves for the WTC to start their first Operational Period in the Plaza Area. They transition out with CA-TF3 Team 1 and start operations at 2000 hours. September 26, 2001: 0700—CA-TF3

Team 1 arrives at the WTC Plaza Area to begin operations. They transition with Team 2 who successfully continued the accountability system as well as the integration with FDNY into field operations.

1900

CA-TF3 Team 2 arrives at the WTC Plaza Area to begin operations. They transition with Team 1. Both teams have been involved with minimal human remains recoveries as well as sub-level searches and cutting and removal of steel and debris in their area of operations.

September 27, 2001

0700

CA-TF3 Team 1 arrives at the WTC Plaza Area to begin operations. They transition with Team 2 who has conducted and a very involved sub-level void exploration with FDNY that took over 3 hours.

1900

CA-TF3 Team 2 arrives at the WTC Plaza Area to begin operations. They transition with Team 1 who has conducted extensive debris removal at the site.

September 28, 2001

0700

CA-TF3 Team 1 arrives at the WTC Plaza Area to begin operations. They transition with Team 2 who has experienced on again, off again work, due to the removal of wall Operations on Tower 1.

1900

CA-TF3 Team 2 arrives at the WTC Plaza Area to begin operations. They transition with Team 1 who has completed their last operational period.

September 29, 2001

0530

Task Force Leader Greene and Plans Officer White attend the morning briefing where the team receives it's demobilization orders. 0700—CA-TF3 Team 2 finishes its last operational period at the WTC Site and return to the Javits Convention Center.

1000

Members of the Task Force 3 Management Team conduct an Operational briefing with members of California Task Force 4 who have just arrived on site.

1000

CA-TF3 Team 1 members perform cache rehabilitation work. Equipment from both Rapid Response Task Force locations and vehicles is returned to the team for cache palletization. Earlier discussions to leave the equipment cache in New York are discontinued.

1700

The team's equipment cache is loaded onto transports for movement to McGuire AFB in New Jersey.

1730

Task Force 3 Team members say their goodbyes at the Javits Convention Center and leave for McGuire AFB in New Jersey where they arrive later that evening and are housed for the night.

September 30, 2001

0530

Task Force members begin the process of final preparations to leave McGuire AFB. After meeting with the Base Commander, the team leaves McGuire with Nevada Task Force 1.

October 1, 2001

Cache rehabilitation starts at FS#77 Media Interviews

October 2, 2001

Media Interviews

October 3, 2001

Media Interviews

October 10, 2001

CISD Debriefing at Fire Station 77, Special Operations

October 16, 2001

Menlo Park Fire Protection District Fire Board Presentation on WTC Deployment

October 20, 2001

Partners only workshop for couples at the Stanford Park Hotel

November 3, 2001

CA-TF3 WTC Picnic for deployed and non-deployed support personnel and their families at the Swanson Family Winery in Napa.

November 1, 2001

Appreciation luncheon for civilian volunteers who assisted during the 9/11 deployment at the Stanford Park Hotel.

December 1, 2001

CISD Debriefing at Fire Station 77, Special Operations

Note: It should be noted that this is only a partial list of related activities that occurred upon the Return of the team.

CA-TF3 WTC Response Mission Evaluation

Alert Phase Evaluation:

Key Task Force 3 members where recalled or came into work upon seeing, or hearing, about the attacks in Washington and New York. When the official FEMA Alert was received, Team Managers were in position to quickly pass this along to all participating Fire Agencies and Civilian Team members.

> Due to the serious nature of the threat against the Nation, the Fire Station and Special Operations Facility were initially secured by locking down the site. In the days following the event, Menlo Park Police were asked to provide additional security patrols for the site and all team members were asked to provide I.D upon entering the compound during periods of time when the cache was being prepared for transport. Prior to the caches departure, the San Mateo County Bomb Squad swept all transport vehicles for explosive devices and a California Highway Patrol escort was provided from point of departure to point of arrival at Travis Air Force Base for security, after this sweep.

> As hours turned into days, the mission began to turn into a "planned" deployment versus an "immediate" emergency deployment. This created several problems with rostering individual team members as schedules changed, and based upon each individual participating agencies personnel rotation model and availability of personnel.

> Two false Task Force Activations occurred during this time frame. Both were generated from the Fire Dispatch center. One created actual personnel movement, the other was quickly found to be a mistake. In both cases the error was caught because no official mission number and request could be provided upon confirmation.

> The movement of the equipment cache in advance of the actual Deployment date to Travis Air Force Base was invaluable to insuring proper palletization, hazardous cargo certifications and approval of the load by the United States Air Force. Shortly after this was accomplished, the Team was requested to fly on a Civilian Air Carrier. This would of course create additional work as each pallets height and configuration would need to be changed. With the help of the California Office of Emergency Services, the Task Force was allowed to fly Military Air.

A Volunteer Civilian Support network was developed in advance of the Task Forces Deployment and blossomed to include Corporate sponsors and a list of people who wanted to just help the team by answering phones and keeping family members informed of the status of their loved ones.

Based upon televised information, and an article in the San Francisco Chronicle on September 18th regarding poor air quality and airborne toxins at Ground Zero, Team Managers opted to purchase the absolute best in respiratory protection for the team members responding to New York. In addition, four additional air-monitoring devices were purchased so that each Rescue Squad would be able to monitor the atmosphere in their area of work. These items were received on September 18thand fit testing was performed on all rostered personnel by that evening.

During the initial days following the attacks on Washington and New York, it became clear that the Federal program staff were overwhelmed, and that not all personnel were familiar with the National Rotation model. This became clear during the initial development of the incidents rotation models. As time progressed, this process improved and was very clear by the teams Activation date.

Activation Phase Evaluation:

The Task Force was activated on September 18that 0800. All participating Fire Agencies and Civilians were notified, and a final roster of selected members pre-mobilized to complete their medical health screening and assemble their personal equipment. Team members were told to report to Special Operations Fire Station 77 at 0300 hours on September 19th, giving the team ample time to load on buses for departure to Travis AFB. This process included a formal team briefing and a last minute DNA sampling from each deployed team member.

In October of 2000, Task Force 3 conducted its first deployment exercise since the Oklahoma City Bombing Deployment in April of 1995. This exercise proved invaluable to the reflex time and lessons learned in preparation for the World Trade Center Deployment.

Deployment Phase Evaluation:

Security of Special Operations Fire Station n 77 was provided by the Menlo Park Police.

Department. A Bomb sniffing dog checked the personnel, equipment bags, and buses prior to departure and the California Highway Patrol provided an escort and security to Travis Air Force Base.

A slight delay occur red upon the arrival of the Task Force at Travis Air Force Base due to the influx of military personnel and increased security level. Once the team was identified, they were given an escort directly into the airfield.

Upon arrival at the Travis Air Force Base, the pre-approved cache was already in the process of being loaded onto a C-141 Aircraft. The logistics personnel were allowed to separate from the main group and coordinate with their military counterparts. This aircraft along with the Logistics personnel was pre-deployed an hour ahead of the main 15 body of the Team which followed in a C-5 Aircraft. The decision to split the team and equipment was approved by the Task Force Leaders.

In flight, and prior to arrival in New Jersey, the Military Air Crew advised the team that they would be going right into the World Trade Center to begin operations. This information turned out to be incorrect and created some disruption.

Upon arrival at McGuire Air Force Base in New Jersey, a minor situation occurred when the trucks transporting the cache choose a different travel route than the buses transporting the team. Since no logistics personnel were accompanying the transport drivers, cell phone contact was used to determine the location of the trucks and their alternative route of travel.

Arrival at the Federal Mobilization Center Evaluation:

Prior to the arrival of the team at the Federal Mobilization Center at the Jacob Javits.

Convention Center, Incident Support Team (IST) Members Fred Endikrat and Rick Warford contacted the Task Force Leaders regarding a new and developing mission, which would later be known as the Rapid Response Task Force System.

On arrival a the Javits Convention Center the Task Force Leaders met with the IST Leaders and discussed this mission while Team members bedded down in an obscure section of the convention center on the floor. Feeding and rest room facilities were not adequate to support the team. The team was advised not to eat at the 24-hour public kitchen, but the on-site feeding kitchen was not open 24 hours and was closed upon the arrival of the team.

Use of the Civilian and Corporate Support Network created prior to leaving California was extremely beneficial to the Team. Within 12 hours of arrival, the team was supported by Random House Publishing who had established 30 person Teams to the support of every 10 Task Force members. Soon care packages including shoes, bedding, books and other comfort items were arriving on site. Other connections were utilized to obtain thick foam mattress pads for all team members to sleep on. These comfort items were invaluable to the well being of the personnel.

Rapid Response Task Force Mission Assignment:

The initial assignment and the roll of the Rapid Response Task Force were somewhat unclear. As the Task Force Leaders met with the IST Leaders, it was became clear that since this had never been done before, no template could be provided and as stated by the IST, Task Force 3 was selected for this mission because of it's prior deployments and reputation for improvising and getting things done.

Initial difficulty in ordering needed equipment for this mission was complicated by the inability of the ESF-9 Leader to understand the missions objectives. In addition, the expectation that the Task Force should arrive with the full authorized Federal 16

Equipment cache was unrealistic based upon prior funding, and had already been outlined in March of 2001 in a report to Congress that showed CA-TF3 having a projected shortfall of $380,000.00 of the 1.8 million dollar cache list.

After a meeting with the Mayors Office of Emergency Management (OEM), the full weight and need for the quick development of the Rapid Response Task Force, or second-strike collapse structure response capability for New York City, became increasingly clear.

What also became clear was the inability of the system to affectively assist the successful implementation of this process under the normal protocols and procedures. Task Force 3 and the Mayors office representative performed a dual pronged approach to this situation in conjunction with the IST Leadership.

For example, the need to obtain vehicles for the immediate and rapid deployment of these units was difficult at best through normal Federal channels. Alternative methods employed by Task Force 3 and OEM provided more immediate results. Using its corporate sponsor Random House Publishing, the Task Force was able to secure two empty beer trucks to be used as Rescue Vehicles to carry equipment within the first 24 hours. While not the first choice, this solution provided a temporary transport platform as Menlo Park Firefighter Rob Dehoney worked with National Fire Apparatus vendors to find a more common Fire Rescue Platform.

Fire Fighter Dehoney and Pierce Manufacturing eventually accomplished this in the form of Volunteer Rescue Company provided by Brookhaven Fire Department and another demonstrator Rescue Body Pickup provided. OEM was able to secure Department of Correction buses and Public works Flat Bed Trucks.

The remoteness of Fort Totten in Queens, where Rapid Response Task Force 2 was assigned also created unique and special logistical and support issues as 32 members of the Task Force were deployed almost an hour away from the World Trade Center Incident on a secured Military Base where they established the first Rapid Response

Capability within the 24 hour goal set by the Mayor and OEM. This site created immediate issues regarding communication, information updates, inclusion and support.

Perhaps the most difficult aspect of the Rapid Response Task Force was the issue surrounding the perception by the members of these units and the estimated value and enthusiasm regarding this detail. While most members understood the need and importance of the mission, the actual human difficulties of this assignment must be understood if this concept is to be successful in the future. Constant focus and vigilance by the Task Force Leaders and IST are crucial, and shorter mission assignments for this type of support function should be cons considered.

Discussions regarding leaving Task Force 3's equipment in place on the Rapid Response Task Forces were ongoing and created unique issues for the Task Force Leaders and the Logistics Group. Eventually the equipment was left in place, with the approval of the 17 Task Force Leaders since the RRTF was an immediate capability and to remove equipment would have created response problems and delays.

Task Force 3 was proud to have been selected for this detail and we believe improvised and overcame tremendous obstacles to make this concept successful. All of the team members and their supporting counterparts are to be commended for this effort.

World Trade Center Assignment Evaluation:

Members of Task Force 3 were assigned to the World Trade Center Plaza Area of Operations starting on September 25th, 2001. Initially Team 2 was to take the Day Shift, but due to their location at Fort Totten, the two Task Force Leaders discussed a change where Team 1 located at the Javits Center would take the first shift.

The Nebraska Task Force at Fort Totten relieved CA-TF3 Team 2. Team 2 ran into extensive problems in transporting the unit into New York City when they lost their Police escort and also ran into almost complete Highway gridlock due to the order to stop and check all trucks entering New York City over either a bridge or through a tunnel.

Help came in the form of a NYPD unit merging off the freeway when the Task Force Leader left the bus to explain the situation. Within minutes the convoy of Military Trucks, a Team bus, and NYPD escort slowly made their way toward the city.

Task Force 3's experiences during the Oklahoma City Bombing where the entire Task Force worked together instead of rotating in twelve hour shifts was more beneficial and cohesive to the Task Forces overall operations. The twelve and twelve schedule created unique communication and continuity challenges which did not exist in Oklahoma.

Both teams, and shifts, established a strong working relationship with FDNY, NYPD and Port Authority as well Contractors on site. This relationship allowed the Task Force to implement and improve personnel tracking in the Plaza Area by establishing a T-Card accountability system that tracked between 250 and 300 workers in the Plaza area from all involved agencies during both shifts. The Task Force also helped to enforce a minimum safety standard in that all personnel only are allowed to enter the debris pile if they had gloves, eye and respiratory protection and a helmet.

In addition the Task Force members worked together with FDNY units to perform extensive sub-level searches, advise them on Technical issues surrounding victim recoveries in stairwells or sub-level areas where victims where found. The teams Structural Engineers, K-9's, Search Technicians, Hazardous Materials Technicians, Safety Officers and Rescue Team Managers were used for special details and consultations on a regular basis throughout each shift.

Rescue Squad members also performed extensive metal cutting and debris removal by hand or with a crane during their shifts. In one instance, team members trained over a hundred personnel from other agencies in the operation and safe use of cutting torches.

The Task Force Leaders worked closely with the IST Field Commanders and the FDNY Sector Commanders to offer a strong example of both a well disciplined, and trained, US&R Operational Unit through the presence of the team members actions and units leadership.

Demobilization Evaluation:

The Task Force began demobilization operations on September 29thand was able to accomplish this with minimal issues or difficulties. The cache was palletized and certified for transport by that evening.

Issues regarding aircraft configuration and load size palletization once again occurred at McGuire Air Force Base where the team packed for Military Transport but were advised on arrival that they may have to reconfigure for Civilian Air Transport. Military Support Personnel and the IST Liaison on site eventually worked out these issues with assistance.

A presentation by the Commander at McGuire Air Force Base thanking the Team Members for their service was well received and appreciated. The team arrived back in the Bay Area at Moffett Field with no incident and the cache was flown into Travis Air Force Base where it was retrieved the next day.

Some confusion regarding the mandatory rest period occurred. After review of the FEMA memo, it was determined that the explanation and interpretation of this information was in error. This was corrected several days later through both phone calling and a memo faxed and e-mailed to all participating Fire agencies and Civilian Team Members.

Critical Incident Stress Debriefing Evaluation:

Effective and timely CISD continues to be a very difficult issue for Task Force Management. In the world of CISD, one shoe does not fit all, and issues for one individual may differ dramatically from another.

Significant improvements in support and coordination have been made since the Oklahoma City Bombing Deployment in 1995, but each deployment nt takes on it's own personality and has it's own very unique stumbling blocks. For example, a family support meeting conducted while the team was in New York which included experiences and issues suffered by individuals who were deployed to the Oklahoma City Incident was thought to be over the top for several families who had their New York City responders come home and tell them that "it just wasn't that way". Most of those issues related to the recovery of human remains create unique challenges in terms of preparation, understanding and the long -term mental well being by team members and their families.

Perhaps the best opportunity for mental well being and healing comes in the form of group interaction. Support from other members who have lived through the same event and understand the dynamics and conditions of what actually occurred lend themselves to an exclusive group of people challenged together through time and place. This bond is very strong and social activities such as gatherings where these individuals can come together in a safe and enjoyable setting help the healing process in ways not fully appreciated. Individual contact and support within the group is also critical as responders experience a variety of emotions on the path back to normalcy.

Health Issues Evaluation:

Issues surrounding health have presented themselves as one of the greatest challenges for the Task Force upon their return. With 70% of the team members reporting some type of illness or problem upon their return from New York City, a tremendous amount of effort and concern continues to be focused on these issues.

Team Managers are working with both State and Federal representatives to keep their personnel informed of any new relevant details and tremendous support and empathy from the general public has been received after news coverage of these issues.

To date, the Task Force continues to monitor individuals, and the Teams Physicians are conducting follow up physicals on each deployed team member. Perhaps the greatest improvement in this area will be the pre and post deployment medical procedures. Team Members deployed to all future incidents will have a more detailed medical base line and comprehensive medical follow up.

Financial Reimbursement Evaluation:

As the smallest Fire Agency in the United States to support a Task Force, issues surrounding financial reimbursement take on significant meaning and have a tremendous affect on the program, and host agency.

The Federal Government can not expect Task Forces to continue the practice of sustaining all deployment costs with no initial, or immediate, financial relief for those agencies To date, the Fire District has received 25% of it's estimated salary costs, and $10,000.00 for alert phase costs which is the maximum allowable amount despite the fact that the alert lasted for 7 days and the pre-positioning of the cache at Travis AFB created related support costs twice the allowable payment amount.

As the Fire District struggles through the laborious claim submittal process with FEMA, costs in excess of the allowable $75,000.00 equipment cap related to the purchase of additional atmospheric monitoring and better respiratory protection, will have to be appealed. Claim appeals also occurred after the Oklahoma City Bombing in 1995 and the appeal process took two years to be resolved in the Fire Districts favor.

The roll of the Task Force in the implementation and creation of the Rapid Response Task Force, or second strike collapsed structure capability for the City of New York, has also created questions regarding costs incurred by the Task Force. This non-traditional assignment was successful due to the creativity of the team's members; many who obtained needed items by purchasing them with their own funds.

The Menlo Park Fire

District upon the teams return reimbursed all of these items, but questions of procedure remain despite the fact that on-site logistical support was problematic at best. These funds are in question, and most likely will also go through the appeal process.

The Menlo Park Fire District Board is to be commended for their actions both before and after this event in terms of support. The Fire Board also authorized expenditures of up to $100,000.00 to support any efforts necessary to assist New York City by the Task Force during this deployment.

The Menlo Park Fire District Board in December 2001 approved the payment of all Civilian Team Members. This compensation, which required a Board resolution to expend over a $150,000.00 prior to receiving any compensation from the Federal Government, was to insure that these individuals who had responded, some who own their own businesses or took non-paid time off from work, would not be adversely impacted by this 13 day deployment. During the Oklahoma City Bombing it took over nine months for the Civilian members to be paid once the Federal Government reimbursed the Fire District for all associated costs.

In a recent meeting, the Menlo Park Fire District Board expressed their concerns to the Fire Chief and Task Force Management about the long-term fiscal impact to the Fire District and Task Force in terms of reimbursement. This lop-sided process clearly is unfair and unreasonable to the host agency and it's participants and partner agencies. 67 personnel responded to New York City and the Pentagon from California Task Force 3. These individuals were compensated by their agencies, which also sustained the cost of backfill during their normal work shifts. In addition, the Fire District initially absorbs all of the equipment costs.

To date, for emergency services rendered during one of the darkest days in our Nations history, the Task Force has received a minimal amount of reimbursement funds in relation to the actual costs sustained by the Team. This process must change dramatically. It is our recommendation the FEMA immediately advanced funds to responding Task Forces within days of deployment to offset the financial impact to the host agencies, their participants and dedicated Civilian professionals.

Lessons Learned

Perhaps the greatest, and most difficult, lessons learned are those experienced in the worst of times! The harsh reality of catastrophic terrorist events and the subsequent mortality rate is difficult to fathom or accept by most people. In addition, the psychological impacts to the general populous are significant.

The simple but difficult truth is that Federal US&R Task Forces confronted with these situations fill a roll that involve operations focused more on human recovery than rescue. While the clear definition, and time, of when these two phases should transcend each other changes from event to event, experiences in New York and Oklahoma City have shown that the window for live victim rescues is very small and usually accomplished by the local first responders within the first 12 to 24 hours. Never the less, hope is always held out for the "miracle" rescue.

Despite this uncomfortable reality, Federal US&R Task Forces continue to play a vital and significant roll in these eve events by raising the bar on operational safety, awareness, capability, intelligence gathering, surveillance or mapping, and by assisting local Incident Commanders with completely foreign situations which require special skills, special resources and an experienced hand in decision making.

Significant issues surrounding exposure and involvement with multiple casualties in conditions which mimic war, create a very difficult personal path for the trained rescuer to navigate. These individuals very quickly come to understand the graphic nature of multiple deaths. While their initial reaction may be frustration that they are rescuers with no one left to rescue, they soon understand that even the most simple of recovery can provide closure to a life, and how important that recovery is to that individuals family members as well as themselves. In comparison, the general nature of human recoveries experienced by Task Force 3 in New York City was far less than that experienced during the Oklahoma City Bombing where individuals where found more intact, and with personal mementoes such as family photographs. In contrast, New York City was a much more sterile and completely destroyed site, and despite thousands on the missing list, actual victim finds experienced by members of Task Force where small, and infrequent, in comparison to the Oklahoma City Bombing.

Similar to the Oklahoma City Bombing, Task Force 3 arrived days into the event and after the initial complicating issues of convergent volunteers, incident control, inter agency coordination, security, feeding, housing, decontamination, and conflicting mission objectives were already either resolved, or being resolved.

This allowed Task Force 3 to build on the earlier experiences and successes of other Federal Task Forces who had responded ahead of us, and develop a solid relationship with the local responders based upon the team's attitude of humility, respect, sympathy and understanding.

Attitude is the trained rescuers best friend or worst enemy. While most Americans ans felt a need to help after September 11th, Task Force members involved with the National US&R Response System had to measure that opportunity, desire and willingness to help, against the harsh realities of what they were trained to do, as well as what they were getting themselves into. In the end, everyone wanted to go, but no one can predict or truly fully understand what that means until you work on the debris pile.

During the World Trade Center deployment, the Task Force attempted to prepare the responding personnel and their families for significant human recovery issues based upon the Oklahoma City model. While well intentioned, this in retrospect caused additional problems when those conditions were not duplicated.

What did develop was a feeling of sorrow and loss experienced through the New York City Firefighters. In addition, the event was personal because of the tremendous number of firefighters killed and the relationship of Task Force personnel with members within New York Cities Urban Search and Rescue Task Force System who lost their lives.

While Critical Incident Stress Debriefing is important and beneficial, informal support among team members is crucial. But in the end it is for each individual to put things into perspective for themselves. Based upon prior experiences or training this may take some time and individuals having problems will need special attention and assistance.

Perhaps the least appreciated and most significant issues surrounding this event were found in the area of team member health and exposure during the World Trade Center deployment. This area continues to concern Team members and managers as we struggle together to understand exactly what it was we were exposed to, and the long term affects of those exposures.

Significant issues surrounding the number of team members that have been ill after this deployment were initially missed due to the number of agencies involved with the team, their various shifts, and the infrequent contact with Civilian participants who responded. The first indication of the extent of this problem was caught during the team's picnic 30

days after the teams return and during a discussion about the health of a Rescue Squad member who had acquired pneumonia and had been off-duty for an extended period of time. This cascading series of events led

Team Managers to contact the State Office Of Emergency Services to encourage them to conduct a State Wide Survey, which was later done.

A more comprehensive pre-medical screening must be done on all pers onnel prior to deployment so that a more extensive base line medical ref- erence point can be established upon the team members return should issues surface.

In addition, the combined efforts of local, State and Federal agencies must be coordinated so that the process of information gathering, and expo- sure or injury reporting is well know, similar and simplified.

In conclusion, another significant lesson learned was the reality that as the Task Force System becomes more well known, and as it's value to the com- munity increases based upon that knowledge and exposure, Team mem- bers must understand that they inadvertently become that communities representative or ambassador representing not only themselves, but their respective agency, the Task Force and the local community.

Recommended Changes

Tiered Response:

Several years ago Task Force 3 was involved with the development of the current National Rotation Deployment model. This system has proven itself to be effective but lacks a crucial component that allows Task Forces to anticipate the actual response plan. In other words, there is no predictable tiered system of response.

The Fire Service uses this system daily to respond to emergencies. Typi- cally this system is based upon alarm response models, which increase, based upon severity, size and scope.

The National US&R System must complete this process to insure that in times of National Crisis, members within the system have a basic under- standing of how the system will respond and system managers respond appropriately.

On Site Support:

It became clear very early in New York that measures to keep costs down by scrutinizing all Task Force requests for support was very important. Perhaps this was done in contrast to the Oklahoma City Bombing where vendor support and associated Task Force expenditures were seen to be out of control.

But this process became so burdensome and counterproductive that we actually believe it compromised the goal of supporting the overall mis- sion objectives and continues to complicate the reimbursement process.

The simple truth is that Federal Task Forces are really local responders and Civilian professionals who only come together under the Federal System during times of crisis. While we are proud of the Federal designation, the annual funding offered by the Federal Government only covers a fraction of the daily operational, management, training and maintenance costs need to adequately support the program. The majority of the programs support is found in the good graces of each involved agency and the dedication of it's individual responders who constantly dedicate their time to meet, train and work together in an attempt to make up for program shortfalls through creative and constructive solutions. Their dedication and ability to perform is the backbone of this system.

More financial latitude and focus on mission specific support must be allowed on-site to Task Forces in terms of their ability to accomplish given goals and objectives related to the overall success of the mission.

Coordination of Medical Issues:

Issues surrounding the complexities associated with health and potential short and long term exposure of team members to a variety of known, and unknown, toxins concerns all of us.

The well being of these Task Force members is of paramount concern to everyone. The system should take this opportunity to develop health related protocols and procedures to insure that future deployments have a more systematic approach, especially in the area of medical health questionnaires, exposure and injury reporting.

In terms of the World Trade Center Incident, Task Force 3 recommends that a quarterly newsletter addressing Health Issues be developed to keep exposed Task Force members informed of findings, results and related issues.

Pre-Funding and Reimbursement:

In the current Memorandum of Understanding with FEMA, the agreement shows pre-funding of up to $100,000.00 to off-set costs incurred by the Task Force. To date, and on prior deployments, this money has ne never materialized. In its place, the Task Force received estimated funding authorizations from FEMA well below information provided on daily 24 hour Task Force personnel costs and the actual total number of days on deployment. It is still unclear how these estimates are generated at FEMA, and we believe a more well understood and comprehensive formula needs to be discussed and agreed upon.

In addition, cost caps on Alert and equipment procurement during Activation are not in line with estimated cache equipment shortfalls referenced in a Report to Congress dated March of 2001. In this report, Task Force 3 showed $380,000.00 of estimated equipment needs, yet during the New York City Deployment was only authorized for $75,000.00 of costs.

The unfortunate fiscal impact of these issues fall squarely on the sponsoring agency and its participants who bear the brunt of response, rehabilitation, personnel issues and a lengthy reimbursement process. This process must change so that it is supportive of the sponsoring agencies and their fiscal responsibilities.

We recommend that this be done through advance funding, more accurate cost estimations, and by fully funding known equipment shortfalls as well as increasing annual grant funds .

Overall Evaluation:

The New York City deployment presented the most complex and difficult mission experienced to date by California Task Force 3.

More attention and appreciation should be given to the roll of the rescuers, those individuals who gladly and nobly answer the call for service, and have much to loose, and very little in comparison to gain. Their dedication to duty is the foundation of this program.

What should also be understood is the difficult dynamics that these incidents create within the Teams Structure. Only one third of the participating team members will be selected for response. This situation creates unique problems that require creative solutions to overcome. The goal is to insure that the team as a unit learns the valuable lessons deployments have to offer, and that the entire team emerges together and intact on the other side of the experience.

In conclusion, Task Force 3 was truly honored to have been involved with this response, and to have stood shoulder to shoulder with some of the finest individuals this Nation can bring together. It is important to understand the value of this experience, because the bright light of goodness, unity, honor, duty, dedication, compassion, resolve and hope, will always eventually overcome the darkness of evil.

End of Report

Discussion Questions:

1) Prevention is the primary focus of a security specialist in regards to disaster management.

   True   False

2) If an emergency develops, the security specialist has no specific role to fulfill until there is a need for after-action security.

True False

3) Contain, control and communicate refers to the security specialist's role in supporting disaster management activities.

   True   False

4) "Size up" is the quick assessment of a situation, which includes the initial decisions that must be made concerning how an emergency will be managed.

   True   False

5) Evacuation decisions are usually pretty simple and straight forward and will not require much consideration from the IC.

   True   False

6) Due to terrorist's propensity to want to take out first responders, command post security is an important priority for the IC.

True False

7) The classification of casualties to determine the priority of need and care is called _____.

8) The _____, _____ and _____ chiefs must keep the IC abreast of resource availability and costs.

9) As with all positions in the IC structure, including the IC, replacement should always be considered if and when _____ responders arrive.

10) An on-going update from on-scene responders is known as a _____.

Answers:

1) True

2) False

3) True

4) True

5) False

6) True

7) Triage

8) Operations, logistics and administration

9) More qualified

10) Situation report

7

Crime Prevention Through Environmental Design (CPTED)

Overview:

So far much of the discussion in this text has focused on emergency preparation. In chapter seven we will begin looking at preventative security measures. Security, in this sense, is defined as protections and safeguards against theft, loss, disclosure or attack. Security measures are at the heart of the prevention model. Effective security is designed to mitigate and prevent losses and avert disasters.

A central concept in security planning is the idea of CPTED—crime prevention through environmental design. We will begin examining the principles and purpose of CPTED as a novel security measure.

Chapter Objectives:
- *Explain the concept of CPTED*
- *State the principles of CPTED*
- *Explain the ideas and principles of defensible space*
- *Define the limitations of CPTED*

What is CPTED?

Crime prevention through environmental design, or CPTED, is a multi-disciplinary approach to reducing crime and increasing perceived safety. CPTED relies upon the influence of offender behavior. It seeks to dissuade offenders from committing crimes by manipulating the physical environment in which those crimes occur. As a result, it relies upon an understanding of what about the environment influences offenders.

CPTED is most effective when involving environmental designers (e.g., Architects, landscape architects), land managers (e.g., Park managers), community action (e.g., Neighborhood watch groups), and law enforcement. If any of the four defender groups are removed it is likely that a CPTED strategy will be less effective than it might otherwise be.

CPTED is used by a variety of groups. Mostly they fall into one of four categories: environmental designers (e.g., architects, landscape architects), land managers (e.g., park managers), community action groups (e.g., neighborhood watch groups), and law enforcement groups (e.g., park rangers, metropolitan police). However each group is not equally equipped to apply CPTED. Instead, each has a unique knowledge base that makes it an important information source for creating effective CPTED strategies. Combined these groups can develop holistic plans that influence offender behavior yet do not neglect other considerations such as preservation of historic landscapes.

CPTED *Principles*

Territoriality

Territoriality is the CPTED principle that is used to clearly delineated private space from semi-private and public spaces. Properly used it creates a sense of ownership in private and semi-private areas.

Territoriality creates an environment where strangers and intruders stand out and are more easily identified. This is accomplished through the effective use of signage, grade changes, fencing, landscape edging, lighting, and any number of imaginative techniques that encourage individuals to take pride in their surroundings and report criminal activity.

Lighting and Natural Surveillance

Natural surveillance is the CPTED concept that encourages an open design. It promotes opportunities for people, as they are engaged in their normal behaviors, to observe the space around them. This principle allows people to feel comfortable as they use a space, maintain distance from intruders that may be in or near the space, and encourage observation of those individuals that may be using the space with criminal intent.

Natural Surveillance encourages the design and placement of physical features so as to maximizes visibility. This includes building orientation, placement of windows, building and site entrance and exit locations, refuse containers, landscaping materials, parking lots, walkways, walls and fences (including the use of wrought iron and similar materials that promote visibility), signage, and other physical obstructions. It may also include the placement of persons or activities to maximize surveillance possibilities.

Minimally maintained lighting standards that provide for nighttime illumination of parking lots, walkways, entrances, exits and related areas, to promote a safe environment, are also Natural Surveillance components of good CPTED design.

Natural Access Control

CPTED features the physical guidance of people coming and going from a space by the judicial placement of entrances, exits, fencing, landscaping, and lighting.

Territorial Reinforcement

CPTED encourages the use of physical attributes that express ownership, such as fences, pavement treatment, art, signage, and landscaping.

Maintenance

CPTED allows for the continued use of a space for its intended purpose and serves as an additional expression of ownership. It prevents any reduction of visibility from landscaping overgrowth and obstructed or inoperative lighting.

The Concept of Defensible Space

All Defensible Space programs have a common purpose: They restructure the physical layout of communities to allow residents to control the areas around their homes. This includes the streets and grounds outside their buildings and the lobbies and corridors within them. The programs help people preserve those areas in which they can realize their commonly held values and lifestyles.

Defensible Space relies on self-help rather than on government intervention, and so it is not vulnerable to government's withdrawal of support.

It depends on resident involvement to reduce crime and remove the presence of criminals. It has the ability to bring people of different incomes and race together in a mutually beneficial union. For lowincome people,

Defensible Space can provide an introduction to the benefits of mainstream life and an opportunity to see how their own actions can better the world around them and lead to upward mobility.

Over the past 25 years, our institute has been using Defensible Space technology to enable residents to take control of their neighborhoods, to reduce crime, and to stimulate private reinvestment. We have been able to do this while maintaining racial and economic integration. The process has also produced inexpensive ways to create housing for the poor, often without government assistance. In this chapter, I will briefly explain the origins and principles of Defensible Space and introduce the reader to the results of our various research projects.

Evolution of the Concept: Pruitt-Igoe and Carr Square Village

The Defensible Space concept evolved about 30 years ago when, as a teacher at Washington University in St. Louis, I was able to witness the newly constructed 2,740-unit public housing highrise development, Pruitt-Igoe, go to ruin. The project was designed by one of the country's most eminent architects and was hailed as the new enlightenment. It followed the planning principles of Le Corbusier and the International Congress of Modern Architects. Even though the density was not very high (50 units to the acre), residents were raised into the air in 11-story buildings. The idea was to keep the grounds and the first floor free for community activity. "A river of trees" was to flow under the buildings. Each building was given communal corridors on every third floor to house a 2,740-unit public housing project, laundry, a communal room, and a garbage room that contained a garbage chute.

Occupied by single-parent, welfare families, the design proved a disaster. Because all the grounds were common and disassociated from the units, residents could not identify with them. The areas proved unsafe. The river of trees soon became a sewer of glass and garbage. The mailboxes on the ground floor were vandalized. The corridors, lobbies, elevators, and stairs were dangerous places to walk. They became covered with graffiti and littered with garbage and human waste. The elevators, laundry, and community rooms were vandalized, and garbage was stacked high around the choked garbage chutes.

Women had to get together in groups to take their children to school and go shopping. The project never achieved more than 60 percent occupancy. It was torn down about 10 years after its construction and be came a precursor of what was to happen elsewhere in the country. Across the street from Pruitt- Igoe was an older, smaller, rowhouse complex, Carr Square Village, occupied by an identical population. It had remained fully occupied and trouble-free throughout the construction, occupancy, and decline of Pruitt-Igoe. With social variables constant in the two developments, what, I asked, was the significance of the physical differences that enabled one to survive while the other was destroyed?

Walking through Pruitt-Igoe in its heyday of pervasive crime and vandalism, one could only ask: What kind of people live here? Excluding the interior areas of the development there were occasional pockets that were clean, safe, and well-tended. Where only two families shared a landing, it was clean and well-maintained. If one could get oneself invited into an apartment, one found it neat and well maintained—modestly furnished perhaps, but with great pride. Why such a difference between the interior of the apartment and the public spaces outside? One could only conclude that residents maintained and controlled those areas that were clearly defined as their own.

Landings shared by only two families were well maintained, whereas corridors shared by 20 families, and lobbies, elevators, and stairs shared by 150 families were a disaster—they evoked no feelings of identity or control. Such anonymous public spaces made it impossible for even neighboring residents to develop an accord about acceptable behavior in these areas. It was impossible to feel or exert proprietary feelings,impossible to tell resident from intruder. Most of us have seen highrise apartments occupied by middle-income people that function very well. Why then do they not work for low-income families? Middle-income apartment buildings have funds available for doormen, porters, elevator operators, and resident superintendents to watch over and maintain the common public areas, but in high-rise public housing, there are barely enough funds for 9-to-5 nonresident maintenance men, let alone for security personnel, elevator operators, or porters. Not surprisingly, therefore, it is within these interior and exterior common public areas that most crime in public housing takes place. Given that funds for doormen, porters, and resident superintendents do not exist for public housing, the question emerged: Is it possible to design public housing without any interior public areas and to have all the grounds assigned to individual families?

Location of Crime in Walkups and Highrises

In interior public spaces	68.0
On outside grounds	37.3
Inside apartments	16.5
Walkups (3 floors)	5.3
Midrises (6–7 floors)	
Highrises (13–30 floors)	

The Private Streets of St. Louis

Also in St. Louis, I came upon a series of turn-of-the-century neighborhoods where homes are replicas of the small chateaux of France. They are the former palaces of St. Louis' commercial barons—the rail, beef, and shipping kings. These chateaux are positioned on privately held streets, closed to through traffic. St. Louis in the mid-1960s was a city coming apart. The influx of people from the rural areas of the South had overwhelmed the city. It had one of the Nation's highest crime rates, but the private streets appeared to be oblivious to the chaos and abandonment taking place around them. They continued to function as peaceful, crime-free environments—nice places to rear children, if you could afford a castle. The residents owned and controlled their own streets, and although anyone was free to drive or walk them (they had no guard booths), one knew that one was intruding into a private world and that one's actions were under constant observation. Why, I asked, could not this model be used to stabilize the adjacent working and middle-class neighborhoods that were undergoing massive decline and abandonment?

Was private ownership the key, or was the operating mechanism the closing-off of streets and the creation of controlled enclaves? Through research funded by the National Science Foundation (Newman, Dean, and Wayne, 1974) we were able to identify the essential ingredients of the private streets and provide a model that could be replicated throughout the city. This was done in both African-American and white areas, and its implementation succeeded in stabilizing communities in transition.

The Effect of Housing Form on Residents' Ability to Control Areas

Over the next few pages I will explain how different building types create spaces outside the dwelling unit that affect residents' ability to control them. Firstly, I should explain what I mean by the dwelling unit: It is the interior of an apartment unit or home. That is the case whether the unit is one among many in a highrise building or sits by itself on the ground. I am interested in learning how the grouping of units in different types of building configurations creates indoor and outdoor "non unit" spaces of different character.

For simplification, I have grouped all buildings into the three categories that capture the essential differences among them. These three categories are: single-family houses; walkups; and highrises. Single-family houses come in three basic types: detached houses; semi-detached houses; and row houses (row houses are also called townhouses).

The fully detached building sits by itself, not touching any other building; the semidetached building has two single-family units sharing a common wall; and the rowhouse building has a few single-family units sharing common walls with other units, one on each side. Although all three types of single-family buildings look different, they share an essential common trait: Within the four walls of each type of building is the private domain of one family. There are no interior spaces that are public or that do not belong to a family. All the interior spaces, therefore, are private. Even the row house is subdivided into a series of distinctly private spaces. There are no interior spaces within any single-family building—whether a row house, a semidetached building, or a fully detached house—that are shared by more than one family. The fundamental difference in the three types of single-family houses shown is the density at which they can be built—which is to say the number of units that can be put on an acre of land in each of these configurations. The upward limit of the detached house is about six units to the acre. The upward limit of the semidetached house is eight units to the acre, but this allows for a driveway to be put between each unit, something that could not be achieved in detached units at six to the acre. Row houses can be built at an upward limit of 16 units to the acre if one also wishes to provide off-street parking on a one-to-one basis.

When one looks at the grounds surrounding these three types of single- family units, one finds that all the grounds are private because they have been assigned to each unit. Regardless of which type of single-family building we examine, each has been designed so that each unit has its own front and rear yard. The front yard of each unit also immediately abuts the street. If we attempt to categorize the grounds as either private, semiprivate, semipublic, or public, we would have to conclude that the rear yards are certainly private because they belong to individual families lies and are only accessible from the interior of each unit. The front yards also belong to individual families, but because they are accessible from the street as well as from the interior of each unit their character is different. I have classed them as semiprivate because of this difference, but some people would say that they are really private.

Looking at the next classification of building—the walkup—one finds that a radical new element has been introduced that totally changes the character of both the inside and outside of the building. We now have circulation areas within the building that are common because they are shared by a few families. The number of families sharing these common areas depends on how the entrances, corridors, and stairs are distributed within the building.

- All interior spaces are within the private domain of the family.

- All grounds around the private unit are for the private use of the family.

- There is a direct abutment between private grounds and the sidewalk.

- The domain of the house encompasses the street.

- Private space exists only within the apartment units.

- The interior circulation areas and the grounds are public.
- There is no association between buildings and street.

The 15-story building at the right has 195 families sharing common interior areas. Because of the large number of people sharing them, these interior areas can only be designated as semipublic or even public. Even the corridors on each floor are shared by 13 families and are accessible from 2 sets of stairs and 2 elevators that are very public. For this reason I would have to designate these corridors as semipublic, if not public.

The outside grounds, because of their disassociation from any of the individual units, and the fact that they are shared by 195 families, can only be designated as public areas

In Figure I–10*, the walkup building is subdivided so that six families share a common entry and interior circulation stair. Two families per floor share a common landing. Entrances from the common staircase usually exit to the outside at both the front and rear.

Such buildings are often called garden apartments. Walkups can be built at a density of 30 to 40 units per acre if they are 3 stories in height, and at a density of 20 to 30 units to the acre if they are only 2 stories in height. Three-story walkups were commonly built in the 1950s and 1960s, but as these are nonelevator buildings, the 3-story walkup has fallen out of favor with the decline in housing demand.

Because the grounds surrounding 3-story walkups, front and back, belong to all the families living in the building, they cannot be considered private. The grounds in the front of the unit are also adjacent to a public street. For this reason I would categorize the grounds in front as semipublic space. The grounds at the rear of the unit are also not assigned to individual families and the rear of the units are often used for parking. In such a case, the grounds at the back would also have to be considered semipublic. It is, however, possible to modify the design of the rear grounds to make some of the areas private and the remainder semiprivate, and I will demonstrate how to do that shortly.

We come now to the last of our three building types: the highrise. These are elevator buildings and commonly come in two sizes, depending on the type of elevator used. The least expensive elevator is the hydraulic, but it has an upward limit of six stories. The electric elevator can comfortably go up to 30 stories, but it is usually used in 10- to 16-story apartment buildings.

Summary of the Effect of Building Type on Behavior

A family's claim to a territory diminishes proportionally as the number of families who share that claim increases. The larger the number of people who share a territory, the less each individual feels rights to it. Therefore, with only a few families sharing an area, whether it be the interior circulation areas of a building or the grounds outside, it is relatively easy for an informal understanding to be reached among the families as to what constitutes acceptable usage.

When the numbers increase, the opportunity for reaching such an implicit understanding diminishes to the point that no usage other than walking through the area is really possible, but any use is permissible.

The larger the number of people who share a communal space, the more difficult it is for people to identify it as theirs or to feel they have a right to control or determine the activity taking place within it. It is easier for outsiders to gain access to and linger in the interior areas of a building shared by 24 to 100 families than it is in a building shared by 6 to 12 families.

The Effect of Building Type on Residents' Control of Streets

If we examine the three building types from the viewpoint of residents' ability to exert control over surrounding streets, we again find marked differences.

Figures I–12, I–13, and I–14 graphically summarize the major differences between residents' ability to control the areas around their homes and public streets. The three illustrations show the same four-block area of a city, each developed using a different building type.

Figure I–12 is an illustration of a row-house development built at a density of 18 units to the acre. Each city block has been subdivided so that all the grounds, except for the streets and sidewalks, are assigned to individual families. The front lawns, because each belongs to an individual family, are designated semiprivate. The rear yards, which are fully enclosed, are private. In fact they are only accessible from the interior of the dwelling units.

The close juxtaposition of each dwelling unit and its entry to the street contributes to the incorporation of the sidewalk into the sphere of influence of the inhabitants of the dwelling. This is further reinforced by the fact that their semiprivate lawn abuts the sidewalk, and the family car is parked at the curb. Residents' attitudes suggest that they consider this sidewalk and parking area as semipublic, rather than public.

Examining the entire four-block area, we find an urban fabric in which most of the outdoor areas and all of the indoor areas are private. In addition, a good portion of what is a legally public street is viewed by residents as an extension of their dwellings and under their sphere of influence: that is, the sidewalk and that portion of the roadbed on which their

are parked. Because of the close juxtaposition of the street to the private front lawn of each dwelling, residents are concerned about ensuring its safety and act to maintain and control it. In actual fact, only the very central portion of each street is truly public in nature. If the street were narrow, even the activity in this central portion would be considered accountable to neighboring residents.

Figure I–13 shows the same four-block area, this time accommodating 3-story garden apartments built at a density of 36 units to the acre. The rear courts within the interior of each cluster have been assigned both to individual families and to all the families sharing the cluster. The families living on the ground floor have been given their own patios within the interior courts, with access to them from the interior of their unit. These patios are therefore private. The remainder of the interior court belongs to all the families sharing a cluster and is only accessible from the semiprivate interior circulation space of each building, making the remainder of the interior cluster semiprivate.

The small front lawn adjacent to each building entry is the collective area for that entry's inhabitants and is therefore semiprivate. As in the rowhouse scheme in figure I–12, all the entries face the street, but each entry now serves six families rather than one and is thus semiprivate rather than private. Parking again is on the street immediately in front of each dwelling. Because of the semiprivate nature of the grounds, the side walk and street are not clear extensions of the realms of individual dwelling units. But even with all these limitations, the neighboring sidewalk and parking zone on the street are considered by many residents as areas over which they exert some control.

Each building entry serves 50 families by means of an interior circulation system consisting of a public lobby, elevators, fire stairs, and corridors. The grounds around the buildings are accessible to everyone and are not assigned to particular buildings. The residents, as a result, feel little association with or responsibility for the grounds and even less association with the surrounding public streets.

Not only are the streets distant from the units, but no building entries face them.

The grounds of the development that abut the sidewalks are also public, and, as a consequence, so are the sidewalks and streets. This design succeeds in making public the entire ground surface of the four-block area. All the grounds of the project must be maintained by management and patrolled by a hired security force. The city streets and sidewalks, in turn, must be maintained by the city sanitation department and patrolled by city police. The placement of the highrise towers on the interior grounds has produced a system of off-street parking and access paths to the building that involves many turns and blind corners. Residents in such developments complain about the dangers of walking into the grounds to get to their buildings at night. The proclivity of landscape designers for positioning shrubs exactly at turns in the paths increases the hazards of these access routes. This problem does not arise in traditional rowhouse or walkup developments where building entries face the street and are set back from the sidewalk no more than 10 to 20 feet. Nor do these fears occur in highrise buildings whose entries face the streets and are only set back slightly from them. In these latter cases, residents are able to move in a straight line from the relative safety of the public street to what they can observe to be the relative safety of the well lighted lobby area in the interior of their buildings.

Figure I–15 shows two housing projects located across the street from one another: a garden apartment complex on the right and a highrise on the left. Both projects are designed at the same density and with similar parking provisions

(40 units to the acre and 1 parking space per unit).

The highrise project has all building entries facing the interior grounds of the development. Parking has been designed as a continuous strip along the street, further disassociating the buildings from the street. The project on the right is only three stories in height and has all the buildings and their entries juxtaposed with the city streets or the interior streets and parking. Each entry faces the street and serves only 6 families, whereas the highrises have 60 families sharing a common entry. Small play and sitting areas have been provided near the entry to each walkup. This serves to extend into the street the sphere of influence of each of the six families.

The residents in the walkup are a very short distance from the surrounding streets, and because of the positioning of the building entries, play areas, and parking, the neighboring streets are brought within the sphere of influence of inhabitants.

Another important lesson to learn from this comparison is that 2 radically different building configurations can be produced at the same density: in this case a density of 40 units to the acre with 1-to-1 parking. This is a very high density that will satisfy the economic demands of high land costs. The walkup development achieves the same density as the highrise by covering more of the grounds (37 percent ground coverage versus 24 percent). Municipalities that wish to reap the benefits of walkup versus highrise buildings must learn to be flexible with their floor-area-ratio requirements to assure that they are not depriving residents of a better housing option in order to get more open ground space that has little purpose.

What is true for site design is also true for building design: The same building envelope can be subdivided in different ways to produce dramatically different results. For instance, figure I–16 shows two ways of configuring a three-story walkup. Both buildings serve a total of 24 families each. In the upper layout, all 24 families share 2 common entrances and 8 families share a common corridor on each floor, although access to the corridors on each floor is open to all 24 families in the building. In the lower design, only 6 families share a common entry, and only 2 families share a common landing on each floor.

In the lower design, the smaller number of families sharing an entry and landing allows the families to control the public spaces better: They can more readily recognize residents from strangers and feel they have a say in determining accepted behavior.

If this were a two-story building rather than a three-story building, it would have been possible, in the lower design, to give each family its own individual entry directly off the street and thus avoid having any interior public spaces at all.

Social Factors and Their Interaction with the Physical

An understanding of the interaction of the social and physical factors that create high crime rates in low- and moderate-income housing developments is useful not only for devising remedies to solve their problems but also for developing strategies for stabilizing neighboring communities composed of single-family housing.

Figure I–17 shows the influence of different social and physical factors on the crime rates in low- and moderate-income projects operated by the New York City

Housing Authority. This analytical technique called stepwise regression analysis is employed when many different factors interact to produce a particular effect, such as, a rise in crime rates. The technique isolates those factors that contribute to the effect most strongly and independently of other factors. In figure I–17 the percentage of population receiving welfare is shown to be the most important factor, followed by building height or the number of families sharing the entry to a building.

Those social variables that correlated highly with different types of crime also correlated highly with each other. These include: the percentage of resident population receiving welfare (excluding the elderly), the percentage of one-parent families receiving Aid to Families with Dependent dent Children (AFDC), and the per capita disposable income of the project's residents.

My interviews with residents, management, and police provide the following explanation for the correlation of these social factors and crime rates: A one-parent household headed by a female is more vulnerable to criminal attack; families with only one adult present are less able to control their teenage children; young teenage AFDC mothers are often victimized by their boyfriends; the criminal activity by the poor is tolerated, if not condoned, among the poor; the poor, and particularly the poor of racial minorities, are unable to demand much in the way of police protection; and the commission of crime against residents in ghetto areas requires minimal skill and risk.

The physical factors that correlate most strongly with crime rates are, in order of importance: the height of the buildings, which in turn correlates highly with the number of apartments sharing the entry to a building; the size of the housing project or "the total number of dwelling units in the project"; and the number of other publicly assisted housing projects in the area.

The above suggests that two classes of physical factors contribute to crime rates: (1) those such as "project size" or the "number of publicly assisted projects in the area" that reinforce social weakness and pathology; and (2) those such as "building height" or "the number of units per entry" that affect the ability of residents to control their environment. The first class of physical factors may also be considered another class of social variable: For instance, if certain social characteristics such as the percentage of AFDC families correlate highly with crime rate, then we can anticipate that a large number of such families gathered together in one area may aggravate the crime problems still further and increase the per capita crime rate.

The significance of this aggregation is not simply that the presence of more potential criminals creates proportionally more crime, but also that a concentration of potential criminals actually increases the rate of crime. Thus, large low-income projects, or low-income projects surrounded by other low-income projects, suffer a higher crime rate than small or isolated projects even when the percentage of AFDC families remains the same in all the projects.

A frequent complaint from residents of communities surrounding large public housing projects is that the teenage criminals living in the projects make use of the large, anonymous environment of the housing project as a place to retreat and hide. For example, there is a particularly notorious project in Jersey City that is located adjacent to U.S. Highway 1 entering New York City. A traffic light at an intersection that borders the project forces truckers to stop there on their way into New York. Teen-age project residents have developed a pattern of hijacking trucks at the stoplight, by throwing the driver out and driving the truck into the project. The truck is then emptied in a matter of minutes and the loot hidden in vacant apartments.

The relationship between the socioeconomic characteristics of residents and a project's crime rate had long been suspected. The most fascinating finding to come out of the data analysis presented in Defensible Space (1972) was, therefore, the influence of building height and number of units per entry in predicting crime rate. Regardless of the social characteristics of inhabitants, the physical form of housing was shown to play an important role in reducing crime and in assisting residents in controlling behavior in their housing environments.

In addition to the fact that buildings with a large number of families sharing an entry experience higher crime rates than those with few families per entry, they are also vulnerable to additional types of criminal activity. Most of the crime experienced by residents of single-family buildings is burglary, committed when members of the family are either away from home or asleep. By contrast the residents of large, multifamily dwellings experience both burglaries and robberies. The higher crime rate experienced by residents in large multifamily dwellings is mostly attributable to the occurrence of robberies in the interior common circulation areas of multifamily buildings: lobbies, hallways, stairs, and elevators. These are also the areas where criminals wait to approach their victims and force them into apartments for the purpose of robbing them.

Of a total of 8,611 felonies reported in all New York City Housing Authority projects in 1969 (excluding intrahousehold incidents), 3,786, or 44 percent, were committed in the interior public areas of buildings. Of the crimes committed in interior public areas, 3,165, or 84 percent, were robberies. The breakdown by location of the felonies taking place in interior public areas was: elevators, 41 percent; hallways, 22 percent; lobbies, 18 percent; stairways, 9 percent; roof landings, 2 percent; and other, 8 percent. Although the socioeconomic charac-teristics of the residents exert a strong influence on crime rate, the physical characteristics of the buildings and the project can exert a counteracting influence. The physical form of residential environment can, in fact, ameliorate the effect of many of the problems created by the concentration of low-income one-parent families with teenage children.

Variations in Crime Rate as Produced by Different Socioeconomic Groups Occupying Different Building Types.

The more complex and anonymous the housing environment, the more difficult it is for a code of behavior following societal norms to become established among residents. It is even difficult for moderate-income families with two adult heads of household to cope with crime and vandalism problems in poorly designed environments, but when poor and broken families are grouped together in such a setting, the results are nothing short of disastrous. The public housing projects now experiencing the highest vacancy rates are those that consist of the worst mixture of social and physical attributes.

The suitability of building types to lifestyle groups I have explained the problems resulting from housing low-income families with children in high-rises buildings. But one should not conclude from this that high-rises are not suitable for other lifestyle groups. For instance, elderly people, even those of low income, do very well in high-rises buildings as long as the buildings are kept exclusively for the elderly.

Elderly people do not like walking stairs and appreciate an elevator building. Retired elderly often live away from their children, and their elderly neighbors become their new extended family. At the push of an elevator button, they can have access to a hundred other families within a high-rise building.

If we also design the ground floor of an elderly high-rise as a communal and recreation area, we can create a security station at the building entry door that can be manned by elderly volunteers. If a problem arises, a push of a button summons the police. With the use of gates and fencing, the grounds surrounding their building can also be secured and defined for their exclusive use.

The lesson we can learn from this is that some of the high-rise stock we have inherited, because it has proven unusable for welfare families with children, may lend itself to conversion for the exclusive use of the elderly.

However, we should not jump for joy too quickly. Many of our high-rise public housing projects in large cities like New York, Chicago, and Boston were built as 1,000-unit agglomerations, and the need for such a concentration of the elderly is, at present, just not there. Also, the community surrounding such a 1,000-unit agglomeration will meanwhile have been devastated—no place to be putting the elderly. It would not be wise to convert 1 of 10 high-rise buildings for the elderly, while keeping the adjacent 9 buildings for families with children. The elderly would be victimized and refuse to live in such an environment.

Finally, even when high rises exist in isolation, the cost of converting a building made up of three-bedroom apartments into one-bedroom units may be prohibitive.

Factors Influencing Crime and Instability

Our institute's study of the Factors Influencing Crime and Instability in Federally-Assisted Housing (Newman and Franck, 1980) involved 44 moderate-income housing sites and 29 public housing sites in three cities: Newark, St. Louis, and San Francisco. It used a path analysis to take into account the influence of other factors, including socioeconomic characteristics, management effectiveness, quality of city police and security services, and form of ownership.

The results showed that two physical factors and two social factors accounted for most of the variation. The two physical factors were the size of the development and the number of families sharing common entries into a building. The two social factors were the percentage of families on AFDC and the ratio of teenagers to adults. As public housing has become housing for the poorest of the poor, the only variables that lend themselves to modification are the physical, project size and the number of apartments sharing common entries.

Project size is a measure of the overall concentration of low-income families in a project or cluster of projects. We found that the larger the concentration, the more residents felt isolated from the rest of society and felt their perceived differences to be greater. Project size affects stigmatization—as perceived both by the outside world and by the project residents themselves. The apathy that comes with stigmatization leads to neglect and withdrawal, first on the part of the residents, then by housing management, and finally by the municipal agencies that service the project: police, education, parks and recreation, refuse collection, and social services. A large project provides a continuous area in which gangs can operate, allowing even one gang or group of drug dealers to contaminate all of its public space.

The larger the number of units sharing common entries is a measure of how public the interior corridors, elevators, and stairs are. The more residents who have to share common areas, the more difficult it is to lay claim to them; the more difficult it is to distinguish other residents from intruders; and the more difficult it is to agree with other residents on the care and control of these areas.

The numbers within the brackets below show the amount of variation in residents' behavior that is explained by building size. If the number is preceded by a minus, it means that an increase in building size has a negative effect on that behavior. In the case of residents' use of public areas, for instance, the numbers in brackets mean that an increase of 1 unit in building size will cause a reduction of 0.50 of a unit in residents' use of public areas. This demonstrates that building form has a very strong predictive capacity on public area use, independent of other factors that are also likely to predict it.

Building size has a statistically significant direct causal effect on residents' behavior as follows:

    (i)   Use of public areas in their development [– 0.50].

    (ii) Social interaction with their neighbors [– 0.31].

    (iii) Sense of control over the interior and exterior public areas of their development [– 0.29].

Further results of our path analysis showed that building size has important causal effects on fear of crime [0.38] and on community instability [0.39], independent of socioeconomic, managerial, ownership, police, and guard service factors. Community instability is measured by apartment turnover and vacancy rates and by residents' desire to move. However, as in the 1970 New York City public housing study discussed earlier, the findings from our study of moderate-income developments showed that the socioeconomic characteristics of residents also have strong causal effects on fear, instability, and crime.

Independent of other factors, the socioeconomic characteristics of residents have a total causal effect on fear of crime of 0.59, on community instability of 0.51, and on crimes against persons of 0.32. These findings can be interpreted as follows: A unit increase in the percentage of AFDC families living in a development will produce 0.59 of a unit increase in fear of crime.

The data from this analysis can be summarized in still another way by looking at the results of the regression analysis. The R is a sign used to represent the percent of variance in one factor that is predicted by all other factors acting together. The effects of building size, socioeconomic characteristics of residents, management performance, form of ownership, and police and guard service together produce the following: R= 0.69 for fear (p < 0.001); R= 0.67 for community instability (p < 0.001); and R= 0.39 for crimes against persons (p < 0.05).

Another way of stating these findings is that the combination of these factors predict 69 percent of the variation in fear, for instance. But more important still, of all the factors in the predictive model, it is the socioeconomic characteristics of residents and building size that together predict most of the variation in fear, instability, and crime.

Reprinted from www.surreycc.gov.uk, Surrey County Council.

Discussion Questions

1) Crime prevention through environmental design, or CPTED, is a _____ approach to reducing crime and increasing perceived safety.

2) CPTED is most effective when involving _____.

3) _____ is the CPTED principle that is used to clearly delineate private space from semi-private and public spaces.

4) _____ is the CPTED concept that encourages an open design. It promotes opportunities for people, as they are engaged in their normal behaviors, to observe the space around them.

5) Defensible Space relies on _____ rather than on government intervention.

6) Territoriality creates an environment where _____ and _____ stand out and are more easily identified.

7) Defensible space programs restructure the physical layout of communities to allow residents to control the areas around their homes.

   True   False

8) Both CPTED and Defensible Space are programs, that have been unequivocally proven to be effective.

   True   False

9) CPTED users generally fall into one of four categories: environmental designers; land managers; community action groups; and law enforcement.

   True   False

10) Natural Surveillance encourages the design and placement of physical features so as to obstruct visibility

    True   False

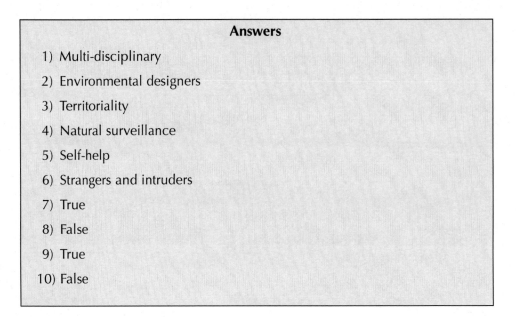

Answers

1) Multi-disciplinary

2) Environmental designers

3) Territoriality

4) Natural surveillance

5) Self-help

6) Strangers and intruders

7) True

8) False

9) True

10) False

Endnote

* Figures referred to in this section were unavailable for reproduction

8 Challenges to the Community

Overview:

In western society, with strong separation of powers, localized governance, civil liberties, privacy expectations, an emphasis on freedom and mobility, historical isolation from global events and a low tolerance for inconvenience, meeting and beating the challenges of homeland security are proving to be a daunting task for public safety planners and first responders.

This chapter will begin to look at these challenges and ask you to start considering the profound questions that homeland security specialists will have to deal with in the new millennium.

Chapter Objectives:

- *Explain the significance of the various settings in the Homeland Security Threat Advisory Systems*
- *State the challenges facing the integration of local law enforcement agencies and homeland security*
- *State the challenges facing public safety and public health systems in upgrading first responder capabilities to address terrorism and large scale catastrophes.*
- *Explain the tenets of the Posse Comitatus Act of 1878 and why this law presents complications to modern homeland security efforts*

Responding to the Homeland Security Threat Advisory System

Understanding the Homeland Security Advisory System

The world has changed since September 11, 2001. We remain a nation at risk to terrorist attacks and will remain at risk for the foreseeable future. At all Threat Conditions, we must remain vigilant, prepared, and ready to deter terrorist attacks.

Guidance for Federal Departments and Agencies

The following Threat Conditions each represent an increasing risk of terrorist attacks. Beneath each Threat Condition are some suggested Protective Measures, recognizing that the heads of Federal departments and agencies are responsible for developing and implementing appropriate agency-specific Protective Measures:

1. **Low Condition (Green).** This condition is declared when there is a low risk of terrorist attacks. Federal departments and agencies should consider the following general measures in addition to the agency-specific Protective Measures they develop and implement: Refining and exercising as appropriate preplanned Protective Measures; Ensuring personnel receive proper training on the Homeland Security Advisory System and specific preplanned department or agency Protective Measures; and Institutionalizing a process to assure that all facilities and regulated sectors are regularly assessed for vulnerabilities to terrorist attacks, and all reasonable measures are taken to mitigate these vulnerabilities.

Courtesy of AP/Wide World Photos

2. **Guarded Condition (Blue).** This condition is declared when there is a general risk of terrorist attacks. In addition to the Protective Measures taken in the previous Threat Condition, Federal departments and agencies should consider the following general measures in addition to the agency-specific Protective Measures that they will develop and implement:

    > Checking communications with designated emergency response or command locations; Reviewing and updating emergency response procedures; and Providing the public with any information that would strengthen its ability to act appropriately.

3. **Elevated Condition (Yellow).** An Elevated Condition is declared when there is a significant risk of terrorist attacks. In addition to the Protective Measures taken in the previous Threat Conditions, Federal departments and agencies should consider the following general measures in addition to the Protective Measures that they will develop and implement:

Increasing surveillance of critical locations; Coordinating emergency plans as appropriate with nearby jurisdictions; Assessing whether the precise characteristics of the threat require the further refinement of preplanned Protective Measures; and Implementing, as appropriate, contingency and emergency response plans.

4. **High Condition (Orange).** A High Condition is declared when there is a high risk of terrorist attacks. In addition to the Protective Measures taken in the previous Threat Conditions, Federal departments and agencies should consider the following general measures in addition to the agency-specific Protective Measures that they will develop and implement:

Coordinating necessary security efforts with Federal, State, and local law enforcement agencies or any National Guard or other appropriate armed forces organizations; Taking additional precautions at public events and possibly considering alternative venues or even cancellation; Preparing to execute contingency procedures, such as moving to an alternate site or dispersing their workforce; and Restricting threatened facility access to essential personnel only.

5. **Severe Condition (Red).** A Severe Condition reflects a severe risk of terrorist attacks. Under most circumstances, the Protective Measures for a Severe Condition are not intended to be sustained for substantial periods of time. In addition to the Protective Measures in the previous Threat Conditions, Federal departments and agencies also should consider the following general measures in addition to the agency-specific Protective Measures that they will develop and implement: Increasing or redirecting personnel to address critical emergency needs; Assigning emergency response personnel and pre-positioning and mobilizing specially trained teams or resources; Monitoring, redirecting, or constraining transportation systems; and Closing public and government facilities.

Synergies and differences between traditional public safety/first response roles vs. security principles.

The Integration of Homeland Security and Law Enforcement[8]

> *"They're a law enforcement agency. They're not in the business of fighting terrorism."*
>
> —*John Edwards*

This lecture directs attention to the challenges of integrating homeland security and law enforcement, especially as those challenges involve redefinition of the police role to encompass more effective surveillance and intelligence functions. The federal government defines homeland security as: "a concerted national effort to prevent terrorist attacks within the United States, reduce America's vulnerability to terrorism, and minimize the damage and recover from attacks that do occur" (Bush 2003). The key part of this definition is "concerted national effort" which means that it is not solely a federal effort, but based on the principle of partnership between governments, the private sector, and the American people. That partner known as law enforcement has always served a first responder role, and it even has some experience at counter-subversive and anti-terrorist (domestic) activities, but today's challenge involves taking on enemies (modern international terrorists) who fight in asymmetric ways that mock constitutional safeguards which balance criminal rights with police powers. Law enforcement has also always been a small-town, decentralized phenomena in American society, and without new models, theories, and laws, it may not be up to the task of collecting, sharing, coordinating, and analyzing the intelligence necessary to successfully assess and respond to modern-day threats. It may be time for a revolution in police affairs, much like the revolution in military affairs toward special, light brigades that are jointly coordinated in real-time. It is definitely the time to reconsider the police role in society, and to what extent police involvement in national defense and domestic security carries a risk of encroachment on civil liberties. We shall begin with an overview of three ways to approach domestic security, and discuss the implications for law enforcement throughout.

The Super-Agency Approach to Domestic Security

The idea of some sort of super-agency that tracks the ideological (American and unAmerican) commitments of its citizens has been around for a long time. It has been implemented in many nations with concerns about internal, or state security. It is implicit in most proposals to federalize, centralize, or consolidate police forces. It is explicit in most proposals to reorganize the intelligence community, such as the 1970 Huston Plan (named after White House staffer Tom Charles Huston) which advocated combining the CIA, FBI, NSA, and DIA. While far from creating a domestic intelligence super-agency (like MI5 in Britain), the creation of the Department of Homeland Security (DHS) is a significant transformation of U.S. government. Formed in the aftermath of terrorist attacks on September 11th, 2001, the new department's first priority became protection of the nation against further terrorist attacks, followed by additional duties for intelligence and threat analysis, guardianship of borders and airports, protection of critical infrastructure, and emergency response coordination. Along with the Coast Guard and Secret Service, twenty-two (22) separate agencies were consolidated into the DHS, and housed in one of four major directorates: Border and Transportation Security, Emergency Preparedness and Response, Science and Technology, and Information Analysis and Infrastructure Protection, as follows:

1. *Border and Transportation Security directorate:* U.S. Customs Service (Treasury); Immigration and Naturalization Service (Justice); Federal Protective Service (GSA); Transportation Security Administration (Transportation); Federal Law Enforcement Training Center (Treasury); Animal and Plant Health Inspection Service (Agriculture); Office for Domestic Preparedness (Justice)

2. *Emergency Preparedness and Response directorate:* Federal Emergency Management Agency (FEMA); Strategic National Stockpile and the National Disaster Medical System (HHS); Nuclear Incident Response Team (Energy); Domestic Emergency Support Teams (Justice); National Domestic Preparedness Office (FBI)

3. *Science and Technology directorate:* CBRN Countermeasures Programs (Energy); Environmental Measurements Laboratory (Energy); National BW Defense Analysis Center (Defense); Plum Island Animal Disease Center (Agriculture);

4. *Information Analysis and Infrastructure Protection directorate:* Critical Infrastructure Assurance Office (Commerce); Federal Computer Incident Response Center (GSA); National Communications System (Defense); National Infrastructure Protection Center (FBI); Energy Security and Assurance Program (Energy)

The most frequent criticism of DHS is not that it's too big (America has had similar super-agencies such as LEAA, the Law Enforcement Assistance Administration, established under the 1968 Crime Control and Safe Streets Act and dismantled in 1980 with NCJRS remaining as a remnant), but that it's too small, and doesn't include two agencies, CIA and FBI, which seem like logical choices for inclusion in DHS due to their poor record of power and information sharing. Apparently, the CIA and FBI are already overwhelmed by a sea of information, and DHS is to go about using new and different intelligence to uncover threats. As the National Strategy for Homeland Security (2003) makes clear, existing agencies like the CIA and FBI are to enhance their analytic capabilities, and new agencies like the DHS are to build new capabilities. Some of those new capabilities the DHS is tasked to develop include the following:

"smart borders" that no longer rely on two oceans and friendly neighbors; change the way we look at travel and immigration

guard against "inside" threats to critical infrastructure and key assets; build a complete list of those assets and involve the private sector which controls or owns 85% of the infrastructure secure cyberspace; not only as a vehicle for terrorist attack, but something along the lines of an Open Secrets Act which other nations have that prevents open-source Internet information from being useful to terrorists

"red team" and dual-use analysis; thinking like a terrorist or how something good could be used for evil; staging drills and simulations of worst-case scenarios

harness scientific knowledge and expertise on countering the proliferation and use of deadly weapons, such as chemical, biological, radiological, and nuclear; develop broad spectrum vaccines and antidotes; rapidly produce prototypes

streamline information sharing among intelligence and law enforcement agencies; connect databases; expand extradition authority; reconsider posse comitatus restrictions on the use of military assistance in domestic security; review obligations to treaties and laws

promote homeland security research; use 21st-century science and technology; built new capabilities to secure the homeland

The most important function of DHS will deal with domestic counter terrorism, an idea that encompasses the notion of an informed and proactive citizenry (informed via new Alertness and Awareness systems) who see something unusual and report it to the appropriate authorities. This is very similar to the voluntary cooperation that police need from citizens for crime reporting, or by another stretch of the imagination, to the idea of community policing. It begs the question, however, of how far law enforcement ought to go with investigating suspicious, noncriminal activity. Clearly, the purpose is to identify, halt, and where appropriate, prosecute terrorists as well as those who provide them logistic support. It primarily involves a tracking mission for law enforcement, and only secondarily a prosecutorial mission, or bringing terrorists to justice. It is, in short, what Jonathan White (2004) calls the "Eyes and Ears" approach to the role of police in intelligence gathering. It is a system of detecting hostile intent. A number of initiatives have been designed to promote individual citizen involvement, such as the following:

Citizen Corps—volunteers who participate in community-level homeland security efforts

Volunteers in Police Service (VIPS)—civilian police who perform nonsworn functions of policing

Medical Reserve Corps-retired healthcare providers who augment disaster responses

Operation TIPS (Terrorist Information and Prevention System)*now-defunct program* for reporting of suspicious activities

Community Emergency Response Teams (CERT)—training programs in local communities

Neighborhood Watch—incorporation of terrorism prevention into its mission via local sheriffs

Infragard—private sector and academic partnering for cyberspace security

National Identification Card schemes—***now-defunct idea*** of high-tech, biometric ID cards

The most frequent criticism of initiatives like the above (especially Operation Tips) is that they smack of police state measures, reminiscent of Nazi Germany, Stalinist Russia, or America's own sorry experience with COINTELPRO ("counter-intelligence program") of the 1960s that collected files on some 62,000 suspicious Americans. The magazine, Mother Jones, has a good retrospective piece on the furor over Operation Tips, if you are interested, and EPIC has a chronology of the National ID Card movement which basically dissolved into a crackdown on driver's licenses. The central dilemma remains of how to incorporate citizen reporting of suspicious behavior into a system of intelligence and law enforcement. Without guidelines, laws, constitutional safeguards, and perhaps training of civilians (Hillyard 2003), the citizen role in domestic counterterrorism may be doomed to defeat on fears that it is dangerous domestic spying.

The Legal Reform Approach to Domestic Security

Some history on the post-Hoover era and Watergate is in order first. In 1967, a Supreme Court decision (the Katz case) condemned warrantless electronic surveillance, and the following year, the Omnibus Crime Control and Safe Streets Act established probable cause as the standard for obtaining a wiretap against U.S. citizens. A 1969 case (the Alderman case) ruled that the methods and transcripts of a wiretap should be open in court for public and adversarial scrutiny. This jeopardized exposure of ongoing intelligence operations, so Attorney General Mitchell established the "Mitchell Doctrine" as it came to be called, which insisted that the President, acting through the Attorney General, had the inherent constitutional power to authorize warrantless, secret surveillance in the name of national security or for purposes of pure or preventive intelligence. A number of court cases followed, all along the lines of the judiciary warning the executive branch of government to avoid using foreign intelligence techniques in domestic cases. In 1972, the Court (in the Keith case) disposed of the Mitchell doctrine, and in the 1973 acquittal of Daniel Ellsberg (who released the Pentagon Papers to the press), the President was determined not to be immune from civil liability for authorizing an illegal wiretap. Watergate, which is closely connected to the Ellsberg case, but technically refers to a 1972—1974 period most remembered for a break-in and bugging of Democratic Party headquarters, signaled an end to abuses in the name of national security along with claims of executive immunity. In 1974, Congress passed the Privacy Act which forbade any federal agency from collecting information about the political and religious beliefs of individuals unless in connection with a bona fide criminal investigation, and in 1975, the Freedom of Information Act, allowed individual access to any personal information which might be secret in the name of national security, and applied it to the FBI. The final separation of domestic and foreign intelligence came in 1978 with the Foreign Intelligence Surveillance Act (FISA), which brings us up to amendments in FISA and the PATRIOT Act of 2001, foundations for modern-day legal approaches to domestic security.

The USA PATRIOT Act of 2001 can be seen as another amendment to FISA because under the latter, agencies don't need probable cause to gather intelligence if their targets are operating as agents of foreign powers, and modern (subnational) terrorists don't usually work for a foreign power, but for some nebulous cause. Specifically, the PATRIOT Act enhances roving surveillance authority and streamlines wiretap authorizations, sets up anti-terrorism asset forfeiture procedures, approves detention of suspected terrorists, removes obstacles to investigating terrorism, increases the penalties for terrorist crimes, removes any statute of limitations, encourages federal involvement in domestic preparedness exercises, and supports activities by the Department of Homeland Security. More significantly, Title I (Intelligence Gathering) of the PATRIOT Act permits disclosure of foreign intelligence information to any domestic or law enforcement intelligence operation. It permits foreign intelligence techniques to be used for criminal justice purposes, and it maintains the secrecy of the intelligence apparatus (the Mitchell Doctrine) as well.

The PATRIOT Act replaces probable cause with a showing of need for an ongoing terrorism investigation, and goes a step further by placing a gag order on the person served with the warrant. They cannot notify the real target of the investigation, or in any way disclose what information law enforcement was seeking. It amends the Family Educational Rights and Privacy Act, and forces school officials to release information, as well as allows law enforcement officials to obtain information on use of library resources, books, and Internet usage. Again, school officials are prohibited from disclosing what law enforcement was looking for. Some experts think the PATRIOT Act was rushed too quickly through Congress, and violates the Fourth Amendment as well as the Balance of Powers principle in the Constitution. When the Department of Justice announced it would eavesdrop on attorney-client conversations with suspected terrorists, many experts thought that crossed the line of reasonableness.

The basic dilemma, as White (2004) points out, is a legal dilemma. Law enforcement has for years been accustomed to working within legal constraints, collecting evidence that can be used for prosecution in a criminal court. There is a natural terminus to a criminal investigation. The intelligence community has for years been accustomed to working with few legal constraints, and there is no natural terminus, or end, to an intelligence investigation. Criminal intelligence is governed by constitutional rules of evidence; national security intelligence is not. Going to trial in a terrorism investigation often means exposing the intelligence sources for the sake of a criminal conviction. This irony, as well as other twists having to do with military tribunals, has produced some rather strange effects in the war on terrorism—American citizens being detained like prisoners of war and foreigners being treated like citizens in criminal courts. To be sure, terrorist groups (according to al Qaeda's training manual) instruct their captured agents to make a mockery of justice systems to insist they were tortured or mistreated, to learn the names of their captors and lie about them, and to use religion at every turn to their advantage. Nonetheless, this is not sufficient reason to proceed in a constitutional vacuum, or make up the rules as you go along. There are other factors that dampen the prospects for successful use of law enforcement for intelligence purposes, and White (2004) implies the following:

POLICE do not have the academic credentials or higher order critical thinking skills to understand the root causes of terrorism, its complexities, or the ability to distinguish between terrorist sympathizers and criminal terrorists

POLICE are trained in reasonable suspicion and probable cause to make stops, ask questions, detain, infiltrate, and collect information, but intelligence work requires neither standard in the ongoing collection of vast amounts of non-criminal information

POLICE agencies are fiercely autonomous, competitive, turf-conscious, mistrustful, and attuned to local politics with little or no interest in thinking outside their jurisdiction and/or partnering with non-police agencies seen as outsiders

POLICE agencies are focused on publicity and getting the word out about their effectiveness at crime-fighting while intelligence work is focused on secrecy and never letting intelligence successes be known

POLICE are taught that criminal justice record keeping should be clear and concise, with writing crisp and to the point, while there is no such thing as too much excess or irrelevant information for intelligence work

POLICE organizations are bureaucracies where power struggles and personal rivalries abound, combined with a stifling tendency toward stagnation and lack of creativity whereas intelligence work rewards eccentricity and creativity

POLICE are prone to negative stereotyping and abuse of power, and any intelligence shared with them may be misused

POLICE are prone to leaks and the leaking of information may occur, tipping the terrorists off about an ongoing operation

POLICE often act officiously and rudely when enforcing security precautions on ordinary citizens, creating a sense of insecurity and giving the public the impression of a police state

POLICE are not psychologically equipped to deal with the kind of massive casualties that weapons of mass destruction can cause

POLICE are not prepared to face a terrorist enemy who uses criminal means to obtain military objectives

The Computer Database Approach to Domestic Security

The National Strategy for Homeland Security (2003) calls for connecting computer databases used in federal law enforcement, immigration, intelligence, public health surveillance, and emergency management, and further, DARPA's plan for Total Information Awareness (TIA) is to merge some of these interconnections into a data mining system of systems involving the private sector, the finance/credit system, and the Internet. Most of the databases involved would be government owned, where they are not so different from one another, and can probably be interconnected. Some, such as CDC's (Center for Disease Control) epidemiology program, continuously scan disease patterns throughout the nation's healthcare system for signs of an outbreak. Others, such as the Department of State's TIPOFF system compiles information on suspected terrorists collected by consular offices overseas, and is already interconnected. There's some rather large databases involved, two of the largest being those from Immigration (the Border Patrol uses a two-finger fingerprint system while the FBI uses a ten-finger fingerprint system) and the FBI (NCIC, or the National Crime Information Center, tracks everything greater than a Class C misdemeanor and is already overburdened by the size of graphics on some items). The following is a list of government databases related to homeland security:

AFIS—Fingerprint system to identify citizens

CCD–Consolidated Consular Database; records of non-immigrant visa entries and exits

CLASS—Consular Lookout and Support System; program for running background checks for visas

CODIS—Combined DNA Index System used for solving crimes

IBIS—Interagency Border Inspection System; immigration program used at ports of entry

IDENT—Fingerprint system to identify aliens

JITF-CT—Joint Intelligence Task Force Combating Terrorism; DIA database

LEO—Law Enforcement Online; VPN with exclusive interactive briefings, alerts, and discussions

NAILS—National Automated Immigration Lookout System

NCIC—Contains criminal justice arrest records, fugitives, stolen property, and missing persons and items

NDPIX—National Drug Pointer Index, DEA records of common targets in investigations

NDSI—National Spatial Data Infrastructure; geomapping records with meta-data tags

NIBIN—National Integrated Ballistics Information Network; unified ATF and FBI database, but mostly ATF

NLETS—National Law Enforcement Telecommunication System; interstate license and registration records

NSEERS—National Security Entry-Exit Registration System

SEVIS—Student Exchange Visitor Information System; monitors foreign students

TECS—Treasury Enforcement Communications System; for suspicious individuals and businesses

TIPOFF—State Department program which searches for known and suspected terrorists

TIPS—Terrorist Information and Prevention System; for anonymous tips

TSC—Terrorist Screening Center; a consolidation of terrorist watch lists

The problem with government databases is not with the federal government's integration of "watch lists," but with any integration at the state and local level of law enforcement. Real-time information sharing may take place among federal agencies, but it's not going to get to the larger law enforcement community in real-time. Some of this is due to federal bias or suspicion against local law enforcement, and another problem is that some state and municipal police departments are as far behind as five years in such basic things as updating parking ticket records. A greater problem arises when one tries to integrate, or commingle (the proper term), government databases with those in the private sector, such as credit card companies, e-commerce firms, retailers, etc.

You would need about 15,000 fields just for merging the header (demographic) information across these databases, which would represent about 300,000 bytes per person. If you multiply this by 500 million people, the header records alone would require approximately 150,000,000,000,000 bytes (136 terabytes) and almost five years to stabilize. Then, there's the key identifier fields (also called crosswalk tables) which contain numerical records such as social security numbers or driver's license numbers which link the different databases together, and one of these has to be a unique identifier (pivot table) to put an interface on it. Since terrorists are likely to use fake IDs, a new unique identifier system may have to be developed, and this will require about ten years of data input time. Then, the transaction data is brought in, which generally produces crashes and errors, generating the need for continual validation, de-duplication, and normalization. The computer database approach is doable, but it will take years to get it right, lots of improvements in technology, and something a whole lot faster than T1 Internet connections for law enforcement. Subcontracting vendors like InferX are already at work on distributed data mining solutions.

Secure intranets (on the .gov domain) and secure videoconferences will most likely remain the federal government's main way of information sharing with state and local governments, along with renaming the 93 Anti-Terrorist Task Forces (ATTFs) throughout the federal court districts into Homeland Security Task Forces (HSTFs). The ATTF/HSTF approach simply involves prosecutors, but Joint Terrorist Task Forces (JTTFs), which have a longer history, going back to Chicago in the late 1970s, are a different thing, and now exist in all 56 FBI field offices where some elite state and local police are picked to be temporarily federalized, and true, joint cooperation exists between the levels of government since the power of arrest is equalized.

A more promising approach to information sharing would build upon what few successes law enforcement has had with "vertical" integration—crossing federal, state, and local levels of government. Bodrero (2002) as well as White (2004) recommend using the six-region information network known as RISS (Regional Information Sharing Systems). The RISS network was designed for sharing criminal intelligence, primarily about gang crime, hate crime, and cybercrime, and would provide a model that works and makes effective use of existing intelligence analysts who work for police departments. RISS is the closest thing to a nationwide criminal investigation network.

Another idea is to build on the War on Drugs as an intelligence model, and NDIC (National Drug Intelligence Center) holds some promise for development because it has always involved excellent cooperation between levels of government. In addition, America has several identified High Intensity Drug Trafficking Areas (HIDTAs), the El Paso Intelligence Center (EPIC) being most notable, which represent excellent working models of how intelligence analysts, from both law enforcement and the military, can come together to work on a common problem.

In addition, there are numerous states with highly-developed criminal intelligence units, such as the New Jersey State Police Intelligence Services which has long had an effective intelligence gathering and analysis capability. Most state police intelligence units maintain liaisons with INTERPOL (International Criminal Police Organization), EUROPOL, the RISS network, FINCEN (Financial Crime Enforcement Network), IALEIA (International Association of Law Enforcement Analysts), and LEIU (Law Enforcement Intelligence Unit, another association that holds annual seminars). It makes little sense for the federal government to ignore these resources as they represent the "best and brightest" that local law enforcement has to offer.

Homeland Security Threat and Vulnerability Analysis

The type of intelligence that DHS hopes to produce is warning intelligence, the kind that eliminates surprise. This kind of intelligence is used by policymakers not so much to inform citizens via reverse-9-1-1 or other civil defense measures, but so that preemptive action can be taken against the would-be attackers. This is an intense form of intelligence that will primarily require informers and infiltrators (HUMINT, or human intelligence) crossing every known subcultural and foreign-language barrier. In the language of risk assessment, this type of intelligence is known as tactical threat analysis, and is sometimes called actionable or flash intelligence. It is the first priority of DHS, and it places the Secretary of DHS on the same footing as the DCI (Director of Central Intelligence) and Attorney General (or Director of FBI as proxy) in being able to order action such as strikes and raids on would-be attackers. It will require data collection and analysis systems that share information in real-time or near-real-time.

The second type of intelligence product sought by DHS is strategic analysis of the enemy, which is a deep, almost-academic understanding of motives, goals, identities, organizational structure, sources of support, capabilities, and points of vulnerability. It is optimistically aimed at the sources of terrorism—those seething hotbeds of extremism and fanaticism that typically characterize the world's trouble spots. At this level, also, the Secretary of DHS is on equal footing with the DCI and AG, but disagreements can be expected on the basis of human differences among interpretations of background information. Where DHS has a monopoly is with the area of vulnerability assessment—the constant measurement and monitoring of how vulnerable America's critical infrastructure is. This is the area that DHS hopes to automate with remote sensors and computer modeling, and it is also the area that is part of the Advisory system for warning the private sector and public. However, the hardest task is going to be involving law enforcement in the intelligence work.

To integrate homeland security with law enforcement, much more training beyond SLATT (State and Local Anti-Terrorism Training) will be needed. Police will need to learn how to collect and analyze intelligence. Police will need to improve their profiling skills, and learn, for example, how to monitor their communities for sudden shifts and expansions in anti-American rhetoric. More bi-lingual and multi-lingual police will surely be needed. Police will have to read a lot of radical literature, and investigate every charity. They will have to infiltrate alienated groups that kill without the slightest compunction, and are often well-financed. They will have to infiltrate religious groups, and pick up on squabbles that go on within such organizations. Police will have to improve their ability at computer forensics, because terrorists often are fairly sophisticated at encryption and computer use. Police will have to become sensitive to trends and indicators in community tension, especially as these tensions are tied into international tensions. If new groups come to town, and keep to themselves, or try hard to blend in, either of these should arouse police suspicion. It will seem like an impossible job, but maybe with a few tweaks, police can do it. In any event, it should portend a new role for police in society—a role that involves America learning how to spy on itself.

Community Response and Homeland Security Challenges in Dealing with Large Scale Terrorism.

Transforming public safety and health mechanisms into effective front line first response systems against a major terror attack is one of the greatest community based challenges in the homeland security effort.

When modeling various community-level catastrophes, the prospect of a successful and well-coordinated chemical or bio-terrorist attack is among the most daunting possibilities. How will first responders, including health facilities and trauma centers, respond and manage such an attack? The following statement from the Center for Disease Control, read before Congress in 2001, does an excellent job of outlining and enumerating the very real and very profound public health challenges of dealing with widespread bio-terror.

STATEMENT OF JAMES M. HUGHES, M.D.
Director, *National Center for Infectious Diseases*
Centers for Disease Control and Prevention

DEPARTMENT OF HEALTH AND HUMAN SERVICES BEFORE THE SUBCOMMITTEE ON NATIONAL SECURITY, VETERANS AFFAIRS, AND INTERNATIONAL RELATIONS COMMITTEE ON GOVERNMENT REFORM U.S. HOUSE OF REPRESENTATIVES

July 23, 2001

Good afternoon, Mr. Chairman and Members of the Subcommittee. I am Dr. James M. Hughes, Director, National Center for Infectious Diseases (NCID), Centers for Disease Control and Prevention (CDC). I am accompanied by Dr. James W. LeDuc, Acting Director of NCID's Division of Viral and Rickettsial Diseases. Thank you for the invitation to update you on CDC's public health response to the threat of bioterrorism. I will discuss the overall goals of our bioterrorism preparedness program, and I will briefly address specific activities aimed at preparedness for a deliberate release of variola virus, the pathogen responsible for smallpox.

Vulnerability of the Civilian Population
In the past, an attack with a biological agent was considered very unlikely; however, now it seems entirely possible. Many experts believe that it is no longer a matter of "if" but "when" such an attack will occur. Unlike an explosion or a tornado, in a biological event, it is unlikely that a single localized place or cluster of people will be identified for traditional first responder activity. The initial responders to such a biological attack will include emergency department and hospital staff, members of the outpatient medical community, and a wide range of response personnel in the public health system, in conjunction with county and city health officers. Increased vigilance and preparedness for unexplained illnesses and injuries are an essential part of the public health effort to protect the American people against bioterrorism.

Public Health Leadership
The Department of Health and Human Services (DHHS) anti-bioterrorism efforts are focused on improving the nation's public health surveillance network to quickly detect and identify the biological agent that has been released; strengthening the capacities for medical response, especially at the local level; expanding the stockpile of pharmaceuticals for use if needed; expanding research on disease agents that might be released, rapid methods for identifying biological agents, and improved treatments and vaccines; and preventing bioterrorism by regulation of the shipment of hazardous biological agents or toxins. On July 10, 2001, Secretary Thompson named CDC's Dr. Scott Lillibridge as his special advisor to lead the Department's coordinated bioterrorism initiative.

As the Nation's disease prevention and control agency, it is CDC's responsibility on behalf of DHHS to provide national leadership in the public health and medical communities in a concerted effort to detect, diagnose, respond to, and prevent illnesses, including those that occur as a result of a deliberate release of biological agents. This task is an integral part of CDC's overall mission to monitor and protect the health of the U.S. population.

In 1998, CDC issued Preventing Emerging Infectious Diseases: A Strategy for the 21st Century, which describes CDC's plan for combating today's emerging diseases and preventing those of tomorrow. It focuses on four goals, each of which has direct relevance to preparedness for bioterrorism: disease surveillance and outbreak response; applied research to develop diagnostic tests, drugs, vaccines, and surveillance tools; infrastructure and training; and disease prevention and control. This plan emphasizes the need to be prepared for the unexpected—whether it is a naturally occurring influenza pandemic or the deliberate release of smallpox by a terrorist. It is within the context of these overall goals that CDC has begun to address preparing our Nation's public health infrastructure to respond to acts of biological terrorism. Copies of this CDC plan have been provided previously to the Subcommittee. In addition, CDC presented in March a report to the Senate entitled "Public Health's Infrastructure: A Status Report." Recommendations in this report complement the strategies outlined for emerging infectious diseases and preparedness and response to bioterrorism. These recommendations include training of the public health workforce, strengthening of data and communications systems, and improving the public health systems at the state and local level.

CDC's Strategic Plan for Bioterrorism

On April 21, 2000, CDC issued a Morbidity and Mortality Weekly Report (MMWR), Biological and Chemical Terrorism: Strategic Plan for Preparedness and Response Recommendations of the CDC Strategic Planning Workgroup, which outlines steps for strengthening public health and healthcare capacity to protect the nation against these threats. This report reinforces the work CDC has been contributing to this effort since 1998 and lays a framework from which to enhance public health infrastructure. In keeping with the message of this report, five key focus areas have been identified which provide the foundation for local, state, and federal planning efforts: Preparedness and Prevention, Detection and Surveillance, Diagnosis and Characterization of Biological and Chemical Agents, Response, and Communication. These areas capture the goals of CDC's Bioterrorism Preparedness and Response Program for general bioterrorism preparedness, as well as the more specific goals targeted towards preparing for the potential intentional reintroduction of smallpox. As was highlighted in the recent Dark Winter exercise, smallpox virus is of particular concern.

- Preparedness and Prevention

  CDC is working to ensure that all levels of the public health community federal, state, and local—are prepared to work in coordination with the medical and emergency response communities to address the public health consequences of biological and chemical terrorism.

CDC is creating diagnostic and epidemiological performance standards for state and local health departments and will help states conduct drills and exercises to assess local readiness for bioterrorism. In addition, CDC, the National Institutes of Health (NIH), the Department of Defense (DOD), and other agencies are supporting and encouraging research to address scientific issues related to bioterrorism. In some cases, new vaccines, antitoxins, or innovative drug treatments need to be developed or stocked. Moreover, we need to learn more about the pathogenesis and epidemiology of the infectious diseases which do not affect the U.S. population currently. We have only limited knowledge about how artificial methods of dispersion may affect the infection rate, virulence, or impact of these biological agents.

In 1999, the Institute of Medicine released its Assessment of Future Scientific Needs for Live Variola Virus, which formed the basis for a phased research agenda to address several scientific issues related to smallpox. This research agenda is a collaboration between CDC, NIH, and DOD and is being undertaken in the high containment laboratory at CDC with the concurrence of WHO. The research addresses: 1) the use of modern serologic and molecular diagnostic techniques to improve diagnostic capabilities for smallpox, 2) the evaluation of antiviral compounds for activity against the smallpox virus, and 3) further study of the pathogenesis of smallpox by the development of an animal model that mimics human smallpox infection. To date, genetic material from 45 different strains of smallpox virus has been extracted and is being evaluated to determine the genetic diversity of different strains of the virus. The NIH, with CDC and DOD collaborators, has funded a Poxvirus Bioinformatics Resource Center (www.poxvirus.org) to facilitate the analysis of sequence data to aid the development of rapid and specific diagnostic assays, antiviral medicines and vaccines. A dedicated sequencing and bio-informatics laboratory also is being developed at CDC to help further these efforts. This laboratory will also be used to help characterize other potential bioterrorism pathogens. In addition, a team of collaborating scientists has screened over 270 antiviral compounds for activity against smallpox virus and other related poxviruses and have found several compounds which merit further evaluation in animal models. These compounds were evaluated initially in cell cultures, and 27 promising candidates are being further evaluated for efficacy. The identification of one currently licensed compound with in vitro and in vivo efficacy against the smallpox virus has led to the development of an Investigational New Drug (IND) application by NIH and CDC to the FDA for use of this drug, cidofovir, in an emergency situation for treating persons who are diagnosed with smallpox. Researchers also have been funded by NIH to design new anti-smallpox medicines and to create human monoclonal antibodies to replace the limited supply of vaccinia immune globulin that is needed to treat vaccine complications that arise during immunization campaigns.

The Advisory Committee for Immunization Practices (ACIP) worked with CDC to develop updated guidelines for the use of smallpox vaccine. These guidelines were published in the MMWR in June 2001 and serve to educate the medical and public health community regarding the recommended routine and emergency uses and medical aspects of the vaccine as well as, the medical aspects of smallpox itself. Several infection control and worker safety issues were also addressed by the ACIP within the updated guidelines.

While we are pursuing the development of additional smallpox vaccine to improve our readiness to respond to a smallpox outbreak, we are also working to ensure that the stores of vaccine that we have in the United States currently are ready for use, including protocols for emergency release and transportation of the vaccine.

• Detection and Surveillance

Because the initial detection of a biological terrorist attack will most likely occur at the local level, it is essential to educate and train members of the medical community—both public and private—who may be the first to examine and treat the victims. It is also necessary to upgrade the surveillance systems of state and local health departments, as well as within healthcare facilities such as hospitals, which will be relied upon to spot unusual patterns of disease occurrence and to identify any additional cases of illness. CDC will provide terrorism-related training to epidemiologists and laboratorians, emergency responders, emergency department personnel and other front-line health-care providers, and health and safety personnel. CDC is working to provide educational materials regarding potential bioterrorism agents to the medical and public health communities on its bioterrorism website at www.bt.cdc.gov. For example, we are preparing a video on smallpox vaccination techniques for public health personnel and healthcare providers who may administer vaccine in an emergency situation. CDC is planning to work with partners such as the Johns Hopkins Center for Civilian Biodefense Studies and the Infectious Diseases Society of America to develop training and educational materials for incorporation into medical and public health graduate and post-graduate curricula. With public health partners, CDC is spearheading the development of the National Electronic Disease Surveillance System, which will facilitate automated, timely electronic capture of data from the healthcare system. CDC has also worked with organizations such as the Council of State and Territorial Epidemiologists to ensure that suspected cases of smallpox are immediately reportable in their jurisdictions and that clear lines of communication are in place.

- Diagnosis and Characterization of Biological and Chemical Agents

To ensure that prevention and treatment measures can be implemented quickly in the event of a biological or chemical terrorist attack, rapid diagnosis will be critical. CDC is developing guidelines and quality assurance standards for the safe and secure collection, storage, transport, and processing of biologic and environmental samples. In collaboration with other federal and non-federal partners, CDC is co-sponsoring a series of training exercises for state public health laboratory personnel on requirements for the safe use, containment, and transport of dangerous biological agents and toxins. CDC is also enhancing its efforts to foster the safe design and operation of Biosafety Level 3 laboratories, which are required for handling many highly dangerous pathogens. In addition, CDC is helping to limit access to potential terrorist agents by continuing to administer the Select Agent Rule, Additional Requirements for Facilities Transferring or Receiving Select Agents (42 CFR Section 72.6), which regulates shipments of certain hazardous biological organisms and toxins. Furthermore, CDC is developing a Rapid Toxic Screen to detect people's exposure to 150 chemical agents using blood or urine samples.

- Response

A decisive and timely response to a biological terrorist event involves a fully documented and well rehearsed plan of detection, epidemiologic investigation, and medical treatment for affected persons, and the initiation of disease prevention measures to minimize illness, injury and death. CDC is addressing this by (1) assisting state and local health agencies in developing their plans for investigating and responding to unusual events and unexplained illnesses and (2) bolstering CDC's capacities within the overall federal bioterrorism response effort. CDC is working to formalize current draft plans for the notification and mobilization of personnel and laboratory resources in response to a bioterrorism emergency, as well as overall strategies for vaccination, and development and implementation of other potential outbreak control measures such as quarantine measures. In addition, CDC is working to develop national standards to ensure that respirators used by first responders to terrorist acts provide adequate protection against weapons of terrorism.

- Communication Systems

In the event of an intentional release of a biological agent, rapid and secure communications will be especially crucial to ensure a prompt and coordinated response. Thus, strengthening communication among clinicians, emergency rooms, infection control practitioners, hospitals, pharmaceutical companies, and public health personnel is of paramount importance. To this end, CDC is making a significant investment in building the nation's public health communications infrastructure through the Health Alert Network, a nationwide program designed to ensure communications capacity at all local and state health departments (full Internet connectivity and training), ensure capacity to receive distance learning offerings from CDC and others, and ensure capacity to broadcast and receive health alerts at every level. CDC has also established the Epidemic Information Exchange (EPI-X), a secure, Web-based communications system to enhance bioterrorism preparedness efforts by facilitating the sharing of preliminary information about disease outbreaks and other health events among public health officials across jurisdictions and provide experience in the use of secure communications.

An act of terrorism is likely to cause widespread panic, and on-going communication of accurate and up-to-date information will help calm public fears and limit collateral effects of the attack. To assure the most effective response to an attack, CDC is working closely with other federal agencies, including the Food and Drug Administration, NIH, DOD, Department of Justice (DOJ), and the Federal Emergency Management Agency (FEMA).

The National Pharmaceutical Stockpile
As CDC recently reported to this Subcommittee, another integral component of public health preparedness at CDC has been the development of a National Pharmaceutical Stockpile (NPS), which can be mobilized in response to an episode caused by a biological or chemical agent. The role of the CDC's NPS program is to maintain a national repository of life-saving pharmaceuticals and medical material that can be delivered to the site or sites of a biological or chemical terrorism event in order to reduce morbidity and mortality in a civilian population. The NPS is a backup and means of support to state and local first responders, healthcare providers, and public health officials. The NPS program consists of a two-tier response: (1) 12-hour push packages, which are pre-assembled arrays of pharmaceuticals and medical supplies that can be delivered to the scene of a terrorism event within 12 hours of the federal decision to deploy the assets and that will make possible the treatment or prophylaxis of disease caused by a variety of threat agents; and (2) a Vendor-Managed Inventory (VMI) that can be tailored to a specific threat agent. Components of the VMI will arrive at the scene 24 to 36 hours after activation. CDC has developed this program in collaboration with federal and private sector partners and with input from the states.

Challenges Highlighted in Dark Winter Exercise
CDC has been addressing issues of detection, epidemiologic investigation, diagnostics, and enhanced infrastructure and communications as part of its overall bioterrorism preparedness strategies. The issues that emerged from the recent Dark Winter exercise reflected similar themes that need to be addressed.

The importance of rapid diagnosis—Rapid and accurate diagnosis of biological agents will require strong linkages between clinical and public health laboratories. In addition, diagnostic specimens will need to be delivered promptly to CDC, where laboratorians will provide diagnostic confirmatory and reference support.

The importance of working through the governors' offices as part of our planning and response efforts—During the exercise this was demonstrated by Governor Keating. During state-wide emergencies the federal government will need to work with a partner in the state who can galvanize the multiple response communities and government sectors that will be needed, such as the National Guard, the state health department, and the state law enforcement communities. These in turn will need to coordinate with their local counterparts. CDC is refining its planning efforts through grants, policy forums such as the National Governors Association and the National Emergency Management Association, and training activities. CDC also participates with partners such as DOJ and FEMA in planning and implementing national drills such as the recent TOPOFF exercise.

Better targeting of limited smallpox vaccine stocks to ensure strategic use of vaccine in persons at highest risk of infection—It was clear that pre-existing guidance regarding strategic use would have been beneficial and would have accelerated the response at Dark Winter. As I mentioned earlier, CDC is working on this issue and is developing guidance for vaccination programs and planning activities.

Federal control of the smallpox vaccine at the inception of a national crisis Currently, the smallpox vaccine is held by the manufacturer. CDC has worked with the U.S. Marshals Service to conduct an initial security assessment related to a future emergency deployment of vaccine to states. CDC is currently addressing the results of this assessment, along with other issues related to security, movement, and initial distribution of smallpox vaccine.

The importance of early technical information on the progress of such an epidemic for consideration by decision makers—In Dark Winter, this required the implementation of various steps at the local, state, and federal levels to control the spread of disease. This is a complex endeavor and may involve measures ranging from directly observed therapy to quarantine, along with consideration as to who would enforce such measures. Because wide-scale federal quarantine measures have not been implemented in the United States in over 50 years, operational protocols to implement a quarantine of significant scope are needed. CDC hosted a forum on state emergency public health legal authorities to encourage state and local public health officers and their attorneys to examine what legal authorities would be needed in a bioterrorism event. In addition, CDC is reviewing foreign and interstate quarantine regulations to update them in light of modern infectious disease and bioterrorism concerns. CDC will continue this preparation to ensure that such measures will be implemented early in the response to an event.

Maintaining effective communications with the media and press during such an emergency—The need for accurate and timely information during a crisis is paramount to maintaining the trust of the community. Those responsible for leadership in such emergencies will need to enhance their capabilities to deal with the media and get their message to the public. It was clear from Dark Winter that large-scale epidemics will generate intense media interest and information needs. CDC has refined its media plan and expanded its communications staff. These personnel will continue to be intimately involved in our planning and response efforts to epidemics.

Expanded local clinical services for victims—DHHS's Office of Emergency Preparedness is working with the other members of the National Disaster Medical System to expand and refine the delivery of medical services for epidemic stricken populations.

CDC will continue to work with partners to address challenges in public health preparedness, such as those raised at Dark Winter. For example, work done by CDC staff to model the effects of control measures such as quarantine and vaccination in a smallpox outbreak have highlighted the importance of both public health measures in controlling such an outbreak. The importance of both quarantine and vaccination as outbreak control measures is also supported by historical experience with smallpox epidemics during the eradication era. These issues, as well as overall preparedness planning at the federal level, are currently being addressed and require additional action to ensure that the nation is fully prepared to respond to all acts of biological terrorism, including those involving smallpox.

Conclusion

In conclusion, CDC has made substantial progress to date in enhancing the nation's capability to prepare for and, if need be, respond to a bioterrorist event. The best public health strategy to protect the health of civilians against biological terrorism is the development, organization, and enhancement of public health prevention systems and tools. Priorities include strengthened public health laboratory capacity, increased surveillance and outbreak investigation capacity, and health communications, education, and training at the federal, state, and local levels. Not only will this approach ensure that we are prepared for deliberate bioterrorist threats, but it will also ensure that we will be able to recognize and control naturally occurring new or re-emerging infectious diseases. A strong and flexible public health infrastructure is the best defense against any disease outbreak.

Thank you very much for your attention. I will be happy to answer any questions you may have.

Preparing for a Terrorist Attack: Mass Casualty Management

Henry J. Siegelson, MD, FACEP
Principal, HAZ/MAT DQE
Principal, Disaster Planning International
Siegelson@mindspring.com
Atlanta, Georgia
October 3, 2003

Introduction

As the country prepares for a possible terrorist attack, communities, businesses, hospitals, elected officials, and children in schools want to know whether they are safe. Can communities protect its citizens from attack? Can hospitals care for biological casualties? Is there a greater threat on the horizon in the form of smallpox or SARS[1]? What can the individual do to protect their home or their family?

It is a reality that, in the event of a mass casualty event, EMS and fire services will not be immediately able to meet the needs of most victims in office buildings, malls, schools, and other soft targets. If several sites are attacked at one time, if a cloud of chemicals or biologic particles blankets a city, first responders will have a response capacity that is limited by personnel resources.

Every potential target must review its current capabilities and assets. Soft targets must take steps to reduce exposure and harm after a terrorist attack. In addition, soft targets must have an internal response capacity that will offer support without the intervention of first responders. Schools, large employers, high rise buildings, military garrisons, athletic arenas, and shopping malls must not only work with the community to support mass casualty plans, but must also develop their own response resources. Our communities must develop plans that enable a vigorous, coordinated, and efficient response from police, fire, and EMS and take advantage of the resources available to industry and the public.

First responder assets (fire, police, HazMat, EMS), hospitals, healthcare workers, and state and regional agencies (Red Cross, Public Health, and Emergency Management) will participate in the community's response to a terrorist attack. The roles of each participant should be specifically described in the community's response plan: a consensus document.

Threat

In the past decade, the intentional release of hazardous chemicals by the Aum Shinrikyo in Japan alerted the world's governments about the threat of mass casualties from chemical exposure. Although the Aum Shinrikyo released anthrax and botulinum toxin without lethal effect, the recent successful use of anthrax as a biologic terror weapon in 2001 epitomizes the ruthlessness and effectiveness of biologic warfare. Chemical weapons used in Moscow, Ricin found in London and Paris, and the threat of nuclear weapons on the Korean Peninsula, South Asia, and Iran complicate these preparations.

There is a very long list of weapons that the terrorist might employ, but the resources with which the community might respond to these threats are finite.

Communities should approach this opportunity to improve preparedness in an "all-threat" or "all-hazards" approach: naturally occurring (earthquakes, floods, hurricanes, tornadoes), man-made (HazMat), intentional (terrorist).

The first step: focus on community chemical preparedness. There is a considerable 24-hour risk from exposure to hazardous chemicals utilized by local industry, transported by rail or truck, sold in hardware stores and grocery stores, and stored on the shelves of our homes.

It is essential that all first responders have the appropriate training and equipment to enable them to operate safely in a potentially hazardous response zone.

In addition, individual businesses, schools, and homes must have plans and equipment in place to decrease the possibility of exposure to these hazards.

A Four-Part Plan for Mass Casualties
1. Hospital: A Minimum level of Preparedness
2. Awareness Training: Hospitals, laboratories, public health, first responders
3. Community Preparedness
4. Off-site Treatment Capability

Hospital Response to Terrorism: A Minimum Level of Preparedness
Hospitals have a community responsibility to offer care to injured HazMat victims.[2-4] In some cases, the injury might be a result of an exposure to a hazardous chemical or infectious hazard. No matter the source of the injury, accidental or intentional, whether it occurs at work, at home, or on the road, the hospital must have the capacity to safely assess for injuries and to safely offer care. This responsibility extends to the victims of a terrorist attack.[5]

A reasonable and cost-effective approach should enable any hospital with an emergency department to reliably and safely care for victims of a HazMat or terrorist event 24 hours a day, 7 days a week. This preparedness should include policies that protect employees, victims, the institution, and the environment.

The hospital should, at the very minimum, be prepared to handle AT LEAST ONE PATIENT EXPOSED TO A HAZARDOUS MATERIAL.[4, 5] If a hospital is prepared for a defined minimum level of risk, then these policies and systems can be used to treat the vast majority of exposures. These systems can be expanded to include the management of mass casualties. Response plans should enable victims to self-decontaminate and thus more efficiently utilize response assets and decrease potential harm to victims. Plan for a few and train for many. Training for hospitals is available.[6]

Chem/Explosives/Radiation: The Sentinel Event

It is important to distinguish between attacks that cause sudden, overt, recognizable injuries-"sentinel events"[2, 4, 7-9]-and those that cause delayed injuries. Attacks using explosives and chemicals generally present as an overt sentinel event with associated "lights and sirens" community response and multiple injuries. The victims and the community will know with certainty that an attack has taken place. A biologic attack will have more delayed effects.

After a sentinel or overt event, it is difficult to rapidly prove that chemicals have NOT been used in the initial moments after an attack. Community and hospital responders must initially assume victims are contaminated. The system must be prepared to protect responders and health facilities from exposure to the "unknown chemical."

Since it is impossible to determine with certainty whether or not the victims have been contaminated, a Minimum Level of Decontamination must be defined. Victims from a sentinel event should not be allowed to enter an adjacent building, bus, ambulance, or the medical center without the removal of clothing. Removal of clothing is the essential first step in the treatment of the contaminated victim. Once the clothing has been removed, the victim will remove 80 to 90% of the contaminant after liquid contamination and nearly 100% after vapor contamination. *This may be the only decontamination procedure that is required for those victims exposed to a chemical (in the form of a gas or vapor) or biologic weapon.*

Officials and decision-makers at schools, high-rise buildings, businesses, military garrisons, and other soft targets can develop the capacity to encourage worried-well and minimally injured survivors to remove their clothing. Clothing removal remains a reliable form of initial gross decontamination. A dry decon kit, such as the Doff-It Kit, will enable the victim to remove their clothing in public without the help of first responders.

Some patients, after a clinical assessment, might require a soap and water shower if liquid or solid exposure is observed or suspected. The victim should remove the contaminated clothing as rapidly as possible to reduce exposure to the hazard. The decontamination facility or shower[6] should enable decon for both ambulatory and non-ambulatory victims. Washing victims in their clothing without subsequent removal of the clothing should be discouraged.

Biologic Attacks

In October and November 2001, the US suffered numerous casualties due to exposure to a highly lethal strain of *Bacillus anthracis* or anthrax. Recently, the threat of an attack utilizing the highly infectious smallpox virus resulted in the production of vast stores of smallpox vaccine: enough to vaccinate the entire US population. Plans are under way, at the behest of President Bush, to plan vaccination of emergency personnel and first responders. Severe Acute Respiratory Syndrome (SARS) preparedness and response is being re-assessed prior to the 2003-2004 flu season.[10]

Hospitals, public health departments, laboratories, and first responders should receive adequate awareness training on the medical consequences of a biologic attack. Every level of worker should have a clear understanding of this threat and the community or statewide plan to respond to this threat. This is important so that:

- Essential workers will go to work after a biologic attack

- Workers understand that reasonable personal protective equipment is available and effective enough to protect them after a Bio attack.

- Workers understand that, if antibiotics or vaccines are required after Bio attack, the employer will be able to deliver these necessary medication most reliably from their place of work (hospital workers and first responders)

Mass Casualty Plan
All communities must have a rational plan to manage casualties after a mass casualty event: it is a matter of national security.[2] The plan should be designed to organize community response resources so that they can be efficiently utilized after a mass casualty incident (MCI). The plan should be generic in scope so that it can be used as a routine planning document to respond to natural events such as storms, tornadoes, hurricanes, floods, and earthquakes, community HazMat releases, and terrorist attacks.

The mass casualty plan must reasonably delineate protocols and procedures for delivering appropriate care to (1) the critically injured, (2) the ambulatory minimally-injured and (3) worried-well survivors. It is essential that the plan address all three clinical groups. The ambulatory victims make up 80-90% of survivors and will likely overwhelm hospital and EMS resources. A mass casualty management and enhanced triage plan can direct these patients away from the hospital and towards a lower level of assessment and care. This necessary triage will enable hospitals to care for the more critically injured survivors.

State-wide efforts to respond to a terrorist attack will require the support of immunity legislation to protect those who triage victims after a mass casualty incident. These triage efforts require creative and aggressive efforts to maximize the efficiency of the community response.

The plans should complement the safety requirements described in OSHA's HAZWOPER 1910.120 standards.[11] The OSHA requirements apply to EMS, fire, police, and hospital personnel.[9, 12]

The mass casualty plan will enable a cost-effective and manpower-efficient response to the attack. The plan is divided into:

- The Scene: Identify and harden soft targets

- The Response Zone: Improve triage for a more efficient response

- The Hospital: Mandate a minimum level of preparedness

The Scene

Potential terrorist targets are often called "soft targets" due to the inherent minimal security precautions undertaken by most large employers, schools, athletic arenas, and transportation facilities. Despite this vulnerability, these soft targets have a significant capacity to participate in the community response.

Identify security personnel in charge of these facilities. Include these personnel in the community plan and the response. After an attack or an event that causes mass casualties, in many cases, response by EMS and Fire will be delayed due to exceptional demand. Soft targets should develop a response plan that assumes an extended period in which they must act on their own. Consider placing specific disaster equipment at these potential sites so that they might have the capacity to decontaminate ambulatory survivors prior to the arrival of first responders. Disaster planners and security professionals can improve terrorism and mass casualty preparedness for their facilities by:

- Developing and exercising evacuation plans.

- Enabling on-site self-decontamination (Dry Decon Kits, Doffit Kits)[13]

- Practicing and enabling shelter-in-place or remain-in-place maneuvers.

- Providing, fit testing, and utilizing N-95 masks

The Response Zone

Alter triage to enable utilization of off-site treatment shelters or Secondary Assessment Centers (SAC). The SAC will have the capacity to receive ambulatory minimally injured victims after an overt attack or Bio victims after a Bio attack in which hospitals have been overwhelmed. The SAC's will have the capacity to manage large numbers of minimally injured or non-injured as tornados, earthquakes, floods, and hurricanes. Utilize off-site treatment areas to preserve the hospital capabilities for the treatment of the critically ill.

The Hospital

All hospitals that have a 24-hour emergency department must have the capacity to safely assess, decontaminate, and treat victims exposed to a hazardous material.[5] Once this minimum level of preparedness has been achieved, expansion of services to include mass casualties can be performed in a rapid and reasonable fashion. Hospitals generally do not have the capacity to manage mass casualties. Thus, communities and public health systems must plan to offer treatment to victims in off-site treatment shelters or secondary assessment centers. The management of mass casualties after a terrorist attack is not merely a hospital problem; it is a community problem.

Dry Decon: A Mass Casualty Decontamination Alternative

Mass casualty HazMat exposures, according to historical sources, usually involve chemicals in the form of vapor or gas. Experience has shown that in such incidents 80-90% of the survivors are ambulatory.[14] Ambulatory survivors can have minimal to severe symptoms. In addition, survivors who are ambulatory and exhibit no symptoms but who are worried that they might have been exposed are referred to as the "worried-well."

The major goal for responding agencies is to quickly identify, evacuate, decontaminate, and treat those victims with obvious exposure to the hazard and with significant injuries. Although water decon is optimal, after a mass casualty attack it will be very difficult to provide timely treatment to the critically ill if water decon, which is heavily reliant upon large manpower and equipment resources, is directed towards the ambulatory survivors with minimal or no symptoms.

Evacuation of victims and removal of their clothing has been proven to be the most important and effective means of decon because nearly all of the contaminant will be in the clothing. This is a reasonable and minimally acceptable level of decontamination. A report from the U.S. Army[14] noted "since the most important aspect of decontamination is the timely and effective removal of the agent, the precise methods used to remove the agent are not nearly as important as the speed by which the agent is removed."

For community or routine HazMat exposures, the personal decon kit or Doffit Kit[13] enables the victim to remove clothing prior to or instead of water decontamination. After liquid or solid HazMat contamination, the removal of clothing will remove 80% or more of the contaminant. This might provide some protection for these patients as they await water decon. These kits enable the victims to rapidly remove their clothing while waiting for water decon.

For mass casualty HazMat incidents in which the victims will likely be exposed to chemicals in the form of vapor or gas, the personal decon kit will enable large numbers of ambulatory, minimally injured, or worried-well victims to remove their clothing in a public setting while protecting their privacy. After evacuation from the scene of the release of a gas or vapor and once the clothing is removed, the chemical is essentially eliminated (see decision tree below).[4]

In October 2001, the Aurora, Colorado emergency management agency utilized dry decon kits in their Domestic Preparedness Chemical Exercise under the supervision of the emergency management agency and the US Department of Justice. Ambulatory minimally ill and worried-well survivors were decontaminated in a matter of minutes using these Doffit Kits.[15] The procedure was well tolerated by the participants and greatly speeded up the decontamination process as seen in the photos below.

It is likely impossible to offer water decon to every victim in a mass casualty incident. To attempt to do so would put seriously ill victims who are non-ambulatory at greater risk since critical resources-both human and logistic-would have to be directed towards the minimally ill and worried-well. In a mass casualty incident, it is reasonable to offer this high level of decon only to those who might benefit most.[16, 17]

Dry decon can be achieved at the scene or the hospital. Local businesses, airports, schools, building security, police, fire, EMS, and hospital triage can all perform decon with this modality.

Summary

Communities must develop the capacity to evaluate, triage, decontaminate, and treat victims of a terrorist attack. This planning should be included in a generic mass casualty plan that enables community response to an "all-hazards" threat. Soft targets can participate in the community response by enabling security personnel to exercise and train with local first responders. Soft targets can develop an evacuation plan and decontamination plan consistent with the community mass casualty plan. Tabletop drills and hands-on exercises will assist in this effort.

References

1. *SARS: Basic Information.* 2003, Centers for Disease Control: Atlanta. p. http://www.cdc.gov/ncidod/sars/factsheet.htm

2. Siegelson, H.J., *Preparing for terrorism and hazardous material exposures: A Matter of Worker Safety.* Health Forum J, 2001. 44(1): p. 32-5.

3. Wetter, D.C., W.E. Daniell, and C.D. Treser, *Hospital preparedness for victims of chemical or biological terrorism.* Am J Public Health, 2001. 91(5): p. 710-6.

4. Levitin, H. and H. Siegelson, *Hazardous Materials Disasters,* in *Disaster Medicine,* D. Hogan, Editor. 2002, Lippincott.

5.   Levitin, H.W. and H.J. Siegelson, *Hazardous materials. Disaster medical planning and response.* Emerg Med Clin North Am, 1996. 14(2): p. 327-48.

6.   *Hospital HazMat and Terrorism Training, decon showers and personal decon kits, regulatory compliance, disaster planning,* HAZ/MAT DQE (www.hazmatdge.com); Indianapolis.

7.   *OSHA Standards Interpretation and Compliance Letters: Emergency response training necessary for hospital physicians/ nurses that may treat contaminated patients.* 1999, US Office for Safety and Health Administration.

8.   *OSHA: Hospitals and Community Emergency Response: What You Need to Know.* 1997, US Department of Labor, Occupational Safety and Health Administration.

9.   Fairfax, D., *OSHA: Emergency response training necessary for hospital physicians/nurses that may treat contaminated patients.,* in *Standard Number: 1910.120.* 1999, Directorate of Compliance Programs, US Department of Labor, Occupational Safety and Health Administration: OSHA Standards Interpretation and Compliance Letters.

10.   *SARS, Information for Clinicians.* 2003, CDC, http://www. cdc.gov/ncidod/sars/clinicians.htm; Atlanta.

11.   *29CFR1910.132, Personal Protective Equipment,* in *Occupational Safety and Health Standards,* US Government Printing Office: Code of Federal Regulations.

12.   Dohms, J., *OSHA safety requirements for hazardous chemicals in the workplace.* Radiol Manage, 1992. **14**(4): p. 76-80.

13.   *HAZ/MAT DQE, Doffit Kit, The Personal Dry Decon Alternative. www.hazmatdge.com,* Indianapolis.

14.   Lake, W., *Guidelines for Mass Casualty Decontamination During a Terrorist Chemical Agent Incident.* 2000, Chemical Weapons Improved Response Program, Domestic Preparedness Program, U. S. Soldier Biological and Chemical Command.

15.   Straight, B., *Emergency Management Specialist, Office of Emergency Management, Aurora, Colorado.* 2001.

16.   Brennan, R.J., et al., *Chemical warfare agents: emergency medical and emergency public health issues.* Ann Emerg Med, 1999. 34(2): p. 191-204.

17.   Sidell, F.R., *Chemical agent terrorism.* Ann Emerg Med, 1996. 28(2): p. 223-4.

Crowd management

Questions of mass terrorism and catastrophic events have restated a number of traditional questions for traditional public safety organizations. One particular question deals with crowd management dynamics.

Dealing with civil unrest, demonstrations and even volatile riots is one thing, but how prepared are first responders in this country to address crowd containment in the event of a terror attack. Imagine a crowd at the scene of a biological weapons release? Naturally the crowd is going to want to move rapidly away from the contaminant, but what if the people in that crowd were now infected with a dangerous microbe? The best first response measure in the interest of public health would be to contain the crowd and prevent them from dispersingor spreading infection to other places. How would first responders manage this crowd? How would police officers or security specialists contain this crowd and convince them to stay at the scene, and for that matter, how willing would first responders be to interact with the crowd at close range risking infection themselves?

Budgetary and overtime concerns

Homeland security costs money. Many local agencies and private businesses are now facing the difficult question of how to pay for ongoing increased security costs. Besides the costs of physical security upgrades, the ongoing costs of additional personnel and overtime can be overwhelming on limited budgets.

Personnel and manpower is the most expensive element in any security program. Although security technology tends to have greater initial investment, the expenditures over time tends to be dramatically less than the costs of on-going wages and salaries to paid first responders. As well, human elements tend to have higher exhaustion factors than technology systems that don't have the same problems of boredom, fatigue and subjective judgment. For this reason there is a push to develop cost effective technology solutions to many homeland security functions traditionally assigned to human providers.

Public/Private Partnerships
"The Importance of Public-Private Partnerships to our Nation's Security"

Remarks of Kenneth I. Juster, Under Secretary of Commerce Bureau of Industry and Security at the Rollout of the National Strategy to Secure Cyberspace

September 18, 2002
Stanford University
Palo Alto, California

In today's world, U.S. industry and U.S. security are inextricably linked, and the public and private sectors must jointly address economic and security issues.

As amply demonstrated by the events of the last year, the health of U.S. industry is dependent on security—the security of our borders, our transportation systems, our mail systems, and our computer networks. At the same time, our security has never been more dependent on a vibrant private sector working in partnership with government at all levels. That is why I would like to speak briefly on the relevance—and the importance—of public-private partnerships to our national security and, in particular, to our efforts to secure cyberspace.

New Targets of Terrorism

Although we must secure cyberspace from all attacks—ranging from the rogue nation to the recreational hacker—let's focus for a moment on what we have learned in recent years about the new targets of terrorism.

It has become quite clear that the ultimate goal of international terrorism is to compel U.S. withdrawal from our global commitments and presence. One of the important lessons from September 11 is that for many terrorists—including Osama bin Laden and al Qaeda—the targets of attack against the United States have gone beyond the physical manifestations of our country overseas—such as our armed forces or our embassies—to our domestic economy and our way of life. By attacking our economy and our infrastructures, terrorists hope to drive us inward—to undermine our national will, to compel us to abandon our global engagement, and to cause us to retreat into isolationism.

Indeed, a principal aim of the terrorists is to attack targets within the United States whose destruction or impairment could disrupt the delivery of services or the performance of functions essential to our national economy or to our government, cause large scale injury or death, or damage our national morale, prestige, or confidence. In attacking these targets, terrorists will exploit vulnerabilities wherever they can find them—whether they be in physical space or in cyberspace.

Homeland Security and National Security

This new terrorist strategy explains why what has become known as "homeland security" is fundamentally different from traditional notions of national security. Traditional national security is largely a governmental responsibility. It involves the joint efforts of the military, the foreign policy establishment, and the intelligence community. It is carried out almost exclusively by the federal government. And it relates to defense of our airspace and national borders, as well as our military, diplomatic, and intelligence operations overseas to maintain global and regional stability. Homeland security, however, is a shared responsibility. It cannot be carried out by the federal government alone. It requires full partnership with the private sector because the private sector owns or operates 85 percent of the nation's critical infrastructures. In light of these considerations, effective protection of homeland security requires a national strategy—not just a federal government strategy.

Such a national strategy includes coordinated action by federal, state, and local governments, along with private industry, as well as with every citizen and resident. The strategy must clarify and, in some instances, redefine the respective roles, responsibilities, and expectations of government and private-sector owners and operators of our critical infrastructures. The strategy also must serve as a vehicle for properly informing and shaping public expectations about future terrorist threats and the roles that government, industry, and each individual must play in defending against those threats. Issuance of the National Strategy

Today, we are presenting to the American people the first-ever National Strategy to Secure Cyberspace. The National Strategy is being released "for comment" by the nation. Providing the nation an opportunity to comment on the National Strategy underscores the importance of having broad support and commitment from the public in order to secure cyberspace.

This document—which was developed by the President's Critical Infrastructure Protection Board—will serve as a starting point for consultations among the federal government, the private sector, and state and local governments on cyber security issues. Indeed, this strategy already reflects a considerable amount of input from the private sector. Many senior executives volunteered considerable time to this enterprise—in addition to performing their regular jobs—and were actively involved in providing input on how to secure our cyberspace. In addition, the Partnership for Critical Infrastructure Security—which is a non-profit organization consisting of over 80 companies and associations as well as federal government agencies involved in many of the infrastructure sectors—has coordinated and summarized common concerns that cut across various sectors, such as infrastructure interdependencies, gaps in research and development, and public policy challenges.

I want to emphasize that it is the strong preference of the U.S. Government—as expressed in the National Strategy—to rely on market solutions rather than regulatory mandates in addressing cyberspace security. Not only are private sector companies the predominant owners and operators of our cyberspace systems and assets, but they have enormous expertise on security matters. Our task, therefore, is to encourage and facilitate your full participation in discussions about the issues and potential solutions outlined in the National Strategy.

Conclusion
In the end, there is no viable alternative to partnership between the public and private sectors. Collaboration, not confrontation, is an essential ingredient to the success of securing cyberspace and our homeland. Leadership must come from both government and corporate America. And I am delighted that there are so many excellent examples of such leadership sitting in this room today. We look forward to working with those of you from the private sector and from state and local governments on further developing and refining this National Strategy.

Military and Homeland Security

When discussing how to effectively combat terrorism and provide a rapid homeland security shield, one very obvious question is why would nations in North America simply not use their existing military apparatus. In the U.S. for example, Air National Guard elements protect the continental air space, and the U.S. Coast Guard patrols the waters and ports, but beyond that there has historically been very little involvement in other forms of domestic security being provided by the armed forces.

One major consideration to having the armed forces participate in ongoing homeland security operations is the Posse Comitatus Act of 1978. This act, enacted during the post civil war reconstruction period specifically bars the federal military from civilian law enforcement functions.

Using the military to police civilian populations within the United States violates many fundamental notions about the separation of power. Historically, as well, in other nations where the military also functions as a civil law enforcement and security force, there tends to be an over-extension of power and resultant corruption. Thus, while the armed forces may possess many of the tools, manpower and training which may assist with Homeland Security, there are great concerns that using the Department of Defense in such a way would fundamentally undermine key aspects of our way of life and governance.

Posse Comitatus Act
20 Stat. L., 145

June 18, 1878

CHAP. 263—An act making appropriations for the support of the Army for the fiscal year ending June thirtieth, eighteen hundred and seventy-nine, and for other purposes.

> *SEC. 15.* From and after the passage of this act it shall not be lawful to employ any part of the Army of the United States, as a posse comitatus, or otherwise, for the purpose of executing the laws, except in such cases and under such circumstances as such employment of said force may be expressly authorized by the Constitution or by act of Congress; and no money appropriated by this act shall be used to pay any of the expenses incurred in the employment of any troops in violation of this section And any person willfully violating the provisions of this section shall be deemed guilty of a misdemeanor and on conviction thereof shall be punished by fine not exceeding ten thousand dollars or imprisonment not exceeding two years or by both such fine and imprisonment.

10 U.S.C. (United States Code) 375

> *Sec. 375. Restriction on direct participation by military personnel:*
> The Secretary of Defense shall prescribe such regulations as may be necessary to ensure that any activity (including the provision of any equipment or facility or the assignment or detail of any personnel)

under this chapter does not include or permit direct participation by a member of the Army, Navy, Air Force, or Marine Corps in a search, seizure, arrest, or other similar activity unless participation in such activity by such member is otherwise authorized by law.

18 U.S.C. 1385

Sec. 1385. Use of Army and Air Force as posse comitatus
Whoever, except in cases and under circumstances expressly authorized by the Constitution or Act of Congress, willfully uses any part of the Army or the Air Force as a posse comitatus or otherwise to execute the laws shall be fined under this title or imprisoned not more than two years, or both.

National Guard Missions

In the U.S the National Guard is modern military force that operates in the tradition of the state militias retained by the original colonies of the United States. Both the Department of the Army and Air Force operate National Guard arms. The National Guard primarily operates in support and under the governance of a each individual state. The governor in each states serves as the commander and chief of the state's army and air national guard. Typically, National Guard units support various state level humanitarian and civil missions such as:

- Supporting natural disaster relief efforts
- Fighting wildfires
- Search and rescue
- Aiding civilian law enforcement with large scale crisis such as quelling riots

In certain situations, the National Guard may be federalized and activated by the President of the United States. In every major conflict the U.S. has been involved in during the last century National Guard units have participated in combat and other operations in theaters of conflict. Due to its civil missions the National Guard possesses several skills that are valuable in modern conflicts such as military police, civil affairs, public health, psychological operations, logistics and transport. Notwithstanding, the National Guard is also trained as a combat force.

This dual nature presents definite challenges to using the National Guard as an ongoing civil security force. Not only in questions related to Posse Comitatus, but also for the fundamental perception of military hardware and equipment and soldiers in battle dress stationed on city streets, airports and public areas.

Since 9–11, National Guard forces have been deployed at U.S. airports, as well as bridges, landmarks and public venues as a means of bolstering security. The long term or permanent transference of homeland security missions to the National Guard remains a question and a challenge.

One area in which the National Guard has been operating in a distinct homeland security capacity has been Civil Support—Weapons of Mass Destruction Teams. Enacted by President Bill Clinton during the 1990's, WMD Teams are Army National Guard units designated to provide rapid response, technical guidance and logistical support to local resources in the event that a weapon of mass destruction is ever used by a nation-state or terrorist organization against U.S. targets.

Mission of Civil Support Teams—WMD

The CST mission is to support civil authorities at a domestic CBRNE incident site by identifying CBRNE* agents/substances, assessing current and projected consequences, advising on response measures, and assisting with appropriate requests for additional support.

In response to a CBRNE situation, the CSTs provide a well-trained team to support the state response as a lead element for the NG. The CSTs provide assessment of the current and projected consequences, technical and analytical consultation, and transmission of the situation to higher headquarters (HQ) to assist in requesting follow-on assets.

The CST is designed to support the state and local emergency response system, but it is not intended to replace those system functions normally performed by the EFR community. Where these systems are in place, formal request for assistance (RFAs) will flow through them and any support provided will be done in conjunction with support being resourced through the incident command system (ICS).

The mission of the CST has been developed and congressionally authorized for CM support for an incident or attack involving WMD. Controlling authorities for the CST (such as the governor or TAG) should carefully consider the impact of deploying (such as team recovery/rest time, resupply) the CST in support of non-CBRNE response situations prior to directing such an employment.

In addition to the response capabilities, the CST brings a number of ancillary capabilities to the state in which it is assigned (or the state to which it is deployed). In particular, the expertise and focus of the unit provides a multidisciplined integration of CBRNE information and a dedicated group assigned to understand the potential response organizations and plans within the state. Preincident coordination with other state and local emergency response agencies and organizations will greatly facilitate a postincident response and can greatly increase statewide preparedness.

Federal Mission of the Army National Guard:

During peacetime each state National Guard answers to the leadership in the 50 states, three territories and the District of Columbia. During national emergencies, however, the President reserves the right to mobilize the National Guard, putting them in federal duty status. While federalized, the units answer to the Combatant Commander of the theatre in which they are operating and, ultimately, to the President. Even when not federalized, the Army National Guard has a federal obligation (or mission.) That mission is to maintain properly trained and equipped units, available for prompt mobilization for war, national emergency, or as otherwise needed. The Army National Guard is a partner with the Active Army and the Army Reserves in fulfilling the country's military needs. In fiscal year 2001, Army Guard soldiers pulled duty in more than 80 countries in a wide variety of operations including peacekeeping, stabilization, security, nation building, etc. Below are a few examples of how the Army National Guard is fulfilling its federal mission.

State Mission of the Army National Guard:

The Army National Guard exists in all 50 states, three territories and the District of Columbia. The state, territory or district leadership are the Commanders in Chief for each Guard. Their Adjutants General are answerable to them for the training and readiness of the units. At the state level, the governors reserve the ability, under the Constitution of the United States, to call up members of the National Guard in time of domestic emergencies or need.

The Army National Guard's state mission is perhaps the most visible and well known. Nearly everyone has seen or heard of Guard units responding to battle fires or helping communities deal with floods, tornadoes, hurricanes, snowstorms or other emergency situations. In times of civil unrest, the citizens of a state can rest assured that the Guard will be ready to respond, if needed. During 2001, 34,855 Guardsmen were called to duty in response to the needs of their community or state.

> *Study: During the Washington DC-area sniper attacks of 2002, a number of investigative resources were utilized in order identify and capture the snipers. One resource the federal government added to the investigation was the use of U.S. Army RC–7 Airborne Reconnaissance—Low (ARL) Aircraft.*
>
> *What unique capabilities did the RC–7 aircraft bring to this investigation? Were the technologies of the RC–7 useful and appropriate for this type of investigation and should they be developed for civilian investigative needs?*
>
> *Did the use of this resource violate the Posse Comitatus Act of 1878, which forbids or restricts the role of the Armed Forces for civil law enforcement?*

Discussion Questions

1) The Homeland Security Threat Advisory System provides highly specific instructions for private enterprise in combating terrorism.

    True   False

2) An _____ Condition is declared when there is a significant risk of terrorist attacks.

3) A Severe Condition reflects a severe risk of terrorist attacks; its corresponding color is _____.

4) The creation of a "super-agency" to combat terrorism such as the Department of Homeland Security is a massive departure for the U.S. Government.

   True   False

5) Public crowd management and containment at the scene of a bio-terror attack would not likely present any new challenges that a normal civil unrest situation would.

   True   False

6) The human element of a security program is usually the most expensive, recurring cost.

   True   False

7) The _____ _____ Act of 1878 prohibits the use of military resources from most law enforcement duties in the United States.

8) The National Guard of a state is usually under the command of the state governor.

   True   False

9) Under special circumstances the National Guard can be federalized.

   True   False

10) The National Guard is banned from participating in civil support missions.

   True   False

Answers:

1) True

2) Elevated

3) Red

4) True

5) False

6) True

7) Posse Comitatus

8) True

9) True

10) False

Homeland Security Program Development Team

Project Director
Daniel Byram, MA

DANIEL BYRAM brings over twenty years of law enforcement experience to his role as educator. He has been involved for more than thirty years in program management, tactical security operations, intelligence operations, and law enforcement.

He has been widely involved in training and program development for law enforcement agencies and business, including the creation of a covert operations training program for law enforcement special operations personnel, the development of hostage rescue and crisis survival responses for covert operations personnel, and the designing of a "blueprint" for corporate terrorism response for the Insurance Education Association.

Daniel, with Dr. Julie Brown, designed the model for the homeland security degree programs offered in the Corinthian College network, and then he brought together experts from across the United States and Canada to develop the program materials.

Daniel holds a Masters Degree in Human Behavior and has provided over fifteen years of leadership in the post secondary educational experience. Mr. Byram is currently the National Director of Security, Justice and Legal Programs for Corinthian Colleges, Inc.

Team Leader
Jeff Hynes

JEFF HYNES has twenty-three years of experience with the Phoenix Police Department and currently serves as Commander. He has managed the advanced training for the Department in defensive tactics, firearms, driving and physical fitness and wellness. He also coordinated and facilitated the yearly forty hour in-service advanced training tactical module for 2700 police officers, handles curriculum review, records keeping, and facilitates the yearly Citizen's Forum. Mr. Hynes has served as a liaison between the Phoenix Police department and other federal, state and local agencies' proficiency related training at the Arizona Law Enforcement Training Academy.

Commander Hynes received his B.S. in Police Science and holds a Masters Degree in Educational Leadership. He is currently finishing his Doctorate in Education from Northern Arizona University and is an adjunct faculty member of several state and community colleges.

Jeff has also received numerous national, state and Phoenix Police Department Excellence Awards and nominations for Outstanding Community Based Policing Initiatives.

Team Leader
Jean Goodall

DR. JEAN GOODALL'S diverse career has been distinguished by the broad range of experiences she has had in her community that have brought her first-hand knowledge of the link between the criminal justice system and government operations. Throughout her efforts in this field, she has interlaced her strong background in public administration and teaching.

Following her study of criminology and public administration, she completed an MA in Criminal Justice. Jean Goodall has worked for over thirty years with legal issues in the criminal justice environment. She has also combined an MA in Management and a Doctorate in Public Administration with knowledge gleaned from numerous FBI, CBI, OEM and weapons seminars, camps and schools. She has received specialized FEMA training regarding Emergency Management and Homeland Security. This in-depth combination provides Dr. Goodall with a unique perspective on the role of the Civil and Criminal Justice System in Homeland Security issues.

Dr. Goodall holds a teaching certificate from the State of Colorado and has twelve years experience in adult education at the university level. She recently served as the chairman of the Criminal Justice Department at Blair College, Colorado Springs, Colorado.

Team Leader
Julie Brown MD

If ready response to disasters is the mark of an exemplary security specialist, DR. JULIE BROWN'S career sets an excellent example. Whether she's been the physician assisting with refugees or a member of the crime-prevention posse for the sheriff's department of Maricopa County, Arizona, Julie has actively engaged in disaster management throughout her career.

An experienced professional in forensic pathology, law enforcement and disaster medicine, Julie is a registered nurse and became a physician in 1988. Dr. Brown serves on several federal disaster teams that respond to a variety of disasters.

Her areas of study include nursing, biology, psychology, human behavior, medicine and general business. She has a teaching certificate in biology, psychology and the medical sciences and has extensive experience as an educator at the college level. She received an MBA in General Business from the University of Phoenix. She formerly served as the program manager for business and accounting for Corinthian College.

Subject Matter Expert
Richard Wilmot, General (retired) United States Army

GENERAL RICHARD WILMOT Wilmot comes from a varied and unusual career in both the government and private sectors. Before retiring from the Army, General Wilmot, a Vietnam War veteran, held several key positions in the defense sector, including Commanding General of the US Army Intelligence Center and School and Director of Intelligence Systems in the Pentagon. General Wilmot commanded troops at every grade from second lieutenant to brigadier general.

Having been in 106 countries, his life story is replete with unusual true adventures. In Afghanistan he was an advisor to the Afghan rebels when they were fighting the Soviet Union in the mid-1980s. This foray alone has resulted in many interesting anecdotes, realizations, and a broad understanding of events that are tied to the international terrorist situation we now face.

Today, General Wilmot is a successful entrepreneur and an international businessman. He practices leadership in tense areas of the world where leading in crisis situations leaves no room for error. He is a motivator, a strategic planner, a consultant, an international speaker and the stories of his adventures provide unusual insight into terrorist situations we face today. He is a graduate of Michigan State University, the US Army War College, the Industrial College of the Armed Forces, and the Command and General Staff College.

Subject Matter Expert
Jane Chung—Examiner, CSC LA Joint Drug Intelligence Group

The analysis of intelligence data is JANE CHUNG'S expertise. As an examiner for the Los Angeles Joint Drug Intelligence Group (LA JDIG), she provides analytical support for narcotics cases for the LA JDIG's Southwest Border Team. She researches commercial and law enforcement databases, evaluates and analyzes the data extracted and presents the findings to the case agent and other analysts.

Jane's experience with data analysis includes work in international intelligence. In Kosovo, she conducted over 800 personnel interviews to determine the threat level against US Forces. She has also developed intelligence threat and damage products focusing on foreign intelligence services, terrorist, paramilitary, law enforcement, political and criminal organizations. Jane managed the classified segment of the Migrated Defense Intelligence Threat Data System (MDITDS) database for the US Army Europe Analytical Control Element.

Jane graduated in 1998 from the University of California, Irvine with her B.A. in Criminology, Law and Society.

Subject Matter Expert
Stewart Kellock, Ost J CD Detective 897, Toronto Police Service

With twenty-six years of policing for the Toronto Police Service and serving with the military, STEWART KELLOCK offers a hands-on perspective to anti-terrorist intelligence. He has a strong and varied investigative background that includes work with a major crime unit, leading multi-unit investigations, investigating several major political incidents, plains clothes experience, and work with Provincial Weapons Enforcement and Intelligence and is currently attached to the anti-terrorist unit of Intelligence Support.

Stewart has extensive military experience. He was commissioned in 1981 and currently holds the rank of Captain. Most recently he was the Leadership Company Commander at 32 CBG Battle School. Previously he was an Intelligence officer at LandForce Central Area Headquarters, which involved him in numerous intelligence operations both domestic and international. His most recent international mission was commanding the Regional Crime Squad as part of the contingent of the United Nation's Mission in Kosovo.

Stewart majored in International Terrorism at Humbar College and has completed numerous courses in military training and policing. He currently serves as the Unit Training Officer for the 53 Division Canadian Regional Unit.

Subject Matter Expert
James McShane MPA—Deputy Chief (retired)—Executive Officer, Narcotics Division New York City Police Department

JAMES MCSHANE was second in command of the 2,300 person Narcotics Division of the New York City Police Department where he was responsible for all narcotics enforcement activities in New York City, including all "Buy and Bust" operations, as well as the investigation of all narcotics complaints. He directed all major narcotic investigations in the City of New York.

James has a law degree and is a member of the Bar of the State of New York and has been admitted to practice in the U.S. Supreme Court and the Federal Courts of New York. He also holds permanent certification as a New York Secondary School Teacher and a New York City teacher's license. James taught Math and served as the Dean of a South Bronx High School where he taught, counseled students and adjudicated conflicts.

James received his BA in Communications from Fordham and was a Fulbright scholar and lecturer at the Police College of Finland in Helsinki. He attended the Police Management Institute at Columbia University School of Business, received a Master of Public Administration from Harvard University's Kennedy School of Government.

Subject Matter Expert
Bruce Tefft—Senior Associate, Orion Scientific Systems

BRUCE TEFFT is a well-seasoned intelligence investigator with twenty-two years of service in foreign affairs and intelligence operations as Headquarters Branch Chief and field Chief of Station in the Central Intelligence Agency's Directorate of Operations. He served in several African countries, Europe, South Asia, and the Middle East. His multiple responsibilities and activities with the CIA varied from developing and teaching intelligence collection and analysis courses, and running intelligence collection and counterterrorist operations against Islamic fundamentalists, to developing and implementing logistics and training programs for over several 1000 U.S. and foreign personnel. He planned and organized the first joint CIA-FBI-US Military operation and successfully captured a foreign terrorist.

Bruce has managed liaison relationships and operations with major Allied Nation intelligence organizations and the U.S. Government Departments such as, State and Defense, the Federal Bureau of Investigation, the Drug Enforcement Agency, Defense Intelligence Agency, Defense HUMINT Service and the U.S. Marine Corps.

He is currently a successful executive as the Senior Associate of Orion Scientific Systems and is the counter-terrorism advisor to New York City Police Department. He has a B.A. and a Master's degree in History and in 1974 received his law degree from the University of Denver.

Subject Matter Expert
Lieutenant Colonel Xavier Stewart

Throughout the last twenty years, LTC STEWART has been widely recognized for distinguished service in his military career and in the field of healthcare. He joined the Army National Guard following the Marine Corps and is the Commander of a Weapons of Mass Destruction Civilian Support Team with the Pennsylvania National Guard. His military duties have included assignments within the Military Police, Military Intelligence, Physical Security, Military Academy and Medical Arena bringing him several prestigious honors including three Meritorious Service Metals and the Guarde Nationale Trophy for Outstanding Service. He is currently a member of the Executive Advisory Board for Homeland Security and has been recognized by Congress with a Congress Special Award.

With a Doctorate in Public Health, LTC Stewart has held numerous faculty positions in respiratory therapy programs, rehabilitation services, biology, physician assistant and nurse practitioner programs. He has been recognized as one of the Top Ten Respiratory Care Practitioners by the AARC Journal and is listed in Who's Who Among College Professors, Who's Who in America and Who's Who in the World. LTC Stewart is a board certified Forensic Examiner and is Board Certified in Forensic Medicine. He is currently a first responder as a nationally registered EMT, HAZMAT firefighter and former deputy sheriff.

He is a graduate of Command and General Staff College and earned a Master's in Education with a Concentration in Health Services.

Subject Matter Expert
Christopher J. Wren

CHRISTOPHER WREN is a Security Specialist whose talents have repeatedly been tested in the field. During the Atlanta Olympic games, where he was responsible for athlete and venue security, he assisted in the design and evaluation of security plans for three high profile locations. While the Director of Security for a large downtown Phoenix Hotel, he was responsible for completely overhauling the hotel security monitoring system to include state-of-the-art camera, motion censors and sound monitors. Christopher's training in dignitary/VIP protection brought him a commendation from the White House Security Detail for his assistance in protection of the President and Vice-President of the United States.

As a commissioned law enforcement officer, Mr. Wren coordinated security efforts with Federal, state and local law enforcement agencies, and he has over four years experience in the planning, set-up and supervision of threat assessment teams. He currently serves on the Homeland Defense Planning and Advisory Team for the City of Phoenix, Arizona.

Christopher served in the U.S. Marine Corps, receiving the rank of Meritorious Sergeant, and was awarded the Navy/Marine Corps Achievement Medal for Excellence. He has studied criminal justice and vocational education and has special training in advanced detective work, media relations, negotiation techniques for first responders and technical aspects of covert operations.

Subject Matter Expert
D. James Stanger

Dr. JAMES STANGER, a prolific author and PhD, is the Director of Certification and Product Development at ProsoftTraining. His credentials include Symantec Technology Architect, Convergence Technology Professional, CIW Master Administrator, Linux+, A+ and he has led certification development efforts in these proficiencies for various organizations including ProsoftTraining, Symantec, and Linux Professional Institute. Dr. Stanger's specialties include network auditing, risk management, business continuity planning, intrusion detection and firewall configuration. He has coordinated audits for various clients, which have recently included Brigham Young University, Fuelzone.com and the William Blake Archive.

As an author, James has created titles for Symantec Education Services, designed executive training seminars concerning firewall and Virtual Private Network (VPN) management, and written other titles concerning security, Cisco routing and system administration for many companies.

In addition to his development work, James finds time to serve on several certification boards and advisory councils where, among his many responsibilities, he works to insure that exams remain relevant and to protect certification exam intellectual property.

Subject Matter Expert
Matt Pope, CPP

MATT POPE is the founder of The Security, Integrity and Perception Standard, a private consultancy, which advises on the impact of global security and business integrity on government and economic stability. He also specializes in identifying and creating cutting edge marketing trends, services and technologies to improve homeland security and public trust.

Matt has sixteen years experience in business, public safety and military force protection. He is certified in professional security management, and holds a degree in political science. Most recently Matt has developed a specific expertise with contemporary issues of public security and integrity, privacy legislation, and security ethics. He has worked with some of the world's leading corporations on a broad range of security and emergency planning projects. Matt also serves as an adjunct instructor of homeland security and has written extensively on topics relating to security, law, contingency planning, ethics, privacy and legislation.

Subject Matter Expert
Lieutenant Kevin Kazmaier

With over 20 years of experience in law enforcement, LIEUTENANT KEVIN KAZMAIER has an extensive background in explosive devices, SWAT and special operations. A member of the International Association of Bomb Technicians and Investigators since his certification as a bomb technician in 1987, he has taught many courses in firearms and advanced explosive technique.

Lieutenant Kazmaier is a graduate of Protective Operations courses from the Association of Chiefs of Police, Secret Service Debriefings, the United States Army Military Police School and the Phoenix Police Department. He has worked as a consultant for America West Airlines and has provided security at such events as the Super Bowl, the Senior PGA Tour and the World Series.

Lieutenant Kazmaier holds an A.A.S. in Law Enforcement and a B.S. in Social Justice Professions.

Subject Matter Expert
Harold M. Spangler, MD

DR. SPANGLER is Chief Resident of Emergency Medicine at North Carolina Baptist Hospital and Bowman-Gray School of Medicine. He is board certified in Emergency Medicine and holds licenses as an Advanced Cardiac Life Support Instructor, an Advanced Trauma Life Support Provider and as a Basic Trauma Life Support Instructor.

After receiving his B.S. degree in Biology, Dr. Spangler went on to receive honors throughout medical school graduating from Jefferson Medical College, Thomas Jefferson University in Philadelphia, Pennsylvania. He is a member of the American Medical Association, the American College of Emergency Physicians, the North Caroline Chapter of ACEP and the National Association of EMS Physicians.

Subject Matter Expert
Alan Pruitt CPP

MR. PRUITT'S extensive expertise has made him an integral part of the development of the Homeland Security Specialist Program at Bryman College in San Jose, California, where he currently serves as the Homeland Security Program Chair. His experiences in the field of intelligence investigation and gathering are diverse. They include his duties as a Marine Corps intelligence officer, his work in corporate security and his service as a licensed private investigator.

In the military, Alan served as a Counterintelligence Agent with the US Army National Guard and as a Counterintelligence Specialist with the U.S. Marine Corps. His military education introduced him to the skill of tactical intelligence photography and he completed courses in counterintelligence and qualified as an anti-terrorist instructor. He was awarded the Navy Commendation Medal from the Secretary of the Navy for superior achievements in security management.

A member of the California Association of Licensed Investigators and the Association of Certified Fraud Examiners, Alan has over 18,000 hours of investigative experience. His many corporate clients have included Paramount Pictures, the Department of Justice and the U.S. Customs Service.

He holds a B.S. in Business Management and is a member of the American Society of Law Enforcement Trainers and the American Society of Industrial Security.

Subject Matter Expert
Steve Martin—Security Operations CEO

MR. MARTIN has over twenty-one years of international experience in the government and private sectors. His career highlights are wide-ranging in the fields of international security, communications, management, business and paralegal.

As a Special Agent with the Defense Department's National Security Agency, Steve faced the complexities of providing physical security for NSA/CSS personnel and facilities. His overall mission was to create and maintain security activities that detected and protected against acts of espionage, sabotage and terrorism. His accomplishments include authoring complex government policies and procedures, team leading for the NSA Strategic Planning Sessions, and coordinating actions and policies on counter-terrorism and counter-intelligence measures. He has trained security officers, managing many of the duties of a 500-man NSA police force. He lectures at home and abroad on security and advanced technology.

When Mr. Martin was with the NSA he maintained a liaison with his counterparts in other government agencies and private industry. In 1993, Mr. Martin founded a private, multi-division company of which he is part owner. From this vantage he is able to provide a very informed analysis of the critical need in homeland security for entrepreneurial enterprise.

Subject Matter Expert
Master Sergeant Rocky Dunlap

MASTER SERGEANT ROCKY DUNLAP retired as Program Manager and Inspector General Team Member for the Air Force Space Command Explosive Ordnance Disposal at Peterson Air Force Base. In this capacity, he oversaw command objectives relating to anti-terrorism issues, homeland defense initiatives, conventional, nuclear and biological improvised devices, weapons of mass destruction and reducing the vulnerability of Air Force Space Command installations within the U.S. and abroad. He was responsible for six major installations and nine remote sites worldwide. Master Sergeant Dunlop established the first regional post 9/11 bomb squad in the Department of Defense to combat weapons of mass destruction. He led NASA's pyrotechnic recovery operations of the Columbia Space shuttle disaster.

He is a graduate of many military courses that deal with weaponry, terrorism and disaster control. He completed courses in anti-terrorism, weapons and ordinance disposal, chemical and biological school, counter insurgency, nuclear, and HAZMAT first responders and has studied to be a post blast investigator.

Master Sergeant Dunlop has completed a BS in Workforce Education and Development, an AS in Explosive Technology and currently holds the highest certification possible for a Department of Defense bomb Technician.

Subject Matter Expert
Mr. William Oberholtzer

WILLIAM OBERHOLTZER, a military consultant with Vector Incorporated, provides expertise on weapons of mass destruction to a variety of security and defense teams. As Chief of Weapons of Mass Destruction Counter Technology Integration, Mr. Oberholtzer provides the National Guard, civilian emergency response agencies and those of the first responder community with recommendations on organization, training and equipment alterations best suited to meet unit requirements.

Credited with making major contributions toward the establishment of the Nation's premier Weapons of Mass Destruction Civil Support Team, he also developed the organization and curriculum requirements for the National Weapons of Mass Destruction and Counter Terrorism Training and Simulation Center in response to initiatives pertaining to homeland defense.

William has a B.S. in Education Administration and Master Degrees in Management and Human Relations. He graduated from Defense Systems Management College and has many FEMA courses and certifications to his credit, including: Emergency Program Manager and Emergency Preparedness, Radiological Emergency Management and Response, Hazardous Material , and the Role of the Emergency Operations Center.

Subject Matter Expert
Dr. Victor Herbert

DR. VICTOR HERBERT has dedicated a lifetime to teaching and administration. He is currently Dean of Instruction for the New York City Fire Department (FDNY) where he coordinates all training for FDNY personnel and directs FDNYC, AmeriCorp, and Fire Safety Education. He came to this position following his work in public and higher education.

With a master's degree in English Education and a Doctorate in Educational Leadership, he taught English and Spanish and went on to win the Fund for the City of New York's award as Educator of the Year in 1983. After obtaining a number of professional certificates in educational administration and Spanish, he received a Fulbright Award to study relationships between Mexico and the United States. He has traveled extensively throughout Latin America.

Besides his teaching positions, Dr. Herbert has assumed many roles in public school administration working as department chair, principal and school superintendent in school districts in New York, Arizona and Connecticut. Dr. Herbert has been an associate faculty member at Chapman University, Arizona State University, Norwalk Community College and St. Joseph's College in New York. His expertise has enabled him to teach both technical and academic subjects. He also has directed several programs for emergency responders in the acquisition of Spanish.

He is a graduate of many military courses that deal with weaponry, terrorism and disaster control. He completed courses in anti-terrorism, weapons and ordinance disposal, chemical and biological school, counter insurgency, nuclear, and HAZMAT first responders and has studied to be a post blast investigator.

Master Sergeant Dunlop has completed a BS in Workforce Education and Development, an AS in Explosive Technology and currently holds the highest certification possible for a Department of Defense bomb Technician.

Subject Matter Expert
Mr. William Oberholtzer

WILLIAM OBERHOLTZER, a military consultant with Vector Incorporated, provides expertise on weapons of mass destruction to a variety of security and defense teams. As Chief of Weapons of Mass Destruction Counter Technology Integration, Mr. Oberholtzer provides the National Guard, civilian emergency response agencies and those of the first responder community with recommendations on organization, training and equipment alterations best suited to meet unit requirements.

Credited with making major contributions toward the establishment of the Nation's premier Weapons of Mass Destruction Civil Support Team, he also developed the organization and curriculum requirements for the National Weapons of Mass Destruction and Counter Terrorism Training and Simulation Center in response to initiatives pertaining to homeland defense.

William has a B.S. in Education Administration and Master Degrees in Management and Human Relations. He graduated from Defense Systems Management College and has many FEMA courses and certifications to his credit, including: Emergency Program Manager and Emergency Preparedness, Radiological Emergency Management and Response, Hazardous Material , and the Role of the Emergency Operations Center.

Subject Matter Expert
Dr. Victor Herbert

DR. VICTOR HERBERT has dedicated a lifetime to teaching and administration. He is currently Dean of Instruction for the New York City Fire Department (FDNY) where he coordinates all training for FDNY personnel and directs FDNYC, AmeriCorp, and Fire Safety Education. He came to this position following his work in public and higher education.

With a master's degree in English Education and a Doctorate in Educational Leadership, he taught English and Spanish and went on to win the Fund for the City of New York's award as Educator of the Year in 1983. After obtaining a number of professional certificates in educational administration and Spanish, he received a Fulbright Award to study relationships between Mexico and the United States. He has traveled extensively throughout Latin America.

Besides his teaching positions, Dr. Herbert has assumed many roles in public school administration working as department chair, principal and school superintendent in school districts in New York, Arizona and Connecticut. Dr. Herbert has been an associate faculty member at Chapman University, Arizona State University, Norwalk Community College and St. Joseph's College in New York. His expertise has enabled him to teach both technical and academic subjects. He also has directed several programs for emergency responders in the acquisition of Spanish.